MICHAEL REED

The Georgian Triumph
1700–1830

PALADIN
Granada Publishing

Paladin Books
Granada Publishing Ltd
8 Grafton Street, London W1X 3LA

Published by Paladin Books 1984

First published in Great Britain by
Routledge & Kegan Paul plc 1983
as a title in THE MAKING OF BRITAIN series

Copyright © Michael Reed 1983

ISBN 0-586-08404-5

Reproduced, printed and bound in Great Britain by
Hazell Watson & Viney Limited,
Aylesbury, Bucks

Set in Palatino

Few themes run with consistency all the way through the history of the British Isles, save the land itself. It is the product of the interaction over time between the internal, mental world of men and women, their hopes, ideas and ambitions, and their external, physical environment.

The five books in this new series examine the varied and complex relationship between man and his environment, and show how the landscape of Britain has acquired its rich historical density. They illustrate the way in which men and women have shaped and occupied the country, and how society has been moulded by the opportunities and constraints imposed by the landscape. Man is the agent of change within the landscape, so that behind a simple hedgerow, a country cottage, a mean street in some grimy industrial town, lie the modes of thought, the unconscious attitudes and the habits and expectations of past generations.

The Author

Michael Reed read history at the University of Birmingham and took his further degrees at the University of London, and the University of Leicester. He is at present Senior Lecturer in Library Studies, Loughborough University. He is the author of *The Buckinghamshire Landscape* (1979), and has published a number of papers on various aspects of economic history, as well as an edition of early seventeenth-century probate inventories for Ipswich.

The Making of Britain
1066–1939

General Editor: Andrew Wheatcroft

Contents

Illustrations

2

4

Acknowledgments

The author and publishers are grateful to the following persons and institutions for permission to reproduce illustrations: Her Majesty the Queen, for her gracious permission to use no. 67; Aerofilms Ltd, nos 1, 3, 10, 19, 23, 24, 28, 29, 39, 41, 60, 61, 62, 70, 75; the Reference Library Department, Birmingham Public Libraries, nos 37, 38, 44 and 65; the Bodleian Library from Gough Gen. top. 57, no. 7; the Trustees of the British Library, nos 6, 8, 12, 31, 49, 66; Cheltenham Art Gallery and Museum Service, no. 21; the Committee for Aerial Photography, University of Cambridge, no. 2; Country Life, nos 27, 34, 35; Crown Copyright, reproduced by permission of the Controller of Her Majesty's Stationery Office, no. 11; Crown Copyright, reproduced by permission of the National Monuments Record, nos 14, 15, 18, 22, 25, 30, 32, 42, 43, 54, 58, 63, 64, 69, 74, 77; Crown Copyright, reproduced by permission of the Royal Commission on Ancient Monuments, Scotland, nos 26, 40, 50, 53, 68, 71, 76; Ironbridge Gorge Museum Trust, no. 45; the Local Studies Department, Manchester City Libraries, no. 73; New Lanark Conservation, no. 52; David Palmer, nos 51 and 55; Philip Reed, no. 47; Stuart and Sons Ltd, Stourbridge, no. 46; T.S.U. City of Aberdeen District Council, no. 20; University of Aberdeen Library for permission to reproduce from the original in the George Washington Wilson Collection, no. 13; Victoria and Albert Museum, no. 59; the Editor of *The Victoria History of the Counties of England* reproduced from *Warwickshire* vol. VIII, no. 72. The remaining photographs are taken from the author's collection. The Greater London Council for permission to redraw a plan from *Survey of London*, vol. XXXIX, figure 13.

Many people have given unstintingly of their help and advice in the preparation of this book. I am very grateful to Andrew Wheatcroft for his suggestions at every stage during its writing. Professor Havard-Williams has continued to provide encouragement and support. I am most grateful to all those scholars and students of the period who have allowed me to draw upon their researches, published and unpublished. They include Professor Ravenhill, Dr A. Harris, Dr David Stevenson, who was at pains to search out Plate 20 for me, Mr Naish, Dr Margaret Davies, Dr George Kay, Dr T. R. Slater, Dr. B. M. W. Third (Mrs Cay), Mrs L. R. Timperley, Dr J. R. Coull and Mrs S. A. Hulland, who allowed me free access to her researches into her family history. Other debts are more particularly acknowledged in their right places. Mrs J. Hey not only typed successive drafts with imperturbable good humour but also helped me to Plate 47. Only my wife and son can know what the writing of this book has cost them, whilst its dedication acknowledges a debt that can never be repaid.

General Editor's Preface

To the archaeologist, the notion of material culture, of a society exemplified by its artefacts, is commonplace. To historians it has traditionally had less appeal, although Professor Fernand Braudel's *Civilisation matérielle et capitalisme* marks a foray into unknown terrain. The intention of this series, which follows chronologically from another of more directly archaeological approach,* is to see the history of Britain from the Norman Conquest to the Second World War, partly in human terms – of changing cultural, social, political and economic patterns – but more specifically in terms of what that society produced, and what remains of it today.

Few themes run with consistency through the history of the British Isles, save the land itself. This series seeks to show the way in which man has shaped and occupied the country, and how society has been moulded by the opportunities and constraints imposed by the landscape. The broad theme is of man's interaction with his environment, which is carried through the series.

As editor, I have tried to allow each author to write his approach to the subject without undue interference. Ideally, such a study would have appeared as a large single volume, but we have sought to make the divisions less arbitrary by allowing authors to cover a broad body of material in more than one book. Thus the volumes dealing with the medieval period come from the same hand, as do those spanning the sixteenth to the nineteenth centuries.

Britain before the Conquest, 5 vols, Routledge & Kegan Paul, 1979–81.

In Michael Reed's study of the Georgian era we move from 'The best of all possible worlds', to use Soane Jenyns's bold phrase, to one where confidence and certainty are sapped. The capacity of man to achieve almost any end comes to its first fruition in this era, and it is interesting to note how many of the innovations and changes usually associated with the Victorian period may more properly be described as Georgian. Urban renewal, model housing, earth moving on a massive scale, major civil engineering projects involving co-ordination of a mass labour force, the mobilisation of capital and financial resources, all fall into this category. For the ready acceptance of innovation, the Scottish Lowlands of the late eighteenth century show as many examples of fervent enterprise as the Victorian advocates of 'high farming'. The fascination of this epoch, so vividly described in this volume, is its fertility and suppleness of spirit.

Andrew Wheatcroft

Preface

The Making of Britain is a story with neither beginning nor end. Its origins are to be found in the remotest period of geological time and it will end only when

> the baseless fabric of this vision,
> The cloud-capp'd towers, the gorgeous palaces,
> The solemn temples, the great globe itself,
> Yea, all which it inherit, shall dissolve,
> And, like this insubstantial pageant faded,
> Leave not a rack behind.

The last clear break in this story came with the passing of the last ice sheets from the landscape of Britain, perhaps twelve thousand years ago. As the glaciers thawed plants, animals and men began slowly to colonise a bleak and desolate wilderness. As they did so they began to modify their environment, a process which has continued ever since and which has produced the landscape of today. But to speak of the 'landscape of today', or, for that matter, of the landscape of the eighteenth century, is to give a 'snap-shot' view of the past, creating an illusion of stability, a stability which in fact has never existed. Such a snapshot is misleading: first of all because it obscures the processes of change, and it is these processes that make history, the story of an infinite becoming, so fascinating; and secondly because it is impossible to provide an accurate and compre-hensive transect through time, whether it is of a brief moment, such as 1 January 1760, or a century or more, even if only because nine-tenths of what happened is either unknown, unknowable or not worth knowing.

This book is not an attempt to provide a snapshot of the

eighteenth century. It is primarily concerned with the infinitely varied and complex relationships between man and his environment during a period in which the pace of change was rapidly accelerating. It was Montesquieu who made the distinction between the internal, that is the social and psychological, and the external or physical milieux of human life, and it was he who suggested that the connecting link between the two was to be found in legal structures, the institutional codification of a society's relationship to its environment. A map of an open-field village is a representation of a remarkably complex structure of rights, obligations and duties governing the way in which a community of men arranged for the exploitation of their environment.

But maps also are only snapshots. They convey nothing of the movement through time that is always taking place and the changes that this movement must inevitably bring. To compare a pre-enclosure map with one drawn after enclosure is to be made forcibly aware of the impact that changes in the internal milieu of men can have on their external one. These changes are brought about by men at work and at play. Fields must be ploughed, sown and harvested, houses must be built and rebuilt, gardens and parks laid out and cricket pitches mown and rolled. Even in the most conservative societies these things are never done exactly the same way twice. Man, at work within a social framework of his own devising, is the agent of change within the landscape, so that going about his everyday affairs he writes and rewrites upon the surface of the external world and in the clearest possible terms his own autobiography. This autobiography reflects the aspirations, ideals and achievements of a society, however elevated or grubby, noble or sordid, in a fashion which is brutally frank and impossible entirely to eliminate. But in order satisfactorily to explain the patterns and processes of human endeavour we must also look at the ideas that have shaped them, and in order to do this we must often travel widely in space and in time. Thus behind a simple hedgerow, a country cottage, a mean street in some grimy industrial town, all distinguishable only by their unremarkable ordinariness, lie the modes of thought, the unconscious attitudes, the habits and the expectations of past generations, and hence much of the history of the western world. It is in this way that the landscape of Britain has acquired its incredibly rich historical density. Here in this book are the main themes in the autobiography of man in eighteenth-century Britain.

To my mother

1 The structure of Britain

When Georg Ludwig, elector of Brunswick-Lüneburg and arch-treasurer of the Holy Roman Empire, reached Greenwich on 18 September 1714, the kingdoms which, by the perverse genetics of the House of Stuart, he came to inherit, were rich, ancient, mature and enormously varied in every strand and fibre of their fabric. In the previous three-quarters of a century Britain had acquired a European reputation for political instability and judicial murder. Only the events of the last ten years, the victories of Marlborough on land and of Rooke at sea, had reversed the reputation for ineptitude and incompetence enjoyed by its soldiers and sailors. His accession as King George I of Great Britain inaugurated a long period in which massive political stability was coupled to profound social change. This political stability is suggested by the leisurely fashion in which he took up his inheritance: it was 20 September before he made his state entry into London, seven weeks after the death of his predecessor, Queen Anne, during which time power was in the hands of regents appointed by George under the terms of the Act of Settlement of 1701 and the Regency Act of four years later. Vacillation and faint-heartedness among those opposed to his accession let slip the chance which this six weeks presented. It was September 1715 before 'Bobbing John', the slippery and unscrupulous Earl of Mar, raised the standard of the Old Pretender at Braemar. Two months later he was outmanoeuvred and defeated at the battle of Sheriff-muir. He had had no real prospect of success, and George's throne was secure.

It is almost impossible satisfactorily to break into the

seamless web of history, more especially if the thread to be followed is spun from the slow evolution of the changing relationship of man with his environment, a pattern of change in which kings are less important than parliamentary enclosure commissioners, and statesmen are significant only because the wars they precipitated led to the felling of ancient woodland to build the ships which their fleets required. Much of the story of man's relationship with his environment is concerned with the processes by which he has come to master it. Even today our mastery is not complete, as an erupting volcano, a storm at sea or a river in full flood can quickly bring home to us. Nevertheless, our mastery is such that it is now necessary to go to Africa or Asia to become fully aware of the way in which men, until quite recently, have had to fit themselves to their environment. Millennia of adaptation and accommodation had, by the beginning of the eighteenth century, led to the creation in Britain of a host of communities unique in their experience and their development. In such communities the design and building materials of houses, churches and barns, the size and shape of farm-carts, ploughs and bill-hooks, the rotation of crops, the nature of manufactures, even the texture of the clothes and boots worn by the inhabitants, were the result of centuries of the most complex and intimate interaction between men and their environments at a local level. Britain at the beginning of the eighteenth century was composed of a congeries of such communities very much more loosely integrated than it is possible to conceive today.

It is because of the fundamental nature of this interaction between man and his environment, and because it has such a long history, that we must begin this account of the making of eighteenth-century Britain with some description of the topography of the island.

The geological structure of Britain upon which its regional and local diversity is based is in detail immensely complex, in broad outline very simple. The basic division is between the Highland Zone of the north and the west where the

Figure 1 The geological structure of Britain

1 The granite tors of Dartmoor. The bleak landscape of the shattered granite rocks of Hay Tor may be contrasted with the wooded valley in the foreground and the fields on the far horizon

rocks are both old and hard, and the Lowland Zone of the south and east where the rocks are young and soft.

Although the rocks of the Highland Zone are the oldest in Britain, and in the Isle of Lewis they are among the oldest known anywhere, their topography is in many respects comparatively young, since they were shaped and moulded by the glaciers of the last Ice Age, glaciers which advanced no further south than the Thames valley. The ice scooped out the lakes and corries of the Lake District, planed almost

16

level large areas of the complex fold structures of the Cairngorms, whilst the bitter cold of peri-glacial conditions shattered the granite tors of Dartmoor. As the ice melted it dumped the masses of material it had scoured from the surfaces over which it had passed to form the drumlins of the Merse of Berwickshire or the moraines of the Vale of York. The lochs of the Trossachs form a pattern of glacial troughs carved by the most powerful centre of ice dispersal in Britain, and only the moraines left behind by the melting ice prevent Loch Lomond from being open to the sea. The amount of material removed by the ice was enormous, as perhaps the structure of the land forms around Suilven in Sutherland makes clear. Aeons of geological time have been removed by the ice from the Scottish landscape, to leave behind only scattered fragments of rocks quite common in England, such as the Mesozoic sedimentary rocks of the Gribun cliffs of the Isle of Mull.

The material dumped by the ice can form heavy intractable boulder clays. In other areas the running melt waters have sorted and sifted the material into finely graded sands and gravels. In yet other areas the ice has left almost nothing save an ancient, naked rock surface, so hard that the weather of the succeeding ten thousand years has made almost no impression on it, producing only a very thin covering of soil, such as Dr Johnson noticed when he visited the Isle of Skye in 1773. The resulting differences in soil type, structure and drainage brought a human response in the form of an intricate pattern of infield, outfield, meadow, moss and bog. Surviving eighteenth-century plans of farms on the Glamis estate of the Earls of Strathmore reflect these differences with astonishing accuracy.

The Highland Zone of Britain also lies in the path of the prevailing winds, with the consequence that it has a very high rainfall, over 100 inches a year in the Lake District, western Inverness-shire, Wester Ross and northern Argyllshire. The heavy rainfall has leached out many of the soil nutrients, leaving them highly acidic, and at the same time creating water-logged conditions in which only bog plants

2   The Suilven (2,399 feet) in Sutherland. The peak is a cap of quartzite. There is a similar cap on Canisp (2,779 feet), the peak in the distance on the left of the picture. Below the quartzite caps are horizontal beds of Torridonian sandstone. Both quartzite and sandstone around and between the two mountains have been eroded by ice to expose the ancient Lewisian gneiss, thus forming a bleak plateau of naked rock and water-filled hollows

and heather can grow. The Highland Zone is also subject to strong winds, much cloud, low temperatures and little sunshine. On the summit of Ben Nevis the mean annual temperature lies below freezing point, ranging from −4.6°C in February to +4.7°C in July, conditions comparable to those of eastern Greenland. In the highest corries snow frequently lasts the summer, and a drop of only 2°C in the average annual temperature would bring back the glaciers.

In the Highland Zone it is likely that altitude has a greater impact upon the range of man's activities than any other single factor. The mean temperature is reduced 1°F for every 300 feet in altitude, and the growing season is shortened by ten days for every 260 feet. Rents on farms in middle Clydesdale of the Duke of Hamilton were reduced in 1760 according to their altitude, the surveyor using a portable barometer to determine the height above sea-level. The north and west generally are better suited to livestock husbandry than to arable farming, not least because animals can be moved, daily if necessary, away from the worst excesses of the weather. Vast tracts of upland Britain can be used only as rough grazing for hardy sheep and cattle. In the Highlands and Islands of north-west Scotland the cattle were driven up into the summer pastures, or shielings, each year, to return again to the shelter of their byres with the onset of winter, a practice which continued until 1939 in the Outer Hebrides. Similar summer pastures were once to be found in Wales and in Cornwall.

But the Highland areas of Britain are not a single, uniform inhospitable plateau. Within the Scottish Highlands there are broad differences between the West Highlands and the East, and then differences more subtle within these two broad regions. Similarly the White Peak and the Dark Peak, Dartmoor and Exmoor, the Brecon Beacons and the Berwyn Mountains, have each their own characteristics. Large areas of Highland Britain are fit for nothing but moor and bog, but when transport was difficult some land had to be cultivated and so, in sheltered glens and straths, in deeply incised river valleys in regions such as Teesdale and Swaledale, especially in south-facing situations where the valley sides are not too steep, and in favourable spots along the coasts where the cliffs do not descend precipitously into the sea, arable farming was carried on. In favourable areas of Strathspey this can reach 1,200 feet above sea level. The island of Tiree enjoys an exceptionally sunny climate, although the constant winds inhibit the growth of trees, and at Kiloran on Colonsay fertile soils have formed on the raised beaches of late glacial shorelines to make one of the most smiling landscapes of the Hebrides. The variation within the broad region of the Highland Zone is almost infinite.

By the beginning of the eighteenth century the trees which in prehistoric times had clothed all but the highest peaks of the Highland Zone had long been removed, a

3 Henfield, Sussex – the intensely cultivated landscape of southern England

process which began in Neolithic times. Constant grazing by livestock, coupled to the soil degradation which centuries of exposure to the elements had produced, meant that woodland could not regenerate. Timber was accordingly scarce and expensive. Houses had to be built of stone or turf and roofed with slates, turf or heather (see Plate 13). Field boundaries, where there were any, were of stone (see Plate 10). It is this use of local materials that gives to so many areas of Highland Britain, even today, a consistency of texture, a sense of organic unity, frequently absent from the more genial Lowland Zone.

The Lowland Zone contains as much diversity as does the Highland Zone, but in broad general terms the underlying rocks here are softer and have weathered more quickly than those of the Highland Zone to produce deeper and more fertile soils and lower, more rounded hills. The climate is less harsh, the rainfall less heavy. Indeed in East Anglia and on the chalk downlands of south-east England water can on occasion be in short supply, with profound effects upon the distribution of villages, farmsteads and hamlets. In other areas where the land is very flat drainage can be a problem, as in the valleys of the Trent and the Great Ouse where flooding after heavy rain is common even today.

However, facile generalisations of this kind conceal an astonishingly wide variety of landscapes where differences are sometimes subtle, as between the individual dry valleys of the Chiltern dip slope, or dramatic, as between the North and South Downs and the Weald. Similarly, the Lowlands of Scotland are by no means a homogeneous region, but rather a series of wide straths separated one from the other by upland formations, the Campsie Fells, the Ochill and Sidlaw Hills, which have glens almost highland in their nature. Even within so restricted an area as the Vale of Monteith there are strong local contrasts.

Such regional differences are based, as in the Highland Zone, upon differences in the underlying geological strata, and these in their turn influence the pattern of local building, to produce the warm golden stone houses of the Cotswolds, the more variegated stone work of Northamptonshire, or, where chalk is the underlying material, the flint work of East Anglia and south Buckinghamshire. Clays suitable for brickmaking are very common, but variations in their composition produce the white bricks of Suffolk, the Staffordshire blues, the brown bricks of the Vale of York or the silver-grey ones of south Oxfordshire and Berkshire. Clay soils often also carry woodland, and at the same time make excellent corn fields. Timber-framed

4 A group of thatched cottages, built of flint with brick dressings, at Monks Risborough in Buckinghamshire

5 A substantial timber-framed, thatched cottage with brick infilling at Shipton, near Winslow, in Buckinghamshire

6 A view of Edinburgh taken from *Theatrum Scotiae* by Thomas Slezer, published in 1693. The castle lies in the centre of the picture. To its left the high tenement blocks characteristic of old Edinburgh can be seen, whilst the Nor'Lock, a little further to the left, has a fringe of single-storey houses. The open nature of the Scottish countryside at this time and the pattern of runrig are apparent. On the far left-hand side is a single-storey water mill with two wheels

cottages with thatched roofs and brick infilling are the consequence.

These local and regional differences, subtle or dramatic, are apparent even today to those with eyes to see. At the beginning of the eighteenth century they were very marked indeed. This was the environment into which George I stepped on 18 September 1714. His new subjects were almost as diverse as the landscapes in which they lived.

There are no accurate figures for the population of Britain before the first census of 1801. However Gregory King, who died in 1712, made a series of well-informed estimates of the population of England and Wales in the last years of the seventeenth century, from which it would seem that the population was then about 5,250,000, with perhaps 350,000 of them living in Wales. For Scotland there are no sources at all before 1755 from which to estimate the population, and the suggestion that in 1700 it may have been about a million is no more than a guess.

These inhabitants were by no means evenly distributed. In Scotland there were particularly sharp regional differences. The south bank of the Firth of Forth was the most densely inhabited region, followed by the lower Clyde valley, the north shore of the Forth and then Tayside. The largest town by far was Edinburgh, with about 40,000 inhabitants crammed into the 'wynds' and tenements of the old town strung along the Royal Mile from the castle to Holyrood House. Next came Glasgow, with perhaps 12,000 inhabitants, followed by Dundee, Perth and Aberdeen, with about 4,000 each.

In the Scottish Highlands immense tracts of upland bog, moor and rough grazing were totally deserted in the winter and inhabited in the summer only by herdsmen and women based in the shielings. However, in sheltered glens, and along the coasts and islands the population could be dense. In the latter part of the eighteenth century there was a population explosion in the Scottish Highlands, based upon cattle rearing, the kelp industry and the potato. The population of Tiree in about 1750 was 1,509. In 1811 it was 3,186, having doubled in sixty years. The kelp industry collapsed after 1815, cattle were replaced by sheep and the potato was hit by blight. The consequences were catastrophic.

In Wales in the eighteenth century Wrexham was the largest town, with about 3,000 inhabitants. Swansea may have had something over 2,000, but Cardiff had fewer than 2,000 as late as 1801. The population of Wales seems to have been fairly evenly distributed, although some concentration of numbers in the Vale of Glamorgan and along the shores of Swansea Bay may already have been discernible.

In England London was by far and away the largest city. There may have been as many as 70,000 inhabitants of the ninety-seven parishes within the walls, and a further half million in the suburbs (see Fig. 12). London was not only the largest city in Britain, it was also the largest in Europe. Its influence over almost every aspect of the national life is impossible to exaggerate, even at the beginning of the eighteenth century. Next in size came Norwich with about 30,000 inhabitants. It was overtaken as England's second largest city by Bristol in the 1730s. Birmingham at the beginning of the eighteenth century had about 12,000 inhabitants, Newcastle upon Tyne perhaps 15,000, Leeds and Manchester about 10,000 each. Brighton, then a fishing village, had 1,500, whilst St Helens was a chapel at a country crossroads.

In the early eighteenth century the most densely populated areas of England lay to the south and east of a line from the Wash to the mouth of the Severn. In the north, especially in Westmorland and the North Riding of Yorkshire, the population was very thinly scattered, although, in contrast, the textile manufacturing regions of the West Riding and the mining areas of Northumberland and Durham were already densely populated, even by the standards of southern England. The eighteenth century saw this distribution pattern change at an accelerating pace as people moved into the rapidly growing industrial towns. This urbanisation was most pronounced, and had the worst social effects, in south Lancashire, north and south Staffordshire, the Black Country and the West Riding, but few towns anywhere in Britain escaped it entirely. In Westmorland, for example, in 1811 no less than a fifth of the population of the county lived in Kendal.

Britain in 1714 was overwhelmingly rural. Most towns were very small so that trees, hedges, corn fields, horses and pigs were all very close to people, and the harvest was a matter of serious concern among all ranks of society. Gregory King thought that there were 794 places in England and Wales deserving to be called towns, but 400 of these had fewer than 700 inhabitants. Less than a quarter of the population lived in towns, and four-fifths lived in towns, villages and hamlets of under 700 inhabitants. Some towns certainly grew very rapidly, more especially in the last two decades of the eighteenth century, but this urban growth

7 A view of Banbury in Oxfordshire drawn in 1724 when the town had less than 1,000 inhabitants. This drawing shows clearly the close and intimate relationship that existed between town and country in the eighteenth century

8 Haddington in 1693, taken from *Theatrum Scotiae*. Runrig, the absence of trees from the Scottish landscape and the close relationship of town and country are all illustrated here

can be exaggerated. In 1801, out of a total population in England and Wales of 9¼ million, only 17½ per cent lived in towns with over 20,000 inhabitants. Not until 1851 were there more people in towns than in the countryside. Change was rapid and widespread in late eighteenth-century Britain, but for long it was little more than a gloss upon a profoundly rural society.

The inhabitants of Britain in 1714 spoke four languages, of which English was the most widely used. George I himself came to read and write English fairly easily, although his command of spoken English was more limited. The 150 years which ended in 1700 had seen English come to full maturity as a literary vehicle, with an astonishing flowering of poetry and drama which was quite unprecedented and in many ways has not been surpassed since. Poets like Robert Herrick and Sir Walter Raleigh can be said to be of the second rank only in an age which produced Spenser, Shakespeare, Milton and Dryden. Before the outbreak of the Civil Wars in 1642 the drama was more truly popular than it had ever been before or would ever be again. By the end of the seventeenth century the massive baroque prose of Milton and Sir Thomas Browne was giving way to the more graceful, supple writing of Addison and the fierce directness of Swift.

A growing proportion of the population was literate, perhaps as much as a half, and demanded amusement, information, emotional experience and spiritual guidance. Much more was written, to survive in manuscript in libraries and muniment rooms, than was ever published, and only a minute fragment has any real aesthetic value. But the sheer quantity of the surviving documentation means that it is possible to see further into the hearts and minds of a greater number of men and women than at any time in the past, and to detect with a little more certainty their attitudes to their environment and to the slow changes which were taking place. During the course of the eighteenth century men and women came to attach increasing significance to Nature, a word of Protean meaning, a movement in taste which can be detected in the literature of the time, and finds reflection in architecture, town planning and landscape gardening. The deliberate search for the Picturesque brought tourists to the Lake District, and, slowly and cautiously, at the very end of the century, to the Scottish Highlands.

English, both written and spoken, preserved wide regional variations that served to underline those based upon topography. One of the strengths of the poetry of John Clare is the sense of the local-ness of his language, based as it is upon the usage of his native Northamptonshire village of Helpston. In addition the English of Lowland Scotland had its own unique characteristics, to be given incomparable literary expression in the poetry of Burns and the novels of Sir Walter Scott.

English was not, however, the only language to be found in eighteenth-century Britain. In Scotland perhaps as many as a third of the population spoke Gaelic. The boundary of the *Gaidhealtachd*, the Gaelic speaking area, began on the west coast less than twenty miles from Glasgow and extended in a great sweeping curve to within thirty miles of Aberdeen before reaching the sea in the vicinity of Nairn on the Moray Firth. This boundary was of course a zone rather than a clearly defined line, but to the north and west of it English-speaking travellers found it increasingly difficult to make themselves understood, and Dr Johnson, when in 1773 he ventured beyond Inverness, had to take an interpreter with him. Much poetry was composed in Gaelic, but Alexander Macdonald was the first Gaelic poet to appear in print, his *Ais-eiridh na Sean Chanion Albannaich* being published in 1751. The publication by James Macpherson in 1762 and 1763 of what he claimed were translations of epic poems by a Gaelic poet called Ossian aroused European interest (they were admired by Goethe) and considerable controversy. Dr Johnson refused to accept them as genuine because Macpherson would not, or could not, produce the originals.

Welsh was also widely spoken throughout Wales. Indeed

the language barrier often served to exacerbate the bad relations which existed between the South Wales ironmasters and their workers, and in 1835, when commissioners enquiring into municipal corporations visited the borough of Aberavon they found that the officers of the borough were farmers and labouring men almost entirely ignorant of English, and it was only with considerable difficulty that any information could be collected from them.

The revival of interest in Welsh had a much earlier origin and a stronger literary basis than that in Scots Gaelic. Edward Lhuyd, Keeper of the Ashmolean Museum at Oxford, published in 1707 *Archaeologia Britannia*, a permanent contribution to the study of Welsh. The Honourable Society of Cymmrodorion was founded by London Welshmen in 1751 and did much to encourage the growing interest in Welsh literature. The poet Goronwy Owen revived the old bardic forms and metres, and the first modern eisteddfod was held at Llangollen in 1789, a symbol of a movement at once literary, antiquarian and Romantic.

The fourth language spoken in Britain was Cornish. Here the story is quite different. Even at the beginning of the seventeenth century Cornish was losing ground rapidly and was spoken only in the western parts of Cornwall. By the end of the eighteenth century it was dead as a spoken language, leaving behind a number of medieval plays, a handful of songs and folk tales, some translations of the Apostle's Creed, and bequeathing to English the word 'gull'.

The linguistic diversity of George I's new subjects was reflected to some extent in the political structure of his new Kingdom. It was just before 1 o'clock in the afternoon of Sunday, 1 August 1714, that George was proclaimed 'by the Grace of God King of Great Britain, France and Ireland'. The claim to be King of France goes back to the reign of Edward III and was not finally abandoned until the Treaty of Amiens of 1802. The title to Ireland originates in Henry II's conquest of that island and the recognition by Pope Alexander III in 1172 of his claim to be Lord of Ireland. We are concerned, however, only with the first of George's three kingdoms, namely Great Britain. This was composed of three parts, England, Wales and Scotland. Wales, at least formally, was assimilated into England by two acts of parliament; one of 1536 divided it up into counties on the English model and gave it representation in the English parliament – one knight of the shire and one burgess from every county town except Merioneth; while an act of 1543 provided for the appointment of justices of the peace and for the replacement of Welsh land law by that of the English common law.

The crowns of England and Scotland were united on the death of Elizabeth in 1603 by the accession of James VI of Scotland as James I of England. A more tangible union between the two countries was delayed for more than a century until in 1707 the Treaty of Union provided for the abolition of the Scottish parliament, free trade between the two countries, uniform coinage, weights and measures and, with some exceptions, a uniform fiscal system. Other Scottish institutions, including the Scottish legal system, were left intact. Thus in 1714 Great Britain was, formally at any rate, the newest of the kingdoms which George inherited.

The distribution of political power is of particular importance for any account of the making of Britain, since it determined what men could do with their own; whether or not they had full liberty to use their property as they pleased or whether this power was restrained or directed in the interests of some public good, however conceived. Under the influence of the writings of John Locke, whose *Essay Concerning the True Original, Extent and End of Civil Government* published in 1690 states clearly and unequivocally that the chief end of society is the preservation of property, the eighteenth century was the great age of private property, almost to the extent of asserting that those without property had no rights in society. In itself this was a reaction against the arbitrary paternalism of the first Stuart kings, and in due course it provoked its own reaction. It is, however, to this tender care for rights of property that the refusal of parliament throughout the eighteenth century to legislate nationally on such matters as the lighting, paving and draining of towns or the enclosure of common fields must be ascribed. Thus do men's ideals shape the fabric of their environment.

The very accession of George I himself is symbolic of the shift of power that had taken place in Britain as a consequence of the political upheavals of the seventeenth century. He succeeded to the throne by act of parliament, not by hereditary succession, since, it was said, there were at the time fifty-seven other persons with a better claim to the throne than he had. It was to parliament that the centre of gravity of power had now moved, although it was to be long before the full implications of this movement were fully realised or worked out. Thus an appreciation of the composition of parliament is crucial for an understanding of almost every facet of the history of the making of Britain in the eighteenth century.

The House of Lords was composed of about 220 peers throughout much of the century, of whom 26 were bishops and 16 were representative peers chosen from among themselves by the 150 or so Scottish peers under the terms of the Act of Union of 1707. The great majority of the members of the House of Lords were wealthy landlords, and some were very wealthy indeed. Their vast territorial possessions, coupled to the respect which the hierarchical nature of society awarded them, gave them an influence, direct and indirect, out of all proportion to their numbers. This influence extended to the House of Commons, first of all because the nature of the parliamentary franchise in the eighteenth century meant that peers could often manipulate the choice of members of parliament through their territorial possessions and secondly because many peers and members were related by blood or marriage.

The House of Commons was composed of two members from each county, elected by the 40-shilling freeholders. This gave a fairly large electorate, perhaps as many as 200,000 at the beginning of the century, but in the absence of a secret ballot the voting could in practice be influenced, either by bribery or by intimidation, or both. Nevertheless elections could not always be rigged in this way, and so it became usual practice for rival political groups in each county to agree to share the county seats, thus avoiding, sometimes for years together, expensive and uncertain elections. On other occasions no amount of bargaining could remove the need for an election contest, and seats were won and lost at enormous expense to all concerned.

In boroughs the electorate varied considerably in its size and in the qualification for the franchise, so that no easy generalisation will serve. For England 203 boroughs returned members of the House of Commons. The total electorate was no more than 85,000, and in only 22 boroughs were there more than 1,000 voters. This meant that boroughs gave far greater scope for corruption than did the counties, and 'rotten' boroughs, with perhaps a dozen voters, were eagerly sought and carefully cultivated by the political managers of the age. Cornish boroughs, such as Launceston and Liskeard, had a particularly bad reputation in this respect.

The Act of Union of 1707 abolished the Scottish parliament. The terms of the act added forty-five new members to the English House of Commons, made up of thirty county representatives and fifteen from royal 'burghs'. This called for some skilful juggling since the Scottish House of Commons had had 159 Members chosen from thirty-three counties and sixty-six royal burghs. One seat was allocated to each of the twenty-seven largest counties, the remaining six small ones were grouped into pairs, Nairn and Cromarty, Clackmannanshire and Kinross, Bute and Caithness. Each pair had one seat, the two counties of each pair electing their member alternately. The electorate was confined to 'freeholders of the old extent', a definition much narrower than that in England and one peculiarly adapted to fraud. In 1788 there were 2,655 registered county voters for the whole of Scotland, of whom 1,318 were fictitious. The burghs were arranged into fourteen groups, each group electing one member, with Edinburgh taking for itself the fifteenth seat. The burgh councils were self-perpetuating oligarchies. Each council chose one representative to meet together with the other representatives of the burghs in its group, and these representatives then proceeded to choose the member of parliament for the group. In 1790 there were 1,289 burgh electors in Scotland, thirty-three of them in Edinburgh: it is no wonder that in 1790 Henry Dundas was returned unopposed for that city.

Supreme political and economic power in eighteenth-century Britain was wielded by parliament, and parliament, until 1832, was firmly in the control of the property-owning, and more especially the land-owning, classes. With hindsight it is possible to criticise eighteenth-century parliaments for failing to provide any central direction for the vast social and economic changes that were taking place, more especially from the 1780s onwards. However it needs constantly to be remembered that these changes were of a nature and direction that was quite unique in human history. Not even the most prescient could have foreseen their full consequences.

At a lower level to parliament power was wielded by institutions working within fixed and known boundaries, whether counties, parishes or boroughs. Such institutions were probably of greater and more immediate importance to the vast majority of those who actually lived within them than was parliament itself. Many of these boundaries were very ancient, deeply engraved into the lives of the communities which they separated, and to be changed only in exceptional and individual circumstances and upon good cause, of which administrative convenience was not one. Thus it was well into the nineteenth century, for instance, before a start was made upon simplifying the tangle of boundaries between Gloucestershire, Worcestershire and Warwickshire. The county of Cromarty, made up of some fourteen separate and detached parts, was not finally amalgamated with Ross until 1889.

Counties in England and Wales were administered by

justices of the peace, required by acts of parliament of 1732 and 1744 to be in possession of landed estates worth at least £100 a year. They exercised wide judicial and administrative powers, including supervision of the repair of roads and bridges, the regulation of wages and the administration of the poor law. The only check upon their power was the requirement that they should act within the law, although in Wales they were supervised to some slight extent by the Courts of Great Session, for which the counties of Wales were divided into four circuits, each of three counties. Each circuit had a judge who visited each of his three counties every six months.

The Act of Union of 1707 and the abolition of the Scottish Privy Council in the following year effectively demolished central government in Scotland and put almost nothing in its place. There was a secretary of state between 1708 and 1725, and again between 1742 and 1746, but in effect Scotland was 'managed', first of all by the brother of the Duke of Argyll, created Earl of Islay in 1705, and then by Henry Dundas, lord advocate between 1775 and 1783. Scotland had almost to govern itself at a local level during much of the eighteenth century. Justices of the peace were first appointed in 1609, but they acquired the power and authority of their English counterparts only very slowly. The position of the Scottish justices of the peace was complemented to a large extent by the commissioners of supply, whose first responsibility was to collect a land tax first imposed in 1667. This tax fell increasingly into arrears and became almost impossible to collect, but the commissioners themselves became more and more involved in running the parish schools and in helping the justices of the peace in their vain attempts to keep Scotland's roads in decent order. The work of both justices and commissioners was made easier, first of all by the abolition of heritable jurisdictions in 1747, and secondly by the fact that frequently justice of the peace and commissioner of supply were one and the same person and a landlord in addition, with very much wider and more clearly defined powers over his tenants than those possessed by English landlords.

In Highland Scotland power and authority rested in the hands of the clan chiefs, and society was organised for war. The chief himself usually leased out portions of his territory to 'tacksmen', frequently his kinsmen, and they in their turn sublet to as many tenants as possible, with the principal object of raising armed men in time of need. The chiefs and their tacksmen were often men of education with an acquaintance with the wider world, whilst their tenants – hardy, proud and poor – had very much narrower horizons. The ancient clan system was already, even before the 1745 Rebellion, slowly breaking up under the solvent of increased appreciation of the pleasures of urban life, in Edinburgh, in London and even on the Continent, and an awareness that this cost money which could be raised only by squeezing the tenants of remote Highland estates. The lengthy process of changing a nexus of ties of kinship and personal loyalties into the commercial relationship of landlord and tenant was accelerated by the '45 and the legislation which followed. A Disarming Act was rigorously enforced, the kilt and the tartan were proscribed, military tenure was abolished. The estates forfeited by those who had rebelled were administered by commissioners who were remarkably enlightened for their time, doing a great deal to encourage trade, manufacture and education.

We have seen already that Gregory King considered that there were 794 towns in England and Wales. Some 200 of these were boroughs, that is they were governed by a corporation composed of mayor, aldermen and burgesses, although there was in practice wide variation in both the titles and the numbers of the members of a corporation. A corporation could have extensive powers, including the right to have a civil court of law and its own Sessions of the Peace, to have a market, to make by-laws for the regulation of trade and manufacture, and to return members of parliament to the House of Commons. Many boroughs, Exeter, Ipswich and Leicester for example, owed their creation to a royal charter. Others, for example Wendover in Buckinghamshire and Wootton-under-Edge in Gloucestershire, were boroughs by prescription, that is they were, by the end of the thirteenth century, so ancient that it was presumed by the lawyers of that time that they must have had a royal grant but had lost it. Boroughs could vary enormously in their size and constitution. Some of the largest towns in England were boroughs, York, Bristol, Norwich and Newcastle upon Tyne, and some of the smallest, Bossiney in Cornwall, Dunwich in Suffolk, Fordwich in Kent and Garstang in Lancashire. On the other hand some of the most rapidly growing towns, such as Manchester, Birmingham and St Helens, were not, and had to rely upon parish or manorial organisations for such local government as they had. The borough corporation exercised its powers within known and defined boundaries that sometimes extended well beyond the built-up area of the town. The borough of Bodmin, for example, had an area of 2,840 acres in which to accommodate a population still under 2,000 in 1801.

In Scotland there were two kinds of burghs: royal burghs, established by the Crown, and burghs of barony, established by the nobility and landlords. Both were governed by a closed, self-renewing corporation. The royal burgh of Dumfries had a corporation composed of the provost, three bailies, fourteen merchant councillors and the deacons of the seven incorporated trades. In some burghs of barony the councillors were appointed by the superior lord, as at Dalkeith for example. In others they were elected by feu-holding inhabitants, as at Macduff in Banffshire which was created a burgh of barony in 1783 by the Earl of Fife with a provost, two bailies and four councillors.

Like English chartered boroughs, Scottish royal burghs included some of the largest towns in Scotland, such as Edinburgh, Glasgow, Dundee, Aberdeen and Perth, as well as some of the smallest, such as Anstruther Easter, Anstruther Wester, Pittenweem and Sanquhar. In theory the royal burghs had a monopoly of trade, both domestic and overseas, and their Convention, an annual assembly of delegates from the sixty-six towns which were royal burghs, did all in its power to maintain this monopoly. By the early eighteenth century it had become impossible to enforce as the burghs of barony, which included towns like Greenock, Kilmarnock and Hawick, drew to themselves an increasing volume of trade and manufacture. However, it was not formally extinguished until 1846.

Many Scottish burghs were quite as corrupt and as mismanaged as any in England. Indeed, in 1819 a committee of the House of Commons found that to all intents and purposes Edinburgh, Aberdeen, Dundee and Dunfermline were bankrupt.

The humblest unit of civil government was the parish, of which there were perhaps 9,000 in England and Wales, and 938 in Scotland. Parishes varied enormously in size. The parish of Weem in Perthshire had eleven detached parts. The main part covered 1,444 acres, the detached portions extended to 40,441 acres. Great Crosthwaite, in the Lake District, covered 60,000 acres, from Helvellyn to Great Gable, from Bowfell to Skiddaw, to include the market town of Keswick. At the other extreme the urban parish of St Lawrence in Ipswich measured 220 yards from east to west and 110 yards from north to south.

For the great majority of the inhabitants of eighteenth-century Britain the parish must have been the most important unit of administration in their lives. In England the parish was governed by the vestry, usually a self-perpetuating group composed of a small number of the most prosperous inhabitants with the parson as chairman. It could make orders on almost every aspect of parish life, from the allocation of the pews in church to making detailed provision for poor and elderly widows and apprenticing pauper children. It also chose the churchwardens, who were responsible for the upkeep of the fabric of the church. The vestry also 'allowed' the accounts of the overseers of the poor and the surveyors of highways, although the county justices of the peace actually appointed these officers and fixed the rates to meet their expenses.

The parish was also the unit for poor relief in Scotland.

Legislation of the Scottish parliament had made the levying of a rate for poor relief discretionary rather than compulsory, with the result that as late as 1800 only one in ten of the Scottish parishes in fact levied a poor rate. Instead, the kirk sessions, in a number of respects the Scottish equivalent to a vestry, using money raised by church door collections and fines, paid minute sums only to the infirm poor and granted licences to beg to a handful of others. Each parish in Scotland was required to establish a school, provide a school house and pay the schoolmaster's salary. In due course most Lowland parishes came to have a school, although they varied considerably in quality. They were established much more slowly in the Scottish Highlands, not least because of the difficulty of obtaining Gaelic-speaking schoolmasters. Whatever their defects these Scottish parish schools were quite without parallel anywhere else in Britain.

In addition to being the basic unit of civil government the parish was also the basic unit of ecclesiastical administration. The energy of religious life in the eighteenth century was directed into rational argument rather than emotional experience and there was considerable intellectual controversy over the fundamentals of Christianity and the justification of an established church. 'Enthusiasm' became a term of abuse. This was at least in part a reaction against the excesses of religious fanaticism of the seventeenth century.

Very many parish priests were content to perform the routine of their office, paying almost no attention to any deeper spiritual significance of what they were doing. Patronage in the church was firmly in the hands of the landed gentry, even in Scotland, and the close physical proximity of church and manor house, as at Staunton Harold in Leicestershire for example, does no more than reflect the interdependence of squire and parson. The parson looked to the squire rather than to his bishop for preferment; the squire looked to the parson for justification of the existing social order.

9 The house and church at Staunton Harold in Leicestershire. The church was built by Sir Robert Shirley between 1653 and 1665, and work on the refacing of the house was undertaken by the fifth Earl Ferrers in 1763

The parson drew his income from fees, from his glebe land, and from tithes. The tithe was a tax consisting of a tenth of the natural increment of flocks, herds, woods and fields. In some parishes the tithe was commuted for a rent charge, in others a carefully drafted *modus decimandi* provided for most eventualities. At Wavendon, in Buckinghamshire, a glebe terrier of 1725 sets out in detail the arrangements for the payment of tithe. Lot meadows were to pay no tithe. Instead the rector had first choice when the meadows were re-allocated each year. Tithe was not to be paid in kind from orchards. Instead owners had to pay a shilling a year. The tithe on 'milch kine' was set at 2½d. a

year for each cow on the commons. For sheep which had
been a year in the parish the rector took the tenth fleece,
otherwise he took a groat per score of sheep for every month
of their time on the commons. If there were only seven
fleeces, he took one, but if there were seventeen he also took
only one. The tithe on pigeons was paid in kind. Each
garden had to pay a penny a year, but if any plants, roots or
herbs were sold out of it then the rector was to have a tenth
part.

Tithes were bitterly resented and proved to be a source of
almost continuous controversy and dissension. By the end
of the eighteenth century they were widely seen as a tax
upon innovation, and the county reports to the Board of
Agriculture state again and again that the tithe was the
biggest single barrier in the way of agricultural improvement. From Northamptonshire, for example, it was reported that the collection of tithes in kind:

> operates very powerfully against the introduction of improve-
> ments in husbandry: whilst at the same time it is attended with
> very disagreeable consequences . . . as it is often the means of
> creating such divisions between the clergyman and his
> parishioners as renders the religious instructions of the former
> of little avail.

It was 1836 before statutory provision was made for the
commutation of tithes and their eventual extinction.

In Scotland, as a consequence of an act of parliament of
1633, tithes, hitherto a tenth of the natural increase of the
land, became a fixed charge, or 'teind', payable in cash or
meal by each estate in the parish. Provision was made for
the commutation of teinds at nine years' purchase, this
being supervised from 1707 by the Court of Session. Pay-
ments in kind came to an end in 1808. Glebe land was of little
significance in Scotland.

The Wavendon glebe terrier with its talk of fleeces, milk,
orchards and pigeons, may give an impression of sleek
plenty. It is, however, an impression that is misleading.
More than half of the benefices of eighteenth-century England carried with them an income of less than £50 a year,

40

and 1,200 of them were worth less than £20. The sycophancy of such poorly paid clergymen is perhaps understandable. There can have been few of the fierce independence of spirit of Mr Crawley of Hogglestock in Trollope's *The Last Chronicle of Barset*.

In Scotland the act of 1633 which made provision for tithes also laid down a minimum stipend for ministers of 800 merks, equivalent to £44 8s. 11d. sterling. By the middle of the eighteenth century the average stipend for Scottish ministers was about £52 a year, but some received as little as £20. Proposals made in 1793 to increase these stipends came to nothing.

England and Wales were further divided for the purposes of ecclesiastical administration into dioceses and provinces. Episcopacy was abolished in Scotland in 1689. The appointment of bishops, in theory in the hands of the Crown, was in practice a matter of politics. Some bishops, like White Kennett, bishop of Peterborough until his death in 1728, carried out their duties conscientiously, whilst others, like Lancelot Blackburne, archbishop of York until his death in 1743, were censured even during their lifetimes for the scandalous conduct of both their public and their private lives. Just as a fortunate minority of parish clergy were wealthy when compared to very many of their threadbare colleagues, so too some bishoprics were well-endowed whilst others were so poor that they were regarded as merely the first steps in what was in effect an unseemly scramble for preferment. The Welsh bishoprics were particularly poorly paid, and Bristol was worth no more than £360 a year, whereas Canterbury was worth £7,000 a year, Durham £6,000 and Winchester £5,000. Stipends of this size, even the smallest, meant that there was in effect an unbridgeable gulf between the episcopate and very many of the parish clergy, with unfortunate effects upon the quality of church life and practice for much of the eighteenth century.

The established Nonconformist sects, after the passions and the perils of the seventeenth century, to a large extent withdrew in upon themselves, although doctrinal controversy could be fierce and uncompromising, leading many into Socinianism or Unitarianism. Barred from grammar schools and the English universities by their religious beliefs, Nonconformists established their own academies, such as that of Philip Doddridge at Northampton, which quickly established an enviable reputation for the education offered, their best students then going on to Edinburgh or Leiden universities instead of to Oxford or Cambridge.

It is, however, possible to exaggerate the spiritual torpor of the eighteenth century. On April 2 1739 John Wesley preached his first open-air sermon to an assembly in Bristol. His message of salvation for all those who would put their faith in Christ, no matter how poor or ignorant, had an enormous impact. The social and ecclesiastical 'establishment' found his emotional methods distasteful, his theology suspect if not impertinent, and, even more important, the large crowds that he attracted, composed as they were of labourers, were seen as a threat to social order. His audiences were invariably well-behaved. It was his opponents who encouraged the mobs whilst magistrates who should have known better made no attempt to intervene. To the poor agricultural labourer, collier or hand-loom weaver he brought hope, and with it the right and the obligation to belong to the local societies that sprang up all over the country, but more especially in the industrial areas of Yorkshire, Durham, Derbyshire, Staffordshire and South Wales. To the end of his long, prodigiously active life (he died in 1791 aged 88, having travelled a quarter of a million miles on horseback) he was a controversial figure, and he has remained so ever since. It is probably impossible to arrive at a judicial, balanced view of his impact on eighteenth-century life, but the ferment of ideas and emotions that he precipitated, both as preacher and as organiser, was of profound and far-reaching significance.

The basic unit in the social structure of eighteenth-century England was the family, composed of man, wife and their children. Very little is known of the structure and composition of the Scottish family during this period, although it seems that it may have been slightly larger on average than the English family. It was very unusual to find any other relatives, whether grandparents, uncles and aunts or brothers- and sisters-in-law, living with this nuclear family. To this relatively simple, uncomplicated structure were added in the eighteenth century apprentices and living-in servants to make up the household. Even with apprentices and servants added in, however, it appears that the household in eighteenth-century England had, on average, fewer than five members. This average of course covers a very wide range of circumstances, from the elderly widow living on her own to the Earl of Lonsdale who, in 1787, was also living on his own at Lowther, in Westmorland, but with forty-nine servants to look after him.

This average of less than five members to a household also conceals a paradox: the mean size of the household was less than five, but in fact more than half of the population lived in households of six or more members, although such households formed only a third of all households. Membership of a large household was the normal experience for the majority of eighteenth-century Englishmen.

But society was not atomistic: it was not composed of thousands of discrete household units. Instead householders were linked across time and space by a complex network of ties of kinship. This kinship network was kept green because it could provide a refuge for orphans, loans for manufacturing enterprise and openings in trade and the professions. It was common practice for children to be sent away from their families to become apprentices and servants in the households of relatives. Households and kinship networks were however composed of human beings. They may have provided support for individual members in time of need, but they could also suffocate or ostracise the individual who refused to conform. Bickering, malice, violence and bullying were as common as generosity, patience and tolerance.

The household is of fundamental importance in the struc-

ture of society since it is the unit of ranking and organisation, determining the social position and opportunities of its
members. The social structure of eighteenth-century Britain
was immensely complex and no generalisations can do
justice to this complexity. It was intensely hierarchical in
that enormous importance was attached to rank, title and
birth, and yet there were no formal barriers in the way of
social mobility. James Brydges, fourth son of an impover-
ished Herefordshire gentleman, was fortunate enough to be
appointed as Paymaster to the Forces Abroad in 1705, an
office providing unequalled opportunities for private gain.
In 1714 he was made Earl of Caernarvon, and in 1719 Duke
of Chandos. Robert 'Parsley' Peel owned a farm at Peel
Fold, Blackburn, worth £100 a year in 1764. By 1794 his son,
also called Robert, had industrial plant insured for £85,370,
had spent £74,880 on buying Drayton Manor near Tam-
worth, and was a member of parliament. His grandson
became prime minister. Such stories of upward social
mobility are commonplace. At the same time the English
rules of primogeniture, under which titles of nobility descended only to the eldest son, gave positive encouragement to downward social mobility. An earl could have a
younger brother in trade and another a country clergyman.

It is customary when analysing the social structure of
eighteenth-century England to rely heavily upon the work
of Gregory King, whose estimates of population have
already been quoted. But his work upon social structure can
be shown to be inaccurate and misleading: for example, he
states that peers had a mean gross income of £2,800 a year in
1688, and yet, in 1641, 121 peers had an average of £6,060 a
year, and by 1710 three dukes, of Bedford, Beaufort and
Newcastle, had over £30,000 each. He even got the number
of peers wrong. He thought there were about 15,000 gentry
families with an average income of less than £500 a year, and
yet the Land Tax Commissioners, drawn from just this
social group, numbered 32,000 in 1702, and it is unlikely
that all the gentry were commissioners, whilst £500 a year as
their average income seems an underestimate, to put it

mildly. Nevertheless, in spite of errors and discrepancies sufficient to cast serious doubt upon the validity of his categories, his survey remains a pioneering study of the greatest interest.

At the top of the social hierarchy, and immediately below the sovereign himself, was the nobility, a small group whose wealth, prestige and influence was out of all proportion to their numbers. There were, until the last decades of the eighteenth century, about 350 English and Scottish peers, almost all connected by an intimate pattern of kinship and intermarriage. Thus Richard, third Earl of Burlington, married Lady Dorothy Savile, daughter of the second Marquess of Halifax. One of his daughters married Lord Euston, son of the Duke of Grafton, although she died before reaching 18, and a second married Lord Hartington, son of the Duke of Devonshire.

Very few, even Scottish, peers lived in conditions that could not be described as affluent, and some were very wealthy indeed. This wealth was based upon huge territorial possessions – the Duke of Argyll owned 500 square miles in northwestern Scotland – and it led to the building and rebuilding of houses both in London and in the country. The Earl of Carlisle spent £78,240 2s. 10d. on the buildings, gardens and plantations at Castle Howard. Gardens were laid out on a prodigious scale. Those at Stowe which Earl Temple left at his death in 1779 covered 440 acres. Vast sums were spent on pictures, books, statuary, dogs, horses and parliamentary elections. Large households were maintained, with gardeners, game-keepers, stewards and chaplains as well as chambermaids and footmen.

There is no clear break in the continuum which extends from the Duke of Bedford or the Duke of Buccleuch, whose gross income in 1770 exceeded £330,000 Scots, about £27,500 a year sterling, to the poorest yeoman freeholder or bonnet laird whose income may not have reached £100 a year. All shared a common characteristic. They owned land, whether measured in hundreds of square miles or in scores of acres. Many were engaged in trade or commerce, promoted manufacture, held government office, but it was to the land that they looked as the basis of their wealth and hence their rank in society, and it was to the land that those successful in business or the law turned in order to enhance their social standing, as, for example, did the banker Henry Hoare, who completed the purchase of Stourhead in 1720 (see Plates 24 and 32). The purchase of an estate could over a couple of generations give admission to the charmed circle of the country gentry and, very occasionally, to the nobility. Upward mobility of this kind was not impossible, but it was enormously expensive, since even a middling estate could cost £30,000, and they were not readily available even if the money was.

Wealthy landlords often took an interest in agricultural improvement, not least because the debts they piled up building their houses compelled them to find means to increase their rent rolls. Many of the middle rank superintended the work on the home or 'mains' farm, whilst the yeoman freeholder or bonnet laird did much of the work himself. On large or middling estates much land was leased out to tenant farmers who could themselves range from the wealthy tenants attracted to the farms of Thomas Coke in Norfolk at the end of the eighteenth century to poor cottagers, labourers, acremen or pendiclers who had little more than a cottage and a garden and had to rely upon wages or upon weaving in order to make a living.

Something like three-quarters of the population of Britain, even at the end of the eighteenth century, was directly dependent upon land, either as owner or as tenant, for its principal means of livelihood; this could mean anything from the luxurious splendours of Chatsworth House (see Plate 31), or Hopetown House, Castle Howard or Inveraray Castle (see Plate 29), to a squalid smoke-filled turf cabin on Tiree or a two-room wattle and daub cottage in Waddesdon. The span from top to bottom of the social hierarchy based on land was enormous, the contrasts beyond simple generalisations, but no clear-cut division can be made anywhere along this continuum, which was composed not of neatly compartmentalised groups but of an infinite number of finely graded interlocking circles.

The remaining quarter of the population of Britain looked away from the land to other sources for their income. Once again, however, no rigid distinctions can be made. Many landowners drew considerable sums from coal mining, government office or East India Company stock. Many yeomen farmers relied as much upon small-scale lead mining, weaving, stocking knitting or nail making as they did upon their crops and livestock, whilst many of those who called themselves manufacturers also kept a cow and some sheep and grew oats and hay. The urban/rural dichotomy, so conspicuous a feature of life at the end of the twentieth century, was at the beginning of the eighteenth only just becoming apparent in those parts of the country most affected by early industrialisation. Towns, even at the end of the eighteenth century, were very much smaller than they are today; merchants and manufacturers, shopkeepers and shoemakers, clergymen, bankers and physicians, quarrymen and fishermen were often also landowners with estates ranging from the 11,000 acres in Wiltshire which Henry Hoare the younger left when he died in 1785 to the rood of ground, including a good garden, on which in 1809 the blacksmith of Ammerton in Staffordshire had built a brick and tile cottage and smithy for which he paid 5 guineas a year in rent to his landlord, Earl Ferrers.

The overwhelming importance given to land, and to the social hierarchy which was erected upon its ownership and possession, meant that the landless, even if they were wealthy, were given a social ranking only very grudgingly, whilst the landless poor were viewed as a positive threat to social order. This meant that communities which were not directly based upon land, such as town dwellers of every kind and the professions, evolved their own social hierarchies – hierarchies which had very little significance at a county or a national level. Thus there were in most towns a number of tradesmen who were sufficiently prosperous to call themselves gentlemen, but their pretensions to gentility aroused derision and hostility among the county gentry, even though their houses were often as elegant as any country house, their sons as well-educated, their daughters as accomplished, their warehouses as richly founded, as anything within the horizons of a country gentleman.

The urban, commercial, professional and manufacturing hierarchies which were in the course of emerging during the eighteenth century had to fight hard for acceptance in a national hierarchy in which land was all important. Hence the almost ludicrous efforts of Sir Richard Arkwright to establish himself as a country gentleman, and the attempts, perhaps only half-conscious, on the part of the first factory owners to make their factories look like country houses, a delusion reinforced by the fact that before the advent of steam power the great majority of factories were built in rural settings.

Increasingly, however, and more especially after 1800, the new hierarchies of urban manufacturing and commercial communities sought acceptance in their own right and without having to make the transition to the landed gentry. The social tensions thus created were exacerbated by the appalling conditions in factories and manufacturing towns, and aggravated by cross-currents of revolutionary fervour and the fear of Jacobinism which the French Revolution had let loose. To many contemporaries revolution in Britain, even as late as 1830, seemed on occasion only a hair's breadth away.

This then was the structure of the Britain into which George I stepped in September of 1714. It was composed of a number of parts which must be treated separately for the sake of convenience: inevitably the separation out of the parts destroys something of the delicate reticulation of linkages between them, but in fact they interlocked and interacted in a thousand subtle and complex ways.

The first of these parts is the land itself, the infinitely varied pattern of underlying rocks, of superimposed soils and drift materials, the altitude and slope of hills and valleys, climate, rainfall, cloud and sunshine. Topography dictates in an infinite number of ways, both crude and subtle, the nature of man's livelihood, the design and structure of his buildings, whether he feasts or fasts.

This may savour overmuch of geographical determinism, but in fact topography is only one part of the fabric. The second part is composed of the structures which men have themselves created for the better regulation of their journey from the cradle to the grave. Since, as Aristotle recognised, man is an animal naturally formed for society, as more than one country gentleman discovered when he could not get his hired hermit to stay very long in the hermitage without which no country estate was considered complete, the relationships between individuals have to be regulated and organised, first of all into families, and then into townships, villages, towns, counties, parishes and kingdoms. The distribution of power, which is part of this regulation, decides who shall be the shearers and who the shorn, and this is reflected in the size and furnishing of houses, the extent and ornament of a park, even the building of a shire hall.

But power is much more than brute force. The structure of society must be given value and significance in a way that the vast majority of its members can accept. The close juxtaposition of church and country mansion to be found the length and breadth of England is not fortuitous. Each reinforces the value and status of the other.

It is possible, too, to trace the impact of artistic and scientific ideas, and changes in them, in the same fabric. The swift development of Palladianism from being the fad of an aristocratic coterie to becoming the norm for more than a generation by which building of every kind was judged, is but one example. The attempt to reproduce the idealised classical landscapes of the Campagna as seen through the eyes of Claude and Poussin or the words of Virgil in the depths of the English and then the Scottish countryside, is another. Torricelli's discovery of atmospheric pressure found embodiment in the steaming, noisy clangour of the Newcomen engine on Durham coalfields and in Cornish tinmines.

2 The rural landscape

Those topographical variations to be found over the land-scape of Britain which were described in the previous chapter brought with them an equally diverse range of rural landscapes. Differences, sometimes subtle and sometimes dramatic, in soil, slope, aspect, drainage and climate had created a similar range of variations in the balance between man, his needs, his resources and his environment. No-where in Britain was in an entirely natural state. Almost everywhere, except perhaps the most rugged mountains of Wales, the Lake District and the Highlands of Scotland, together with the limestone platforms of the Pennines, had been cultivated at some period in the past, even if it had long reverted to rough moorland pasture, waste or woodland. Soils in particular had been much modified by centuries of ploughing, marling, liming, paring, burning and grazing, so that by the beginning of the eighteenth century they had everywhere made at least some progress along the road towards domestication and the agricultural soils that we know today. Those who had to wrest a living from the land were well aware of the advantages physical factors could offer and the limitations it could impose. Long experience had taught them that they could ignore these factors only at the risk of poor crops, emaciated animals and consequent hunger. In Devonshire, for example, it was common know-ledge that the best cider came from apple trees growing on loam soils with a south-east facing slope, whilst the pre-judice of the farmers of Graystock in Cumberland against wheat was due to the coldness of the climate and the altitude of their lands. They knew that it would not ripen, and so there was no point in attempting to grow it.

Millennia of empirical practice, observation, trial and error had created a balance in which specialisation was based upon physical and climatic factors, a balance expressed not only through differences in the kinds of crops grown and animals kept, but also in the layout of fields and farmsteads, the design of implements and waggons, and local differences in the rhythm of the agricultural year. Agricultural specialisation today, with its emphasis either upon large-scale cereal production or else upon dairying, is quite unlike agricultural specialisation at the beginning of the eighteenth century, when it would have been very unusual to have found farms either without livestock or without arable. Even in the most mountainous areas, where the climate was at its harshest, oats were grown to provide food for men rather than animals. At Bewcastle in Cumberland, for example, it was noted in 1794 that it was very mountainous and barren, and that the chief crop was oats. The oatmeal was mixed with water and flattened out by hand to form a thin, unleavened bread called 'haver' or clapbread. Enough was baked in a day to last the family for at least a month, being stored in the carved oak bread cupboards which formed a prominent feature of many Cumberland homes in the seventeenth and eighteenth centuries. Only improvements in transport and communications could effectively break down traditional specialisations based upon environmental differences, and only wide-ranging scientific, industrial and technical developments could in due course replace them with specialisations based upon the fertilisers, machinery and genetics of 'high' farming.

Wide diversity between the regions of Britain and subtle differences within the regions means that it is almost impossible to generalise at all accurately about them. Instead it may be more to the point to look at individual farming communities within some of these regions and to watch them at work.

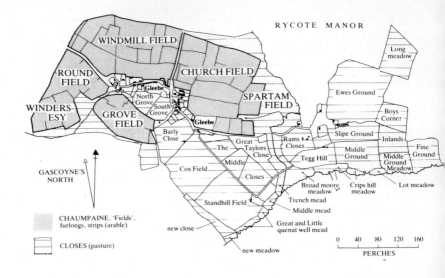

Figure 2 Great Haseley and Latchford, Oxfordshire in 1701 (based on a map from 'An Early Eighteenth Century Cartographic Record of an Oxfordshire Manor' by W. Ravenhill in *Oxoniensia*, vol. 39, 1974)

The common field system of husbandry was, at the beginning of the eighteenth century, to be found widely distributed over much of central, midland and southern England, although locally it had been much modified by enclosure so that it had all but disappeared from some districts, such as the Cheshire Plain, or from individual parishes such as Packington in Leicestershire or Haselbeach in Northamptonshire. Some parishes, Padbury in Buckinghamshire, for example, remained unaffected by enclosure until they were totally and rapidly enclosed by an act of parliament, whilst in others piecemeal enclosure had been going on for at least three centuries, modifying slowly and gradually the open-field patterns. This had been taking place at Great Haseley and Latchford in Oxfordshire, for example.

In brief, the common open-field system meant that the arable lands of a township were divided into at least two great open fields, on occasion as many as ten, although three was a more usual number. Some would be cultivated whilst others lay fallow. These fields were in turn divided into furlongs, and the furlongs into strips. An individual farmer could find his holding scattered over the length and breadth of the arable, an arrangement that must have entailed much walking to and fro from one strip to the next. After the crops had been harvested the livestock of the village was turned into the field to graze on the stubble. Meadow and pasture were often scarce. Meadow almost always lay near a stream in order to ensure a good supply of water for the growing grass, and each villager could find himself with a new strip of meadow each year, since it was normal practice in many townships to reallocate the meadow each year by lot. In so far as there is such a thing as a 'typical' open-field village then Thornborough in Buckinghamshire may serve as an example.

The traditional structure of the common field system is often reflected in the terms of the leases granted to those who had actually to make it work. Thus in 1735 Francis Fortescue granted to John Sims, a yeoman, a lease for three lives of a farm at Idbury in Oxfordshire consisting of the farmhouse, two yardlands, a traditional measure of land that could contain anything from 25 to 40 acres, common of pasture for eight beasts, sixty sheep and four horses, a barn of two bays and a garden. For this Sims paid a fine of £320, and a rent of 40s. a year. In addition he had to give two capons at Easter, pay a heriot on his death of his best beast or £5, render one day's carriage of hay with a team of cart horses and two men or pay 3s., the carriage of 100 furze faggots from Idbury Heath to the manor house or 2s., one day's reaping wheat with one man at corn harvest or 2s., and one day's raking barley or 1d. Terms such as these differ only in detail from those demanded of tenants before the Norman Conquest.

The lands of individual farms were scattered, sometimes

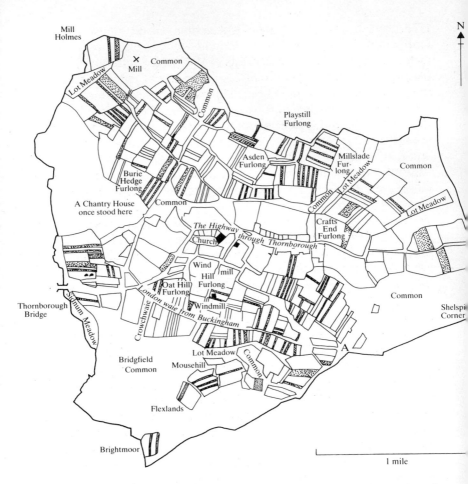

Figure 3 Thornborough, Buckinghamshire before enclosure, adapted from a map of 1613. The strips marked are those that belonged to Magdalen College, Oxford. There has been some consolidation, but the only area of ancient enclosure is that where the Chantry House once stood. There are extensive commons, and four areas of Lot Meadow. See also Figure 7

in very small parcels indeed, and consequently they must have been difficult and expensive to manage. Thus a survey made of the Manor Farm, Ashley, Northamptonshire, in

54

1778, shows that it contained 154 acres of land and was worth £145 a year. There were 29 acres of old enclosures, including the Wood Close of 20 acres and the largest single piece of land in the farm. There were two pieces of meadow of 9 and 5 acres. The remaining 113 acres were arable and grass leys. They were scattered over the three open fields of the township. In Bridge Field there were 42 acres in at least seventeen parcels; in Tedding Field there were 29 acres in nineteen parcels, including one of a fifth of an acre, and in Wood Field there were 37 acres in fourteen parcels. Such minute subdivision may have spread the risks inherent in any agricultural enterprise over a variety of soils and micro-climates, but at great cost in wasted time, energy and resources.

Probate inventories throw further light upon the activities of those who had to make a living from the open-field system. Edward Moss senior of Desford in Leicestershire died in 1712, leaving personal possessions worth £65. Desford was still an open, unenclosed township at this time, with three fields. In West Field, Moss kept eight heifers, thirty-three ewes and lambs, thirty lamb hogs, a mare and a foal. This was clearly the fallow field, being grazed by the livestock of the villagers. In Forest Field he had 2 lands of growing wheat, and in the Bull Field he had 1 land of growing peas. These were the two fields under crops, one carrying winter sown wheat, and the other spring sown peas.

The open-field system could be made to work, and to yield handsomely to those with enterprise. Another Leices-tershire yeoman, Thomas Elliott, was worth £510 when he died in 1710. He accumulated this considerable sum of money by straddling two open-field villages, Walton and Sketchley. In Sketchley he cultivated 3 yardlands and kept eighty-nine sheep as well as, very unusually, having geese worth £10. In Walton he also had 3 yardlands, together with seventy-two sheep, nineteen beasts and two swine.

Yeomen were, if one leaves aside the gentry and the clergy, generally at the apex of the social pyramid in many of those villages where the open-field system was still practised early in the eighteenth century, and their probate inventories often reveal large farmsteads, well-stocked with both animals and implements. Lewis Russell of Great Bowden, yeoman, for example, had in his house at the time of his death in 1710 a hall, parlour and kitchen, each with a chamber over, a buttery, a cheese chamber, a malt-house and a barn. He had two waggons, two carts, three harrows and two ploughs. His wheat lately sown in the field was worth £12. He had eight cows, two calves and thirty sheep in the fallow field. In total his personal possessions were worth £250 18s.

Occasionally the documents give a glimpse of the humanity behind the numbers, prices and acres. Thomas Parker, yeoman, of Little Appleby, at the time of his death in 1735 had a cow called Young Jeremy, a red cow called Parson and another called Cherry, as well as four horses, called Dick, Flower, White Foot and Dobben. His horses and cows must have been more to Thomas Parker than simply four-legged money-makers.

The term yeoman is a status indicator, a title of respect afforded to a man by his neighbours. It is no certain guide to the wealth of its bearer, and some yeomen, if their probate inventories are any sure guide, were quite poor. This means that in fact there could be considerable over-lapping between the social categories into which rural society was traditionally divided, with well-to-do husbandmen, the next category below that of yeomen, sometimes better off than poor yeomen. But to reduce everything to economic terms is to miss the nice distinctions of social acceptance based upon birth, kinship, esteem and achievement, as well as wealth, which have always characterised social organisation. Nor were yeomen always exclusively engaged in farming. George Fisher, a yeoman, of Barrow-upon-Soar in Leicestershire left personal possessions worth £147 in 1726. He had a glass decanter and some Delftware in his house, rye, peas, wheat and barley growing in the fields and three hives of bees, as well as ashes and ashballs and materials in the fields for the lime trade.

Even those generally considered to be at the bottom of the social organisation, the agricultural day labourers, could in fact show considerable variation in the range of their wealth and possessions. Thomas Marler, day labourer, of Willoughby Waterless, had in 1712 a house, parlour, dairy and chamber, four lambs and no more than £4 18s. 6d. in goods. John Smith, labourer, of Woodhouse, on the other hand, had house, chamber over, parlour and dairy, five cows, four yearlings, four reared calves, an old mare and a foal, seventeen ewes and lambs and thirteen barren sheep; in all, possessions worth £46. Clearly there were labourers and labourers!

Even at the beginning of the eighteenth century, with at least three centuries of enclosure behind it, the common field system could be found from Yorkshire to Dorset, and from Staffordshire to Norfolk. In spite of a basic underlying unity of practice no two villages were exactly alike. There was almost infinite variety of detail as the members of each community responded over time, as much to the hazards set by their own environment as to the problems created by their own past decisions. Figure 4 shows how the inhabitants of the parish of Micheldever adapted this system to the environmental conditions peculiar to the Hampshire chalklands. The parish contained two townships, Northbrook and Weston Colley, each with three open fields. The thin soils of the downs themselves meant that even in Northbrook little more than half of the area of the township was given over to arable. It was possible to cultivate small areas of the downland by paring off the turf, burning it and sowing corn in the ashes. Yields could be spectacular in the first year but then they tended to fall away very rapidly, so that after about five years the land should have been returned to pasture for at least twenty years. In times of high corn prices, especially during the Napoleonic Wars, the temptation to over-crop was on occasion irresistible, and these 'baked lands' became exhausted and derelict. Landlords were well aware of the dangers and frequently inserted clauses in leases prohibiting such practices.

The downs themselves provided common grazing for sheep during the day, with, at Weston, an area set aside for cattle. At night the sheep were folded on the arable, where

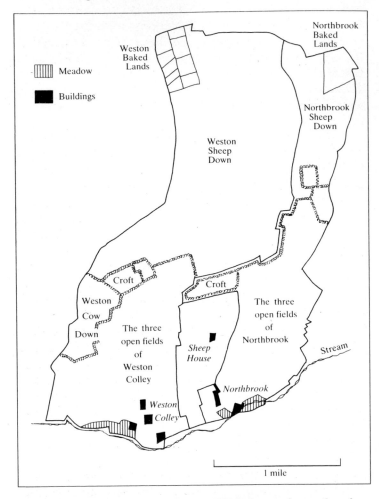

Figure 4 Micheldever, Hampshire in 1730 before enclosure (based on map from M. C. Naish's 'The Agricultural Landscape of the Hampshire Chalklands, 1700–1840', unpublished MA thesis, University of London, 1961)

58

they dropped their dung which was trampled into the soil, thus keeping the land in good heart. More manure was produced when the sheep were fed on turnips, clover and sainfoin, crops which were introduced into Hampshire from the beginning of the eighteenth century, thus breaking the need for a fallow. In this way sheep folding became an integral part of a delicately balanced rotation designed to produce heavy crops of wheat and barley, complemented by sales of mutton and wool from the sheep.

The introduction of new crops and new rotations into the traditional open-field system was a slow and uncertain process and was by no means complete even at the end of the eighteenth century. Only enclosure could bring any large-scale, radical change, but for many communities this was too drastic a solution and so they sought ever more minute and detailed regulation of their open fields and in particular of the all-important balance between crops and animals. The code of by-laws adopted by the inhabitants of Sherington in 1682 ran to twenty-six articles, nearly all of which were concerned with laying down exactly when cows, sheep and horses might be allowed into the cornfields after harvest, when they were to be excluded, when a lamb was to be counted as a sheep and when pigs were to be ringed. Similar regulations were drawn up for Padbury in 1779. They are to be found wherever the common field system persisted. They were so elaborate that they required the services, often full-time, of fieldsmen, haywards or fieldkeepers to see to their enforcement. Joseph Mayett, son of a farm labourer of Quainton, records in his autobiography how, after serving for thirteen years in the Peninsular War he returned in 1815 to his native village to serve for three years as hayward of the open fields, which were not finally enclosed until 1843.

In some townships the common field system remained almost unchanged until it was transformed, almost overnight, by parliamentary enclosure at some time during the eighteenth or nineteenth centuries. In other townships piecemeal enclosure had been going on for centuries and indeed, even within Lowland Britain topographical difficulties may have precluded the establishment of common fields in the first place. At Wendover in Buckinghamshire the parish encompassed both low-lying lands in the Vale of Aylesbury and steep hills in the Chiltern scarp. The pattern of closes and open fields in the parish in the eighteenth century reflects closely these topographical constraints. In the neighbouring parish of Halton, where similar conditions prevailed, a survey made in 1794 shows farmers coping with both sets of conditions with apparent ease. Thomas Higgs had 54 acres of enclosed arable, 22 acres of enclosed pasture and 119 acres in the common fields. Henry Baldwin had only 4 acres of enclosed arable, 22 acres of enclosed pasture and 157 acres in the common fields. A five-course rotation was recommended: fallow, barley, clover, beans and wheat.

The common field system was to be found all over Lowland Britain wherever topography permitted the laying out of fields and a genial climate allowed the wheat to ripen. In much of the north and the west of the country, however, high rainfall made it impossible to grow wheat, which simply would not ripen in the short, cool and wet summers, and a difficult topography imposed restrictions upon the size of fields. This meant that farmers had to earn their livings by raising cattle and sheep and growing oats in the more level, sheltered spots, thus creating an agricultural system which was finely tuned to the environment.

In Aspatria in Cumberland there was in 1576 an infield laid out in strips, called locally 'riggs' or dales. It contained both arable and meadow land. The only cereal crop grown was oats. This was sown in the spring, thus permitting a winter fallow, but the infield was probably permanently under cultivation. There was in addition an outfield of about 80 acres. This was divided into quarters, each quarter being ploughed and cropped in turn, the other three being used for grazing. In addition there were 4,300 acres of moorland pasture and grazing. This pattern of an intensively cultivated town or infield, an occasionally ploughed

60

outfield and immense areas of common moor and pasture is to be found all over the north and north-west. The pastures were frequently divided into two: the more accessible, lying near to the hamlet or village and generally of better quality, were stinted. The more remote and inaccessible, often of poor quality and where only the hardiest of sheep could stand being blown over with snow in the winter, were common to all. The infield was divided up into clearly marked strips, but because there was no fallow there was no common of pasture over the arable. Some townships may in fact have had more than one town field. Lancaster, for instance, had sixteen, but it seems that they were almost always cultivated independently of each other and not in rotation. At Eggleston in Northumberland there were three common fields in 1608, but of the forty-nine tenants at that time only five had lands in all three. The implication must be that each field was cropped independently, without reference to what was going on in the other two.

The absence of common of pasture over the arable meant that the strips could be enclosed with none of the opposition that this would have aroused in the Midland Plain, where common of pasture was valuable and important. Enclosure was often accompanied by exchange and consolidation of individual dales, a process known as 'flatting'. The resulting compact blocks could then be cropped individually. Enclosure of this kind was widespread in the sixteenth, seventeenth and eighteenth centuries over much of northern England, and one of its consequences was that parliamentary enclosure played only a minor part in the enclosure of arable in the north and north-west in the eighteenth century, it being very much more concerned with the common moors and wastes.

Even when enclosure had taken place it was not unusual for the grazing of the closes to be shared among neighbours. This seems to have occurred in Wensleydale, for example, where, under the stimulus of demand from the rapidly growing Yorkshire industrial towns, the grazing of dairy cattle became of increasing importance, the locally produced cheese being bought off the farms by factors who then resold it at the market at Yarm. As in Leicestershire so here in Wensleydale peasant farmers combined two or three occupations – mining and stocking knitting, for example, with the keeping of two or three cows. Over what has been called the great Pennine knitting belt, covering Wensleydale, Swaledale, Ravenstone Dale, Stainmore and beyond, the knitting of gloves, mittens, caps, jerseys and above all stockings, was probably the most important occupation after agriculture. It was from the inhabitants of these dales and hills that Abraham Dent, shopkeeper of Kirby Stephen, bought immense quantities of stockings to send south to London for the army. In 1780, in the month of February alone he sent no less than 5,000 pairs of stockings off by the carrier to London.

Piecemeal enclosure could affect not only the arable but also the waste and commons, whether stinted or not. Large areas of common could be enclosed by agreement. At Hayton in Cumberland, for example, there were 1,478 acres of infield, and 3,178 acres of common. An agreement of 1704 provided that the High Common of 2,125 acres should be set aside for pasture, whilst the Low Common of 1,053 acres should be enclosed and divided up amongst the inhabitants.

Enclosure of the pastures, whether common or stinted, led in due course to the slow extension of settlement away from the original village or hamlet and up on to the moors themselves. One by one the better favoured spots were enclosed, the pastures improved, sheepfolds were built, to be followed by barns, and then in due course other farm buildings and finally houses. By the end of the eighteenth century there were two farmsteads standing 1,500 feet up on Shining Tor, right on the Cheshire and Derbyshire border, and Whitehill farmhouse, over 1,300 feet up and just over a mile to the south-west, has 1750 engraved on the front. A similar pattern of piecemeal encroachment and dispersal of farmsteads into higher and more inhospitable districts has been noticed elsewhere. At Eggleston, in Tees-

10 Troutbeck, Westmorland, a view looking north. The stone walls rippling up the sides of the valley can be clearly seen

dale, for example, the eighteenth century witnessed new farmhouses moving gradually away from the comparative shelter of the hamlet itself, situated as it was on a fairly level, south-facing site overlooking the Tees, out on to the fells. At Troutbeck the village itself is strung out for over a mile along the eastern-facing slopes of the valley, its ancient enclosures showing up clearly on the aerial photograph as a patchwork of small, irregular-shaped fields, some of which are long and narrow. On the other side of the valley more recent, successive enclosures show up as lines of stone walls, looking like the ripples of an advancing tide, each stage marked by an isolated farmstead sheltered by a belt of trees.

63

To suggest, or merely to imply, that the north and west of England were given over entirely to pastoral farming is to be guilty of gross over-simplification. The hills of western Northumberland, for example, were characterised by scattered farms and hamlets, small areas of intensely cultivated arable and wide expanses of unenclosed pastures. In the eastern lowlands of the county, however, were to be found the large open arable fields and nucleated villages typical of the Midland Plain. A similar pattern has been noticed for the lower Dearne valley in Yorkshire, where in the eastern downstream townships such as Mexborough there were still large open fields in the eighteenth century, whilst in those further upstream, where the topography becomes increasingly difficult, the proportion of open fields declined steadily, so that at Adwick-upon-Dearne, two-thirds had been enclosed by 1737 and the strips had been flatted into compact blocks.

In the Vale of Glamorgan and the Vale of Clwyd, the Gower peninsula, the coastal plains of Pembrokeshire and Cardiganshire, wherever the terrain was sufficiently flat to allow them to be laid out, then common arable fields divided into strips on the English pattern were once to be found. By the beginning of the eighteenth century a great deal of piecemeal enclosure and consolidation had taken place, and continued to take place during the course of the century. Churchstoke in Montgomeryshire, for example, had three open fields in 1754, but they had been almost totally enclosed by the end of the century. Similarly, many common field parishes in Pembrokeshire were enclosed by agreement in the middle decades of the century.

Enclosure of this kind very frequently followed closely the existing pattern of strips, so that many fields of the Welsh lowlands, even today, are long and narrow, an echo down the centuries of a system of husbandry that has long since passed into history. Parliamentary enclosure of common arable fields was of far less importance in Wales than it was in England, and only comparatively small, isolated areas of common fields, in Breconshire and the Vale of

Clwyd for example, still remained to be enclosed by act of parliament in the nineteenth century. Even so, not all Welsh common fields have been enclosed. The strip fields of Rhosili Vile, on the Gower peninsula, are still cultivated in common even today.

Even in lowland Wales topography compelled an intensely local response to differences in soil, slope, altitude and drainage. The coastal plain of Cardiganshire and the valley of the river Teifi, for example, were a patchwork of arable and grassland, small woods, bogs and unenclosed heathland, reflecting closely the structure and the drainage of the underlying soils.

Away from the coastlands and the river valleys were vast areas of uplands given over to grazing. At the end of the eighteenth century almost half of Cardiganshire was unenclosed wasteland. The driving of livestock from winter quarters up to these mountain pastures for the summer was once a common practice throughout Wales, and persisted in Snowdonia into the 1770s. It seems to have been discontinued by the end of the century, due largely to two reasons. First of all the cattle were replaced by sheep. Since these require far less attention than cattle the summer migration of herdsmen became unnecessary. Secondly the *hafotai*, the upland shelters where the herdsmen lived during the summer, were themselves replaced by permanent farmsteads.

Nevertheless, although the annual summer migration to mountain pastures came to an end, the rearing and grazing of cattle and sheep remained of the first importance, and the droving trade into England brought relative wealth and prosperity. When Matthew Pugh, a drover of Llandyssil in Montgomeryshire, died in 1725 he left possessions worth £309. He had 665 sheep and 44 cattle, together with £10 worth of implements of husbandry and 15 acres of rye and 18 acres of 'Lent grain'. His implements and grain serve to draw attention to the way in which in Wales, as in the rest of Britain before the Transport Revolution, the rural landscape was influenced by topography. Even in the mountain heartland some grain, normally oats, had to be grown in favour-

11 A corn barn at Cors-y-Gedol, Llanddwywe-is-y-graig, Merioneth-shire, built in 1685. The slits in the walls were to provide ventilation. The door in the centre of the long wall is matched by one on the opposite wall. This gave a through draught for winnowing the grain

able localities, as the wide distribution of corn barns shows. To transport grain to remote hamlets and farmsteads was physically almost impossible and economically very expensive. There could have been very few farmers, even in the wettest and most mountainous districts, who did not grow some corn for their own and their animals' consumption.

The Scottish rural landscape of the eighteenth century was quite unlike that of England. At the beginning of the century enclosure and improvement had scarcely begun. Large areas of the countryside were almost totally devoid of trees, and the nucleated village so characteristic of midland England was entirely unknown. Improvement began very slowly in the first decades of the century and was completed in something of a rush between 1780 and 1820. It brought with it an almost total recasting of the landscape. This was the great age of the surveyor. Something like 30,000 estate maps were made in Scotland between 1700 and 1850, and the rectilinear landscape that came off the surveyor's drawing board is far more conspicuous here than it is in many parts of England.

Traditional Scottish husbandry was carried on through an outfield-infield system, a distinction of land use that may go no further back than the thirteenth century. The infield was an area of land which was under continuous cultivation. It was divided into anything between two and five 'breaks'. Each break was sown with oats and barley, sometimes with pease, rye and, in the Lothians at any rate, with wheat. Occasionally a break was allowed to lie fallow for a year, but usually the only period of fallow came during the winter months. The ploughing was done with the heavy traditional Scots plough, which was much criticised by improvers during the century, but Lord Kames declared that 'of all forms it is the fittest for breaking up stiff and rough land, especially where stones abound.' It took a team of from ten to twelve oxen to pull it and perhaps four men to manage it. In some parts of Scotland, especially the Highlands, the terrain was too intractable even for this plough, and so the caschrom and spade were used in conjunction with 'lazy beds', a system in which the strip of land upon which oats or potatoes had been placed was covered with earth from the adjacent strip, thus creating a series of narrow ridges and furrows.

The land of individual farmers was distributed runrig, that is it lay dispersed throughout the infield in strips (see Plates 8 and 12). There is a little evidence to suggest that in some parts of Scotland these strips were periodically redistributed amongst the tenants. Some consolidation of these strips had already taken place before improvement became widespread. The strips themselves formed massive ridges, sometimes 6 feet high, 30 feet across and as much as 1,000 yards in length. The heavy rainfall over much of Scotland means that much soil is water-logged, and it was often impossible to sow grain anywhere but on the tops of the ridges, the furrows being overgrown with rank vegetation that provided coarse pasture for livestock. Weeds were almost unchecked, the wild chrysanthemum, or 'gool',

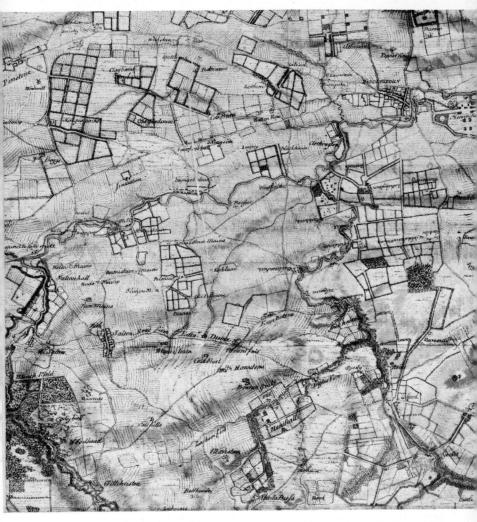

12 Part of William Roy's military survey of Scotland compiled from 1746 onwards. Paul Sandby, who drew Plate 67, was the chief draughtsman. Haddington lies in the top right-hand corner. Runrig, interspersed with moor and rough grazing, is widespread though some enclosure has already taken place. There is very little woodland and a windmill is marked in the top left-hand corner. In the bottom right-hand corner is Yester, where the formal gardens were laid out for the Marquess of Tweeddale in the late seventeenth century being particularly widespread.

The outfield was an area of land generally poorer in quality than the infield and further from the farm. A small part, perhaps a tenth, was manured by folding livestock on it during the summer months. This 'tathed break' was then ploughed and sown with oats, and cropped until it was exhausted. It was then allowed to revert to rough pasture and could remain as such for up to twenty years before once again coming under the plough. This system of shifting cultivation bears many resemblances to the 'breck' system practised on the sandlands of Nottinghamshire and the 'baked' lands of the Hampshire chalklands.

Neither infield nor outfield lay in large consolidated blocks. The nature of the terrain meant that patches of both lay interspersed with pasture, meadow, bog and peat moss, a pattern reflecting very closely the composition of the underlying soils and their drainage. In the Howe of Angus, for example, the arable was sited on the glacial drumlins, the hollows or howes between being taken up with bog and moss. At the same time, in more favoured spots, it was not unknown for outfield to be converted into infield, principally by the application of lime to improve the quality of the soil.

The infield and outfield were often surrounded with a head dyke, sometimes a stone wall, sometimes a turf bank and ditch, designed to keep livestock away from the growing crops. Beyond the head dyke lay the common moor, providing rough grazing. In the southern uplands much hill pasture had by the beginning of the eighteenth century been divided up into separate 'gerss', farms specialising in livestock husbandry. In the Highlands, however, the uplands were given over to shielings or summer pastures. These were often to be found on south-facing slopes and were rarely more than about five miles from the parent settlement, usually referred to as the 'wintertown'. Many were less than a quarter of a mile away, although, at the other extreme, twenty miles was not unknown. On Tayside shielings were often over 2,000 feet up in the hills, whilst on

North Uist some were at sea level. The shieling 'bothy' was a small oval or circular cabin made of stone and turf with a separate dairy room and an enclosure in which the cattle could be milked. The shieling grounds themselves were sometimes enclosed within a wall, and in particularly sheltered spots oats were sown. The movement from the wintertown up to the shielings could often involve the entire population and all their livestock – cattle, horses, sheep and goats – the men returning from time to time to the wintertown to look after the crops. As the demand for cattle developed during the eighteenth century so the return from the shielings, hitherto timed to coincide with the beginning of harvest, was brought forward to mid-August so that the cattle could be driven to the September fairs at Falkirk or Crieff, the first stages on their long road south to London and Smithfield market.

The land was cultivated from farms. Individual farmsteads were often loosely grouped together to form a 'fermtoun', but it was the end of the eighteenth century before anything resembling a nucleated village made its appearance in the Scottish landscape. It was said of the parish of Holywood, Dumfries, in 1791, for example, that there were neither towns nor villages in the parish, the inhabitants living in detached houses.

The farms themselves differed considerably in size and in their proportion of infield to outfield. Farms on Lochtayside generally had more infield than outfield. On the other hand, in the parish of Assynt, on the west coast of Sutherland, there were 2,202 acres of infield, 1,506 acres of shielings, 2,902 acres of natural woodland, and no less than 83,421 acres of hills, moss, 'rocky muirish pasture' and lochs. In this mountainous and inhospitable landscape there were forty-three farms. The largest was Ledbeg, with 10,813 acres, larger than the majority of English lowland parishes, but it had only 183 acres of infield. The smallest farm was Badnaban, of 49 acres, only 9 of which were infield.

A farm was often worked by a group of tenants. Occasionally these tenants held a single lease and paid their rent jointly. More often they held a specific fraction of a farm, a quarter or a third, and paid their rents separately. Yet other farms were held by a single tenant, especially in Lowland Scotland. These tenants in their turn sublet small parts of the farm to people variously called acremen, crofters, cottars, cottagers, grassmen, mailers and pendiclers. Crofters held a small piece of infield but no outfield. Grassmen had a cottage, byre and kailyard, a right to pasture but no arable land. Whatever the theoretical distinctions between them subtenants of this kind shared a common characteristic: their plots of land were too small to support their families, and so they worked for wages for the tenant farmers and were often also part-time weavers. When a tenant left his holding, renouncing his tack or lease, then he had to 'flitt', along with all his subtenants.

Subdivision of farms among tenants and their subtenants could sometimes reach ridiculous proportions. Blarliargan Farm on the north side of Loch Tay had in 1769 a total of 120 acres of land attached to it, of which 31 acres were infield and 42 were outfield. It supported ten tenants, three crofters and their families. In Assynt there were, in the two farms just mentioned, twenty people in five families living on Badnaban, and forty people in eight families living on Ledbeg. The harsh conditions of Scottish rural life meant, however, that a farm divided in this way was in fact a very successful adaptation to the environment. In an age of primitive technology and widespread poverty, the 'fellowship' of the farm provided a better chance of survival than that which would have been enjoyed, or endured, by a tenant living and working in isolation.

The main tenants of farms had to pay their rents to their landlords or superiors in a varied mix of cash, services and cain, or kind. In addition they had to contribute to the stipends of the minister and the schoolmaster, and they were also thirled to the mill, which meant that they had to grind their grain at the lord's mill and pay the tolls imposed by the lord and the miller.

At the beginning of the eighteenth century written leases were unusual, but they were gradually introduced during the course of the century, a process much eased by the passing of the Entail Act of 1770, which permitted the proprietors of entailed estates to grant leases of up to thirty-one years, and to become the creditors of the succeeding heirs of entail to the extent of three-quarters of the money spent on improvements. Leases gave security of tenure and often laid down the course of husbandry to be followed as well as restricting the number of subtenants. Leases on the Monymusk estate of Sir Archibald Grant, near Aberdeen, show tenants paying rents in oats and barley of such quality 'as will please the merchant'. This grain they then had to carry to Aberdeen at their own expense. Other items included linen yarn, geese and capons, whilst carriage services included the carting of lime, timber and slate. Tenants were also expected to repair dykes and ditches, to plant a stated number of trees each year, and to enclose and bring into cultivation a certain minimum area of moorland every year.

These finely wrought patterns of fields and farms, arable, meadow, pasture and rough grazing to be found the length of Britain at the beginning of the eighteenth century, reflecting closely local topographical differences, were echoed by similar variations in traditional styles of buildings, whether of farmhouses, cottages or barns, again reflecting in the same fashion the underlying topographical structures.

The farmhouses of Scottish tenant farmers and the cottages of their subtenants were frequently built of turf, often of stone and sometimes of alternate layers of turf and stone, and occasionally of stake and rise (wattle and daub). Walls were rarely more than 6 feet high and upper storeys almost entirely unknown. It was usual for door and window openings to be cut out after the walls were completed. The roof was supported on cruck blades, called 'couples' in Scotland. These were naturally curved timbers resting on stones about 2 feet from the ground in the side walls and curving

13 A photograph of a clachan on the shores of Loch Duich, Wester Ross, taken in about 1880

over to meet at the apex of the roof. The roof itself was covered with turfs laid like slates on wooden purlins, thatched with straw, rushes or heather, and often secured against storms by means of straw ropes. It was common for men and animals to share the same roof, the partition between them often being of the flimsiest kind, and it was usual for them to share the same entrance. Human dwelling accommodation was usually of the 'but and ben' type. The 'but' was the kitchen, entered by the common doorway. Beyond lay the 'ben', an inner room used as a bedroom and storeroom. Occasionally some larger farmhouses had three rooms, whilst smaller ones often had only one. In the Lothians and Berwickshire the garret space was used as a storeroom and as sleeping accommodation for the young men of the household. The house had a barn at one end and a byre at the other, the whole forming a building that could be as much as 40 feet long and 16 feet wide.

Only very gradually, and as part of the improvements introduced by Scottish landlords during the eighteenth century, were these traditional cottages replaced by more sanitary, more regularly built, two-storey farmhouses, and the livestock banished to separate stables and byres built round a courtyard (see Plate 19). A survey of the barony of Lasswade near Edinburgh made in 1694 reveals some tenants in possession of two-storey farmhouses with glass windows and with ancillary buildings set round a farmyard, but it seems very likely that these were unique in Scotland at this date.

Longhouses, in which human beings and their domestic livestock lived in the same building, had once been common over most of Britain, but by the beginning of the eighteenth century they were largely confined in England to Devonshire, the Lake District and the Pennines. In England, unlike the Scottish longhouses just described, it was usual for the building to be divided between animals and men by means of a cross passage. Such longhouses continued to be built in Devonshire down to the end of the seventeenth century, and thereafter they were much altered and modified to improve living standards. At about this time, however, and through much of the eighteenth century a large number of long houses were built in the Lake District. Here the separation between men and animals becomes even more pronounced and they often have their own entrances. The Lake District longhouse had a distinctive and massive chimney and fire hood, with a fire window on the adjacent wall. Here on the hearth a peat fire was kept burning night and day, and there is a well-authenticated account of one such fire being kept burning for well over two hundred years.

Even later than the longhouses of the Lake District are the laithe houses of the West Riding, built in considerable numbers from the end of the seventeenth century to the end of the nineteenth. Here a byre, with a hay loft over, was attached to dwelling accommodation, but men and animals had their own entrances to their respective parts of the building.

Longhouses are a striking example of the close adaptation of men's needs and capacities to particular local circumstances. They appear to be especially appropriate in regions of pastoral farming, and some, notably in Devonshire, were clearly the property of fairly prosperous men. But they did not develop, or persist, in every pastoral region. In

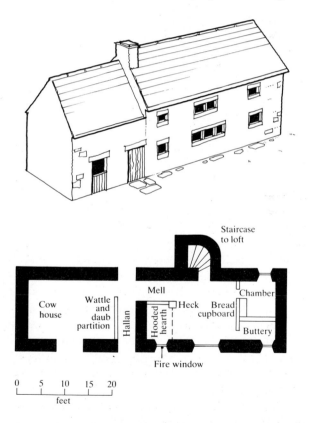

Figure 5   A Lakeland longhouse in the early eighteenth century

75

Swaledale, Wensleydale and Wharfedale they are unknown; instead the field barn evolved. This was a barn, with a hay loft over, isolated in the fields at some distance from the farmstead. It is this purely local response to broadly similar problems that gives to the fabric of Britain, even over a comparatively brief span of years, its incredibly rich density and diversity, making the historian who would attempt to grasp something of this richness and diversity seem at times less than convincing.

In Lowland England the range and variety of traditional farmhouses and cottages is immense, not least because here were the most prosperous parts of the country and those most open to continental influences. The wealth of the Kentish yeoman was proverbial, and found its expression in some of the finest houses ever built anywhere. One of the most splendid examples still surviving is Synyards at Otham built in the late fifteenth century. It would be a long time before its opulent self-assurance would be matched anywhere else at this level in society.

Houses such as Synyards were firmly rooted in a vernacular tradition of building that has its ultimate origins in the early medieval centuries. By the opening years of the eighteenth century this tradition was under attack, and this attack was coming from two directions.

First of all the changes in polite architecture at the country mansion level which we shall be discussing in the next chapter gradually and almost imperceptibly percolated down the social scale, via masons' yards and carpenters' workshops and, after 1682 with the publication of Joseph Moxon's *Mechanick Exercise*, through pattern books. These books gave examples of the new fashionable styles in ornaments, mouldings, window frames and doorways, together with details of the classical orders, so that country builders were gradually introduced to cornices and pilasters, architraves and entablatures, and the niceties of Doric, Ionic and Corinthian. Many of these details were clumsily applied, but there were two innovations which were of greater practical importance. First there was an increasing search

14 Synyards, Otham, Kent – one of the finest surviving late fifteenth-century timber-framed houses. The hall was floored over in about 1603, and the attic was floored and a dormer window inserted in 1663

for symmetry of façade. Synyards would by the end of the seventeenth century have been considered old-fashioned because its door was not in the centre and its windows were of different sizes. Newly built farmhouses and cottages were from now on given a regularity of external appearance quite at variance with the old traditions. The second practical innovation was the adoption by country masons and builders of the idea of the 'double pile' house. Hitherto the rooms of farmhouses and cottages had extended the width of the building, and it was possible to make houses larger only by adding rooms at either end or as wings. By the end

77

15 Sycamore Farmhouse, Hopton, Derbyshire – an eighteenth-century farmhouse with a regular façade and Venetian windows in the central bow

of the seventeenth century it had become usual practice to build houses which were two rooms deep, the rooms connected by passage ways and corridors.

The second attack on the vernacular tradition came from the rising standards of comfort and amenity which were apparent in very many districts of Lowland Britain from the last half of the seventeenth century. By the end of the century village shops were stocking tobacco and sugar as a matter of course. New tastes developed which called for changes in the functions of rooms. The hall, once the principal room in the house, became only an entrance passage and the most convenient place in which to build the staircase. The kitchen, even in the seventeenth century often a separate building a short distance from the house because of the fire risk, became an integral part of the house. First-floor rooms ceased to be miscellaneous store rooms and became properly and fully furnished bedrooms. The parlour was no longer a ground-floor sleeping room. Probate inventories show prosperous yeomen farmers sitting in their parlours in Russian leather chairs, drinking tea from china cups, their glazed windows decently curtained, a coal fire blazing in a hearth furnished with brass fire tongs, whilst a long-case clock ticked somnolently in one corner of the room.

Standards of comfort were increased by changes in plan and in materials. The introduction of the 'double pile' plan meant greater privacy for individual members of the family. Windows were glazed as a matter of course, and the sash window, introduced from the Netherlands at the end of the

16 A sixteenth-century jettied house at Winslow, Buckinghamshire, with brick nogging arranged in a herring-bone pattern in the gable end

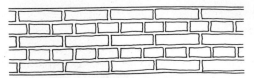

English Bond: alternate courses of headers and stretchers, giving a very strong bond.

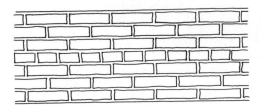

English Garden Bond: has either three or five courses of stretchers to one course of headers.

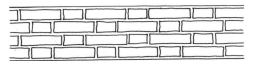

Flemish Bond: Courses of alternate headers and stretchers. Not so strong as English Bond, but more economical. Introduced into England in c.17, although Flemish stretcher bond, in which courses of alternate headers and stretchers are separated by several courses of stretchers only, was in use from mid c.17.

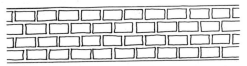

Header Bond: Courses of nothing but headers, Expensive because it used so many bricks, it was used mainly for decorative work and for curved walls. Its great strength meant that it was also used for engineering work.

Figure 6 Varieties of brick bonding in use in the eighteenth century

seventeenth century, spread very quickly. Cleanliness and warmth increased when brick became the usual building material over much of Lowland England, except on the lime-stone belt from Dorset into Lincolnshire where stone became the normal material. The wattle and daub technique used in many timber-framed houses and cottages was replaced by brick nogging, often in a herring-bone pattern, providing some of the most attractive textures in towns and villages even today.

By the end of the seventeenth century house builders had learnt to use brick on its own, without the supporting crutch of a timber frame. Many used it with skill and virtuosity. Brick was cut and rubbed to provide ornament of every kind, even the capitals of pilasters, the work being so fine that it is almost impossible to detect the joints between the bricks. Different coloured bricks were used to provide contrast, and to pick out doors and windows. Different bonds were employed – English, English Garden and Flemish – to exploit the decorative possibilities in the patterns thus created. When the bricks were of the same colour the result is quiet and subdued. When one colour is used for the headers and another for the stretchers the result is often very pleasing, sometimes bizarre, but never monotonous. Many windows were certainly blocked up after the imposition of the Window Tax in 1696, but blind windows were also used for decorative purposes.

It is important, however, that we should not exaggerate the range, extent or pace of these changes. A newly built well-to-do farmer's house might incorporate them all, but a great deal of patching, facing and rebuilding also went on. A new wing might be added, window frames replaced, earthen floors remade in brick or wood, a timber-framed façade faced with brick, but the medieval or Tudor shell of the house still remained. Brick did not everywhere replace traditional building materials. Clay lump, that is unbaked bricks of clay two or three times the size of fired bricks, continued to be used in Suffolk, Norfolk and Cambridgeshire. Over a hundred examples still survive in the

Solway Plain of the traditional clay-walled houses of Cumberland, and there are still numerous cottages in Haddenham in Buckinghamshire where the wichert, made of a local chalky clay, is as sound as when it was first erected, three hundred years ago.

Finally, we should not forget the one- or two-roomed cabins, often built of turf, and sometimes partially sunk in the ground, which were the homes of the very poorest sections of the community. Insanitary, poorly heated, badly ventilated and over-crowded, they were as far removed from the comfort of a newly-built farmhouse as it was possible to be. They persisted in some districts of Lowland Britain until well into the nineteenth century.

We must not underestimate the achievements of traditional agriculture. It established a fine, subtle balance between environment and technology. Charles Vancouver, writing in 1808, had to admit that the common Devonshire plough, made for 15s. by a hedgerow carpenter, was far superior in its performance to what might be expected from the very rude appearance it made. Local breeds of sheep and cattle were often admirably adapted to local conditions. The Exmoor sheep was extraordinarily hardy: it had to be, to withstand the Exmoor winters. Over much of Lowland Britain, where the grain harvest was the first consideration and it had to be brought home from comparatively level open fields, the four-wheeled farm waggon, taking six months to make and costing anything between £20 and £40, was to be found on the farms. They were unknown in hilly and mountainous regions, first of all because the grain harvest was of lesser significance and so there was no call for them, and secondly because wheeled vehicles were difficult to manage on steeply sloping ground and would easily topple over. A sledge was much more suitable.

Change took place slowly within the patterns of the traditional rural landscape and the patterns themselves have their own history. Farm waggons appeared in England in the sixteenth century. Open fields in the Welsh lowlands replaced older, Celtic, systems of husbandry in the years

82

after the Norman Conquest. Scottish runrig, as we have seen, may be no older than the thirteenth century. The origins of the open-field system in England are a matter for some controversy but it also may not have reached its full maturity before the thirteenth century.

To describe the traditional patterns of husbandry as 'systems' may suggest that they had an iron rigidity that was inimical to all change. This is not so. The long-term decline in grain prices that took place throughout Britain generally during the seventeenth and the first half of the eighteenth century compelled more and more attention to methods of increasing production as one way to offset falling incomes. Enclosure was one answer, and it was certainly widespread over much of Lowland Britain. The new closes could be used for industrial crops such as woad, madder, saffron or tobacco, or they could be laid down to pasture for sheep and cattle. Another answer was the insertion of new crops into the traditional rotations without going to the expense and the risk of enclosure.

Nevertheless, when every allowance has been made for its achievements, traditional agriculture was undoubtedly rigid and wasteful, its structures inimicable to good husbandry. Change would have to be radical and upon a large scale if there was to be any real improvement in standards of husbandry, and such change, when it came, would bring equally radical change into the landscape as a whole.

3 Rural change

Farming covers a very wide range of functions, both managerial and manual, and they all call for considerable skill. The process of change across these functions is little understood, even today, but it is clear that purely economic considerations play only a part, and not always the major part. The temperament, age, education and background of farmers are equally important in explaining the differences between farms, and great weight must also be given to the influence of a farmer's neighbours. All of these factors, which are discernible today, were also present in the eighteenth century, and the history of Mr Pringle of Coldstream in Northumberland shows them all at work together. He had been a surgeon in the army, and in about 1756 he introduced the cultivation of the turnip into his district, but none of his neighbours would follow his example. It was only when Mr Dawson, described, significantly, as an 'actual' farmer, adopted the system that it began to make headway. At first his practice was also ridiculed – by the old, the ignorant and the prejudiced – but his superior crops and profits soon made converts.

Much innovation came from wealthy landowners who could afford to experiment and to take the risks that experiment entailed. As John Holt, writing in 1795, noted of Lancashire farmers 'the hazards they have to encounter, from seasons, and other causes, leave little room for trials of uncertain experiments.' Charles Vancouver made much the same kind of remark about Devonshire: 'in truth the farmer has by far too much at stake to be easily seduced from the course of husbandry pursued by his forefathers.' Thomas

Coke of Holkham undoubtedly took a keen interest in the administration of his Norfolk estates and had as shrewd an eye as any for the finer points of a good cow or sheep, but his Park Farm made a profit in only four out of the ten years between 1817 and 1826. The losses were the price he paid for his reputation as an improving landlord and the standing and influence in county politics that it brought him. John Curwen was an active propagandist for agricultural improvement both in practice (his farm at Schoose, near Workington, was a model of its kind), and by precept. He wrote and published on the subject and founded an agricultural society, but it was only after he married an heiress that he could afford to become an agricultural improver, his farm becoming his favourite hobby.

The neighbours of such enthusiasts as Curwen were often reluctant to adopt new projects uncritically, and frequently show a hard-headed realism in taking up only those improvements which they were sure would pay. George Culley of Glendale in Northumberland, for example, achieved a national reputation as a breeder of sheep, and he made a great deal of money by letting out his rams. His neighbours cannot fail to have been impressed by his evident prosperity, but they were not impressed by all of his ideas. He continued to favour oxen for ploughing when his neighbours were switching to horses, and his attempts to introduce water meadows into Northumberland were quite unsuccessful. A reluctance to change may have been based upon a shrewd assessment of the likely success of some new scheme within the context of local conditions of soil and climate rather than upon ignorance or stupidity or a disposition to reject a proposal simply because it was new, something which Arthur Young called 'the sleep of so many countries'. Change is not necessarily always for the better, nor is it always seen as desirable or beneficial, and in any case there were so many new ideas floating about at the end of the eighteenth century that it must have been very difficult to tell the good from the bad. Any change has an inherent risk of failure, and eighteenth-century yeomen farmers had too much to lose to go chasing after every hare-brained scheme of some wealthy gentleman would-be agricultural improver with more money than practical experience.

That new crops and new techniques could spread quickly among yeomen, husbandmen and cottagers once they had been shown to be worthwhile is apparent from the speed with which the cultivation of tobacco swept through Gloucestershire in the seventeenth century, or the potato through the Highlands of Scotland in the late eighteenth century. Similarly in Herefordshire the use of clover and the construction of water meadows spread very rapidly in the seventeenth century, but it was the very end of the eighteenth before farmers on the light soils around Ross were finally convinced of the value of turnips as a full course in an arable rotation, and then they rapidly replaced their traditional Ryeland sheep, which yielded a fine fleece, with a turnip-fed breed that gave a heavier but coarser one.

Agricultural improvement has a very long history. Much small-scale change had already taken place long before the enthusiasm of a comparatively small number of wealthy landlords made it fashionable. Farmers were aware in the thirteenth century of the importance of bringing fresh seed and livestock into their farms, and long before the end of the seventeenth century they were travelling widely in search of new strains. Edward James, who lived at Kinvaston in Staffordshire at the end of the seventeenth century, bought his cattle from Newcastle under Lyme, Stafford, Eccleshall, Wolverhampton, Cannock, Bromley, Brewood, Stone and Newport. Albeit unconsciously he was exploiting the possibilities of hybridisation rather than following the more static policy of Robert Bakewell and those who followed him of fragmenting the gene pool among uniform breeds in order to maintain established standards. The minute book of the commissioners for the Northamptonshire estates of the Duke of Grafton shows them paying careful attention to crop rotation, including the sowing of turnips, clover, ryegrass, trefoil and sainfoin, the repair of farm buildings and the terms of leases in the 1720s, a quarter of a century before Thomas Coke was born. It is very easy to be mesmerised by the Norfolk experience, something partly due no doubt to the skilful propaganda of its advocates, but it was by no means suitable for every district, as Arthur Young noted: 'One fault', he wrote, with a touch of acerbity unusual for him, 'in the husbandry of the county and of Norfolk farmers when they move into very different districts, is that of being wedded too closely to practices which derive their chief merit from a right application to very dry or sandy soils.'

Landed proprietors ranged from the cottager owning no more than a garden to the Dukes of Bedford and Buccleuch, whose landed estates would have aroused the jealousy of many a petty German prince. The larger the landed estate then the more scope there was for introducing change and the deeper the purse to pay for it, and the more complex, professional and efficient was the estate organisation that conceived, nurtured and developed that change. Many country gentlemen with an estate of under 1,000 acres managed it for themselves. The great landowners required a body of full-time officials, officials whose skill and degree of specialisation develop noticeably during the course of the century, and whose advice was increasingly sought and relied upon by their employers.

Thus as early as the 1720s the Northamptonshire estates of the Duke of Grafton were managed by a committee composed of Colonel Whitworth, Mr Blythman, Mr Sherd, Mr Watlington and Mr Walter. They met as occasion required, both in London and in Northamptonshire. They decided the terms of leases and the repair of farm buildings. When the enclosure of Grafton itself was being planned it was Mr Blythman who waited upon the bishop of Peterborough to negotiate suitable terms for the enclosure of the glebe. The duke himself attended their meetings from time to time and it was he who took the final decision in difficult or controversial matters. When the surveyors for the enclosure of Grafton complained that they could not continue to work at the agreed fee of 6d. an acre because the common fields lay in such small parcels, making it very difficult to measure and map them, their case was referred to the duke and it was he who consented to an increase in the fee. When the enclosure was complete they rode over the new fields and deliberated long over the most appropriate crops and rotations for each.

The Dukes of Argyll owned more than 500 square miles of Argyllshire in the eighteenth century, in addition to estates in Dunbartonshire, Clackmannanshire and West Lothian. The fifth duke, John, who died in 1806, in particular took a minute interest in the administration of his vast estates. He had chamberlains for Mull and Morvern, for Tiree, Argyll and Kintyre, as well as a receiver-general in Edinburgh. His Grace issued detailed instructions to his chamberlains in the October of each year, when they assembled at Inveraray Castle to clear their accounts, and he expected an equally detailed reply in the following year. He was very well aware of the enormous problems that mounting population pressure was creating in the Scottish Highlands, and did all that he could to mitigate them. In 1771, for example, he wrote that the island of Tiree was overpopulated, and that the farms had far too many tenants, subtenants and cottars. He wished to relieve the farms of these 'supernumeraries' but he had no inclination to subject them to any sort of distress. He would encourage them to settle in a fishing village which he proposed to establish. He ordered a quay to be built at Scarinish, the first in the island. He brought in a blacksmith and a cartwright. He ordered the enclosure with stone dykes of two of the three commons on the island. He encouraged the sowing of flax and insisted that part of his rent should be paid in linen yarn, which was then exported to a linen factory at Dunoon.

In fact the Dukes of Argyll spent most of their time in or near London, rarely passing more than a month or two each year at Inveraray Castle. Nevertheless they maintained a firm grip on estate administration, and it is due to the immense amount of paper work that their absence engendered that we know so much about the contribution they made to the profound changes that took place on their estates in the eighteenth century as they moved people from the countryside into new towns and villages, enclosed, dyked and drained lochs and mosses, built roads, bridges, schools, harbours and inns, established industries and planted trees by the tens of thousands in the hitherto largely open Scottish countryside.

Indeed it is often due to the absence of the landlord from his estates that we know so much about his attempts to improve it, as a constant stream of letters would pass between him and his steward, bailiff, factor or gardener. Sir Marmaduke Constable of Everingham in Yorkshire spent the years between 1730 and 1744 on the Continent, since he was a Roman Catholic and as such he was excluded from the wide range of social and political activities open to his Protestant peers. In spite of his long absence from his estates he was, and remained, thoroughly familiar with every facet of their administration. He seems to have known every tenant, and every building, tree, ditch and field of their farms. He entrusted the care of his estates to Dom John Bede Potts, OSB, who spent most of his time at Everingham, with a subordinate steward, Thomas Champney, in charge of Sir Marmaduke's Lincolnshire estates. Administration at a distance created its own problems. In November 1732 Potts reported that Daniel Decow's house was in need of repair. In June 1733 he wrote that it was nothing but Providence that preserved the inhabitants' lives as it was a wonder that it had not fallen down. Not until January 1737 could he write that it had at last been repaired.

The impact of the landlord upon his estate clearly depended upon a number of factors: the size of the estate and hence its resources and the degree of full-time professional personnel such as stewards, land agents, surveyors and lawyers needed to run it; whether or not he himself was resident for all or a greater part of the year; and finally the extent of his own personal involvement in the management of the affairs of his property. This last was often provoked and sustained by the pressure of debt and the need to

17 This house at Great Limber is typical of the architectural style adopted for many of the Brocklesby estate buildings in the first part of the nineteenth century

increase estate income by raising rents on improved farms, by opening mines, the commercial exploitation of woodland and the systematic development of urban and suburban properties. The debt itself was often incurred by expenditure on the very improvements which were to pay it off, as well as on the building and rebuilding of country houses, on horses, gambling and even more reprehensible pleasures.

As the Spirit of Improvement made its presence ever increasingly felt so the impact of a landlord upon his estate became ever more marked and pervasive. By the end of the eighteenth century, for example, the first Baron (1748–1823) and the first Earl of Yarborough (1781–1846) had amassed an estate of over 55,000 acres, centred on Brocklesby, in Lincolnshire. They carried out a great deal of improvement to the farms, villages and cottages on their estates, many being rebuilt in a quite distinctive and individual style using bricks made in kilns on the estate. The style of these estate buildings has, not inappropriately, been called 'rural Gothic'. Farmhouses and cottages were often given a great deal of rather fussy ornamentation. Gable ends were decorated with carved barge boards, posts and finials. Windows were provided with drip mouldings which were of no practical use because eaves were so wide. Doors were panelled and studded with nails, and chimneys were often elaborately ornamented. Houses and buildings at the centre of the estate were usually more elaborate than those further away. An entirely new landscape was created, a landscape with its own distinctive style and one in which it is very difficult to trace any substantial vestige of its medieval predecessor.

The Holkham estates in west Norfolk are similar to those at Brocklesby in Lincolnshire in that the landscape created there by Thomas Coke in the last years of the eighteenth century has all but submerged the earlier medieval landscape.

When Thomas Coke succeeded to his inheritance in 1776 his estate covered just over 30,000 acres. Enclosure and improvement had been going on steadily since the beginning of the century, sometimes by means of a private act of parliament, sometimes by the systematic buying out of small proprietors. At the same time large farms were being created. Edmund Skipton held a farm of 1,000 acres in Fulmodestone in 1707, paying £300 a year rent. There were, however, still large areas of unenclosed common land remaining in 1776, much of it inherently poor quality. Coke spent a great deal of money on consolidating and enclosing the estate, and then on the improvement of the land. At Fulmodestone again, the Great Common covered 556 acres. At its enclosure Coke received 406 acres. This had then to be clayed, drained, divided up into fields and provided with fences and access roads. Between 1790 and about 1820 there were some thirty major building and rebuilding projects on the estate as new farmsteads were brought into existence on the newly reclaimed lands, and old farmsteads were modernised. Grenstein Farm, for example, in Tittleshall, was carved out of reclaimed common and marshland in about 1800. The actual farmhouse and farm buildings were built of locally made brick and roofed with locally made pantiles. The farmstead was sited in the middle of its lands and given a new access road. The farmstead still remains, with its barns, stables, hay house, cowhouse, piggeries and yards. In this way an entirely new landscape was brought into being, the creation of one generation of men, and one that still bears the unmistakable ethos of the age that created it.

It would be misleading, however, to suggest that it was only great landed proprietors who were interested in enclosure and improvement, or even that all of them were. Seventeenth-century articles of agreement to enclose, drawn up by communities of peasant farmers, so frequently give the monumental inconveniences of the open-field system and the quarrels and disputes that it engendered as the principal reason for enclosure that we must believe that in many cases this was indeed a genuine reason. In contrast, the third Duke of Bridgewater was so immersed in the development of his Lancashire coal mines and the building and financing of the Worsley canal that he had neither the time nor the money to develop his Buckinghamshire estates, and so villages like Ivinghoe, Cheddington, Edlesborough and Pitstone remained unenclosed until long after his death.

The Holkham and Brocklesby estates are but two examples of the process of change that was transforming many parts of Britain at an accelerating pace over the course of the eighteenth century. But the extent of this change must not be exaggerated. The new landscapes of the Lincolnshire Wolds and of West Norfolk were the consequences of factors working within purely local and regional constraints. Only during the course of the eighteenth century were the agricultural practices developed that could turn their thin, poor soils from sheep walks and rabbit warrens into highly productive arable farms and fields. The rich diversity of the British landscape means that in many other parts of the country landlords, however rich and powerful, had to be content with a far less radical redrawing of the landscape. In Buckinghamshire, for example, the Marquess of Buckingham had as large an estate as that at Brocklesby or Holkham, but the pattern of evolution on the heavy clays of north Buckinghamshire gave him far less scope for large-scale landscape replanning. Many villages had a long history of piece-meal enclosure, and so parliamentary enclosure was often no more than a tidying-up process. There were no large heaths or commons. None the less where parliamentary enclosure did take place upon the Marquess's estates, as at Maids Morton or Thornborough, the effects could be far-reaching.

The act for the enclosure of Thornborough was passed in 1797 and the award by the parliamentary commissioners appointed to carry out the enclosure was signed and sealed in 1800. In other words the enclosure itself was completed fairly expeditiously. Occasionally there could be widespread opposition before the passing of the act, and prolonged delays between the passing of the act and the sealing of the award. At Quainton, also in Buckinghamshire, opposition held up the passing of the act for almost forty years – from 1801, the date of the first petition to parliament for an act, to 1840, when it was at last passed. At Meltham in Yorkshire the actual enclosure itself was a lengthy, expensive and bitterly contested affair: the act was passed in 1817; in 1830 an amending act was necessary to appoint auditors of the commissioners' accounts, one of whom was in prison for debt, and it was 1832 before the award was finally completed.

When the parliamentary enclosure commissioners had completed their work, and all the evidence points to the fact that the great majority of them did their work scrupulously fairly and without unnecessary expense, each proprietor found himself in possession of a consolidated block of land in place of his scattered strips in the open fields. These blocks had then to be enclosed with hedges and ditches. This was to be done at the expense of the individual proprietors, and the commissioners in their award would lay down responsibility for each particular length of fencing. The act frequently prescribed how the boundary fences were to be constructed. The act for Stewkley, also in Buckinghamshire, passed in 1811, required the fencing to be quickset hedges, ditched on one side, with a substantial post and rail fence on both sides, this fence to be maintained until the hedge had become well-established. It was usual to plant hawthorn in the new hedges, although in Worcestershire crab and holly were also used. In contrast, great difficulty was found in establishing hawthorn on the dry soils of the Hampshire chalklands, and so dead fences, of hazel rods, were widely employed. Nurseries were established all over the country to supply the tens of thousands of seedlings that were required. In October of 1800 the Marquess of Buckingham paid 6s. 6d. per thousand for 49,000 quicksets for the enclosures at Weston Turville, and this is but one bill for one proprietor. Mr Billingsley, on his farm at Ashwick Court, Oakhill, in Somerset, is said to have planted 1½ million hawthorn seedlings.

It was left to the individual proprietor to divide up and fence his block of land as he wished. This could take several years to complete and be very expensive. The ½d. a perch that the Marquess of Buckingham paid on three occasions for the weeding of 1,237½ perches of quickset hedge at Thornborough probably meant very little to his lordship, but to a small proprietor it could be a considerable sum indeed, and some undoubtedly sold land in order to meet the heavy expenses that enclosure entailed, while some certainly sold out entirely, but enclosure did not bring any mass exodus from the land. Indeed enclosure could create a demand for labour for years to come. Hedges had to be planted and then weeded, the protective fences had to be erected, painted and then maintained, field gates had to be made and hung, ditches had to be dug and then kept scoured, roads had to be laid out, the new farms that appeared in the newly enclosed fields had to be built. It could take ten to fifteen years for the new landscape to mature, and then only after the expenditure of tens of thousands of pounds, of which the cost of obtaining the act and meeting the expenses of the parliamentary commissioners was only a part.

Figure 3 (p. 54) shows Thornborough before enclosure. Figure 7 shows the same village after enclosure. To compare the two maps is to discover just how radical the change has been. Roads have been straightened and more clearly defined. The areas of common land and the open arable fields

Figure 7 Thornborough, Buckinghamshire after enclosure in about 1800

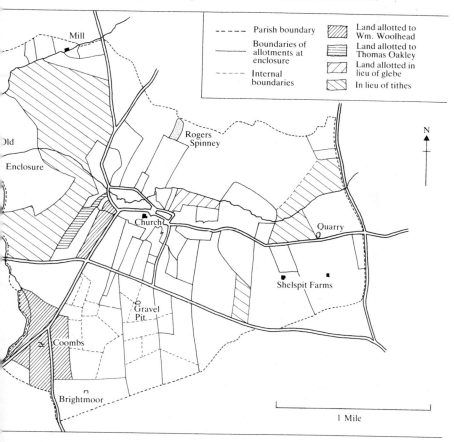

have both been enclosed and divided up into rectilinear closes, their straight hedges marching purposefully across the landscape. New, isolated, farmsteads – Western Green, Shelspit, Brightmoor and Coombs – have been built out in the fields, away from the village itself. The old self-contained community of the open-field village has been destroyed for ever.

Once enclosure was complete, there could be extensive changes in land use. The ancient arable fields were often turned down to pasture, with considerable variations within individual farms as to the rotation patterns of crops and grass. The commons and wastes were converted from rough grazing either to arable or to cultivated grasses for hay or pasture. What had been a bare, brown, open, often very untidy landscape of ant-hills, weeds, rushes and mole-hills became a greener, neatly compartmentalised one, often with very many more trees, one that was more sternly directed towards the production of food.

Parliamentary enclosure was responsible for the biggest single landscape change in English history. Between the first, for Radipole in Dorset, in 1604, and the last, passed in 1914, there were in all 5,265 enclosure acts affecting a little over 6¾ million acres in England, almost 21 per cent of the total area of the country. Of these acts, only twenty-six were passed before 1727. The two most important periods were from 1760 to 1780, and then from 1793 to 1815, during which two periods 80 per cent of all enclosure acts were passed, no less than 547 of them in the five years 1810 to 1814.

The enclosure of Thornborough was primarily concerned with open-field arable, but about a quarter of the area of the parish was common waste. This proportion of arable to waste seems also to have applied, approximately, at a national level. In fact, of the 6¾ million acres enclosed by act of parliament, almost a third, at least 2,307,000 acres, were common and waste. It is very easy to overlook this side of the enclosure movement, but in some counties, especially Cumberland, Westmorland, Northumberland and the Holland division of Lincolnshire, there was very little open-field arable to enclose, and none at all in Kent and Lancashire. Instead there were vast areas of common moor, woodland, heath and fen. In Westmorland 79 per cent of the total area of the county was common waste, and at the beginning of the eighteenth century a quarter of the area of the West Riding of Yorkshire was common land, some 425,000 acres. Only 75,000 acres of this was common arable. In Northumberland 15 per cent of the area of the county was enclosed by act of parliament, but of this area so enclosed only 3 per cent was common arable. The five largest areas awarded under an enclosure act were Hexham Manor and Allendale Common in Northumberland (40,322 acres, including some arable), Whittlesey Mere in Cambridgeshire (23,950 acres), Exmoor, in Devon and Somerset (20,014 acres), Dent in Sedbergh, Yorkshire (20,000 acres) and Holland Fen in Lincolnshire (18,052 acres). Areas such as these may serve to correct any impression that this chapter may have given that eighteenth-century England was everywhere tamed and neatly cultivated.

The enclosure of common moorland and fen was always very much more expensive than the enclosure of common arable. Moorland frequently had to be drained. Then the coarse vegetation had to be pared off and burnt. The land had to be cleared of stones before ploughing could begin, and it often took four or five ploughings and a dressing with lime before the first crops could be sown. Because of the huge areas so frequently involved, miles of new fences and roads were required. The new fences were often of stone; hundreds of miles of drystone walling in Derbyshire, Yorkshire and the Lake District date from this time.

Much of the incentive for the enclosure and cultivation of the more inhospitable regions came from the very high grain prices of the period of the Napoleonic Wars. With the coming of peace in 1815, and a series of slumps in grain prices, there was a long slow withdrawal from the most marginal of these lands, and they were abandoned to the heather and the curlew once more. Reclamation of this kind was not always successful, and failure was not uncommon, even before 1815. It was noted of Croglin in Cumberland in 1794 that many tracts of common land bear ancient marks of ploughing, whilst at Wolsingham, in Durham, of the 11,128 acres of moorland allotted in the award of 1765, 6,106 acres were not taken up at all and they remained as moorland.

Enclosure of marsh and fen was probably even more difficult and expensive than the enclosure of high moorland, and little permanent progress could be made in the Lincolnshire fens until the steam engine was applied in the 1820s to the pumping of water. The fens before enclosure supported one of the most highly specialised communities in Britain, one peculiarly adapted to its environment. The main emphasis was upon fishing, fowling and reed cutting, and the grazing of livestock, especially cattle. Drainage and enclosure destroyed an entire way of life, and there were serious riots during the draining of Holland Fen between 1768 and 1773. However, some of the richest farmland to be found anywhere in Britain emerged from the reeds once the draining was completed. By the end of the century rich crops of wheat, carrots, onions and flax were being harvested, and in the early nineteenth century new villages, including Langriville, Eastville and Frithville, were established, linked by a distinctive gridiron pattern of roads, with drainage ditches as field boundaries rather than hedges.

Commons and waste were not only to be found in high moorlands. The thin poor soils of the Yorkshire and Lincolnshire wolds, the Mendips, west Suffolk and the chalklands of Hampshire were given over to extensive common sheep walks and rabbit warrens. In the East Riding of Yorkshire it was estimated that there were 10,000 acres of rabbit warrens in 1808. Given the state of agricultural techniques in the first part of the eighteenth century a rabbit warren provided a reasonable return from poor soils, but the rabbits could never be kept inside the warren, they caused enormous damage to neighbouring crops, and a large area (600 or 700 acres) was required if the warren was to be at all profitable. From about 1780 onwards the warrens were ploughed up and new farmsteads laid out. Their

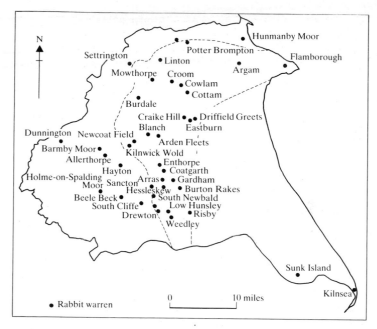

Figure 8 Rabbit warrens in the East Riding of Yorkshire, *c.* 1600–1850 (based on map by A. Harris in 'The Rabbit Warrens of East Yorkshire in the Eighteenth and Nineteenth Centuries', *Yorkshire Archaeological Journal*, vol. 42, 1967–70) and later personal information

memory survives in the quite common place-name of Warren House, Warren Farm or Warren Lodge. The common sheep walks disappeared at about the same time and in much the same way, but there are no place-names to commemorate them.

Enclosure in Wales has been far less exhaustively studied than it has in England, but it seems clear that far more common moorland and waste than arable was enclosed by act of parliament in Wales. None of the eighteen enclosure acts for Cardiganshire, for example, refer to arable. All were instead concerned with waste, and, as in England, large areas of it at one time. An act of 1812 for Anhuniog Common covered 5,000 acres of land in seven parishes. In North Wales coastal marsh as well as mountain moorland was enclosed. The draining of Malldraeth Marsh in Anglesey was completed early in the nineteenth century. Large areas of marshland along the Dee estuary in Flintshire were reclaimed during the course of the eighteenth century. An act for enclosing and reclaiming Dinas Dinlle marsh in Caernarvonshire was passed in 1806. An embankment round 2,560 acres was finished ten years later, but a further fourteen years elapsed before the work was finally completed.

Enclosure was the most potent catalyst for rural change in the eighteenth century. Landscapes within individual parishes could be almost completely redrawn within the space of five or six years, a pace of change for which 'revolutionary' is not too strong a word. Once enclosure itself was complete then improvements in husbandry practices followed swiftly. Rents rose, often as much as three times, and tenant farmers had to exploit their new fields accordingly. It was not, however, until the 1770s that these improvements became widespread or conspicuous. Many

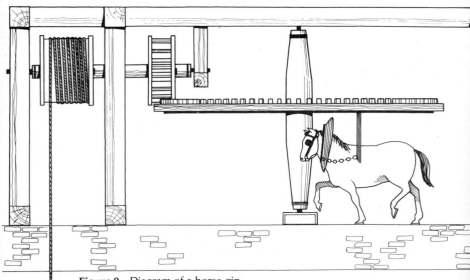

Figure 9 Diagram of a horse-gin

of the writers on agricultural improvement paid great attention to the proper rotation of crops, and it is certainly true that new rotations, particularly those incorporating the turnip, were of considerable importance. But there were other strands to the Agricultural Improvement movement.

First of all mechanisation of farm work made its first tentative beginnings. A cutting box for hay, chaff and straw was in use from the 1760s. The first practical threshing machine was invented in 1786 by Andrew Meikle, a miller living near Dunbar, and its use spread rapidly. In 1798 the ironmaster John Wilkinson had a steam-powered one at work on his estate at Brymbo in Denbighshire, but it was the 1820s before steam power was at all common on farms. Much more usual as a source of motive power was the horse-gin, of which over 1,300 still survive in Britain. They seem to have been built chiefly between 1780 and about 1850. The energy of the horse, walking round in a circle, was transmitted to machinery which could be used for a wide variety of purposes: crushing apples for cider, driving a threshing machine, pumping water, even for turning the end-over-end butter churn which was invented in the eighteenth century.

Secondly enclosure brought new farms into existence, and by the end of the eighteenth century much attention was being paid to the layout and design of farm buildings. The buildings were often grouped round a square yard which contained the dunghill. The stables for horses were usually placed opposite the cowsheds, on the west and east sides respectively, the stables being sometimes divided into stalls which would each take two horses that normally worked together. The barns would then be on the north and the farmhouse itself on the south, but in fact there was considerable variation in the layout of a farmstead, and many architects, such as Samuel Wyatt, gave a good deal of attention to the designing of farmsteads in the interests of efficient management. Piggeries were often placed at a distance from the main farmstead because it was thought that horses found the odour from pigs objectionable. Barns were occasionally built away from the farmyard in order to take advantage of a stream to drive the threshing machine. Barns were also from time to time given quite astonishingly elaborate architectural treatment. The Great Barn at Holkham, said to be the largest in England, was designed by Samuel Wyatt in about 1790, and he went on to provide complete designs and plans for at least half a dozen Holkham estate farmsteads. Dairy buildings were often treated almost as picturesque cottages, and Henry Holland designed one in the Chinese style at Woburn for the Duke of Bedford. Farm offices at Roseneath, Dunbartonshire, were

18 The Chinese Dairy at Woburn Abbey, Bedfordshire, designed by Henry Holland for the Duke of Bedford

planned in 1811 in an elaborate Gothic style, with a three-storey central tower and crenellated round towers at each end, and a dairy at Home Farm, Kinfauns Castle, Perthshire, was given an octagonal ogee roof.

Farmhouses themselves became substantial private residences. This meant that the ancient practice of farm servants and labourers living in the farmhouse was gradually discontinued. Arthur Young, writing in 1804 of Waterden in Norfolk, describes rather primly some of the consequences of this, including 'an increased neglect of the Sabbath, and looseness of morals: they [the farm servants] are free from the master's eye, sleep where and with whom they please, and are rarely seen at church.' A further consequence was that it became necessary to provide cottages for farm labourers. Newly built ones could only improve on those already in existence, many of which were small, cramped, dark and insanitary. A new cottage with a principal room about 14 feet square, two small rooms behind for storage purposes, and two first-floor bedrooms cost about £60 in north Devon early in the nineteenth century. It may have been marginally more habitable than many of the old ones. It was certainly far removed from the *cottage orné* being built at about the same time for the Duke of Bedford at Endsleigh, also in Devonshire.

In some ways the improving landlord in Scotland in the eighteenth century faced a more difficult task than his English contemporaries. The climate was generally harsher, the soils more infertile and more in need of draining, the terrain steeper and rougher. Communication was often very difficult since Scottish roads were very much worse than English ones. Nor was there in Scotland any long or widespread tradition of agricultural innovation such as that which in England stretched back to the last years of the sixteenth century, although there is evidence of improvements being introduced in the Lothians from the early seventeenth century. Scottish landlords had to begin from a very much lower base line of agricultural practice.

On the other hand there were far fewer obstacles in the

way of enclosure in Scotland. There were fewer trees and almost no well-made roads or substantial cottages in the way. There were no rights of common of pasture over the arable in Scotland and the landlord could abolish runrig himself. An act of 1661 protected landlords who enclosed, and required those with estates worth £1,000 Scots (£83 6s. 8d. sterling) to enclose 4 acres a year for ten years.

(a)

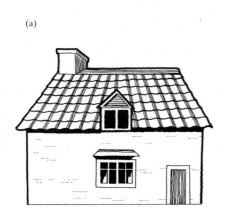

(b)

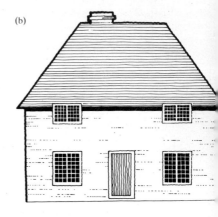

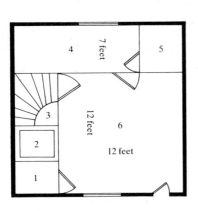

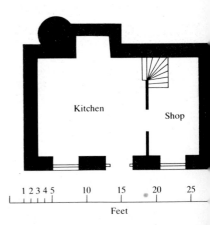

Key

1... A closet 4 & 5... A Leanto
2... Chimney ... One chamber over
3... Stairs 6... The keep room
Cost about £40. Rent £3. 3s 0d

Plan of a Cottage
Built on Oldridge Wood in the Parish of St Thom.
near Exeter by John Prawl for Mr Sillifant of Coor
near Crediton, Devon

Another act of 1695 permitted proprietors whose land lay in runrig to apply to the sheriff or justices of the peace to divide and re-allot such land. Another act of the same year permitted proprietors who had rights of commonty over the waste to apply to the Court of Session for its division, although it was the 1760s before the enclosure of commons in Scotland really got under way. Thus in Scotland there were not the legal obstacles in the path of enclosure that there were in England. Enclosure was entirely at the discretion of the landlord, and no agreement among the tenants or private act of parliament was necessary.

Scottish landlords frequently showed a genuine concern

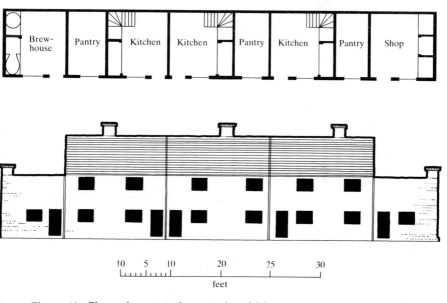

Figure 10 Plans of cottages for agricultural labourers (a) A cottage at Dereham in Norfolk (from A. Young, *General View of the Agriculture of the County of Norfolk*, 1804) (b) Plan of a cottage built near Exeter, Devon (from C. Vancouver, *General View of the Agriculture of the County of Devon*, 1808) (c) Plans for three cottages erected in Worcestershire. All three are supplied by the same pump, and one small room serves them all for washing and baking; the tenements have two private lodging rooms over each kitchen and pantry respectively (from W. Pitt, *General View of the Agriculture of the County of Worcester*, 1813)

105

for the welfare of their tenants, and although some were evicted from their farms much was done to resettle them, even in the Highlands. All change provokes opposition, and many Scottish tenant farmers refused to accept that any change in their traditional ways of doing things could ever bring any benefits. There are several recorded instances of tenants on the farms of the Duke of Hamilton in middle Clydesdale who, from behind the security of a long lease, refused to have their lands reduced from runrig into consolidated blocks. There were in the 1720s in Kirkcudbrightshire some early large-scale enclosures for cattle raising. These provoked disturbances that led to the violent destruction of some of the enclosing dykes. There was much opposition to the improvements introduced by the Duke of Argyll into his estates in Tiree at the end of the eighteenth century, some tenants declaring that they would rather emigrate than give up their traditional runrig, but much of this hostility was due to the fact that the duke had succeeded to estates forfeited to the Earl of Argyll as principal creditor of Sir Allan Maclean of Tiree as long ago as 1659. The old clan loyalties were very powerful and much more important than changes in traditional and well-tried practices.

It was usual to begin improvements with the Mains Farm or home farm, and as in England many of these farms were run at a loss. Attention was also given to the laying out of the grounds, or policies, around the mansion house, often with the avowed intention of 'civilising the prospect'. An act of parliament of 1503 required landowners to have parks and to plant at least 1 acre of woodland, but the word 'park' never developed in Scotland the rather specialised meaning it acquired in England and so a mansion could have several 'parks' in its vicinity which were essentially enclosed areas of meadow and pasture. A number of villages were built or rebuilt as part of this programme of improving the policies. Thus Kenmore was rebuilt when the policies to Taymouth Castle were remodelled in the 1760s, and Atholl was moved across the road when Blair Castle policies were improved in the 1750s (see also Fig. 11, p. 135).

The first enclosures were strongly influenced by topography, and fields in some parts of Scotland, around Gabroc Hill in Ayrshire for example, show in their long narrow shapes the influence of the runrig strips. Only in the latter part of the century, when large-scale enclosure was undertaken, were the new fields laid out without regard to local landform conditions. Runrig and the system of leasing to tacksmen were abolished. The farm, with its joint tenants and numerous subtenants, was divided up and enclosed, sometimes with hedges, as in the central lowlands and

19 Morton House, Fairmilehead, Midlothian – a substantial farmhouse rebuilt in the late eighteenth century with its farm buildings arranged round a square yard, and a hexagonal horse-gin shed. The tower to the left of the farmstead dates from the late seventeenth or early eighteenth centuries

Ayrshire, sometimes with immense dykes, made of the stones collected from the newly laid out fields, such as the Kingswells dyke, west of Aberdeen, which is half a mile long and varies from 6 to 25 feet in width. The fermtoun itself was replaced by individual farmsteads. Enclosure and improvement pushed up the hillsides far beyond the head-dyke, the ancient division between outfield and common 'muir'. Much of this improvement of marginal lands was done, as in England, under the stimulus of very high grain prices during the Napoleonic Wars, and much reverted to moorland again when this stimulus was withdrawn. In the Lammermuir Hills, for example, in what has been defined as the 'moorland core', that is the area of moorland mapped

20 Kingswells Consumption Dyke, near Aberdeen, built to 'consume' stones cleared from land that was being enclosed and improved

as such on the earliest Ordnance Survey maps about 1860, there is evidence from aerial photographs of at least 12,000 acres of land which had once been cultivated and had then been abandoned before 1860, together with 248 abandoned farmsteads.

For much of the eighteenth century improvement depended upon the initiative and enthusiasm of the landlord. Only he had the necessary capital to meet the expense and risk of experiment. Sir Archibald Grant spent a long life and much money gradually improving his estate at Monymusk. He planted trees on a large scale; in 1754 he estimated that he had 2 million. He had his own nurseries in which saplings were raised from seed. In 1718–19 he bought two pecks of acorns, as well as fir and pine seed. In June 1722 he was preparing ground in which to sow elm seed, and in August 1723 he could write that the fir and birch seed had come up well but not the silver fir or the horse chestnut. By 1729 he was inserting in the tacks he was granting to tenants clauses to the effect that they should plant a given number of trees each year. In 1735, for example, the tack granting the whole of Afforske Farm to James Moore required him to plant 100 trees each year of ash, elm, allars (alder), birch or plane. In addition he was to plant trees, not more than 6 feet apart, upon the ditches and dykes the lease required him to make.

Sir Archibald was by no means the only landlord to plant trees on this scale and in this way. At Linton, by the very end of the eighteenth century, the Duke of Queensbury was granting 57-year leases to his tenants. This encouraged tenants to plant belts of trees as shelter for their sheep, something that they refused to do when the leases were only for nineteen years. In 1733 at Blairadam in Kinross there was scarcely a tree. By 1792 there were 1,144 acres of plantations. By the mid-eighteenth century the Duke of Atholl had over 4,000 acres of plantations at Blair Atholl. This policy of deliberately planting tens of thousands of trees over thousands of acres introduced an entirely new element into the Scottish landscape. When Thomas Winter rode from Peterhead to Monymusk in 1726, a distance of thirty miles, he did not see a single tree. By the end of the eighteenth century much of the lowlands and border country had become as well-wooded as many parts of England. In this process of enclosing, planting, draining, ditching and dyking, followed by the introduction of new crops, including the inevitable turnip, and improvements in livestock that led to the emergence of the Ayrshire breed at the end of the eighteenth and the Aberdeen–Angus at the beginning of the nineteenth century, Scottish landlords were adapting to their own special circumstances practices already well-established in England. Some of the best-known of Scottish improvers spent long periods in England. Sir Archibald Grant of Monymusk was a member of parliament at Westminster from 1722 to 1732. This meant that much improvement on his estate had to be conducted by means of correspondence. In fact, although landlords may have provided the initial stimulus, the ideas and the money, much of the detailed work was in the hands of factors and gardeners – men like Thomas McAlla, gardener to the Earl of Stair, and John Burrell, principal advisor to the commissioners who administered the estates of the Duke of Hamilton. Sir Archibald Grant brought Thomas Winter from England to Monymusk in 1726. Winter proposed to manage the estate in the best English fashion. He thought the ploughs best suited to Scottish conditions were made near Stow on the Wold. They could easily be obtained, he wrote, by the Winchcombe carrier, who would bring them to London, and they then could be sent by sea to Aberdeen. He hoped by 'often repeated conversation' with Sir Archibald's tenants 'to bring them to see their errours'. He was likely to have an uphill task. Sir Archibald thought his labourers hardworking, but 'ignorant and stubborn in it'.

Improvement could be a lengthy and expensive business, and more than one landlord found that the debts accumulated during the course of such improvements compelled him to sell out before he was able to reap the benefits from his efforts. This happened to John Cockburn of Ormistown, who, after more than twenty years of careful effort had to sell his estate at Ormistown to the Earl of Hopetoun in 1747. Even the wealthy Dukes of Argyll were at times hard pressed. Improvements at Inveraray were costing £10,000 a year by 1800, and in 1802–3 land had to be sold to meet the most pressing debts. It was often the stimulus of debt which provided the motive for yet further improvement.

Thus by example and precept improvement was established and diffused. But the structure of traditional Scottish rural society presented Scottish landlords with a very real problem, one which English landlords did not have to face. The enclosure and realignment of traditional fermtouns meant that large numbers of subtenants could find themselves homeless. The benevolent paternalism so characteristic of the eighteenth century meant that many landlords felt themselves obliged to make some provision for the dispossessed. This was done by the establishment of new villages which, it was hoped, would be centres of trade and manufacture, providing homes and employment and, incidentally, increased rents to the landlord. At Ormistoun John Cockburn was laying out the new town by 1735. He provided building plots, timber and stone, and required that the new houses should be two storeys high, in itself a revolution in the pattern of traditional Scottish rural domestic building. Crieff was laid out on a gridiron plan by the Duke of Perth in 1731. Grantown on Spey was begun in 1776. Altogether something like 350 new towns and villages were established. Artisans, especially weavers, were deliberately attracted to them, and some, such as Beauly in Inverness, were built on peat mosses as part of a programme of improving waste. Landlords built saw mills, paper mills, waulk mills, breweries and laid out bleach fields. By the end of the eighteenth century, however, it seems that Scottish landlords were losing interest in industrial investment, more particularly as industry itself was moving away from the countryside and into the towns, and hence out of their control. In the nineteenth century they confined themselves much more exclusively to agricultural improvement.

This chapter has been concerned with rural change. Enclosure has figured prominently because this was the most important single factor at work in promoting change. But we must be very careful not to exaggerate either the pace, the direction or the extent of this change. The open-field system persisted in many parishes and townships until the 1840s. The mechanisation of farming spread very slowly indeed. Jethro Tull published his *Horse Hoeing Husbandry* in 1733, but it took a century for the horse-drawn hoes and seed drills that he advocated to become at all common. In 1813 Arthur Young could report it as something unusual that Mr Simpson of Ottley in Suffolk, having met with Mr Tull's books, was making a trial of his methods in a 6-acre field. A reaping machine was invented in the early nineteenth century, but it was mid-century before they were to be found in any numbers.

Very many of the heaviest, most important tasks of the agricultural year had still to be performed by hand. Weeding was generally done by gangs of women and children. Oxen were widely used for ploughing, and they continued to be used in Sussex until the end of the nineteenth century. In Devonshire it cost between 18d. and 20d. to shoe an ox, and three yoke of them were the equal to the heaviest work in the country. Wheat was reaped by means of the sickle or scythe, and large numbers of men, women and children were employed at harvest time. Charles Vancouver, writing in 1808, gives a vivid description of the wheat harvest in north Devon. An entire neighbourhood would turn out to harvest a field of perhaps 20 acres. The farmer was expected to provide ample food and drink throughout the day to all who came, and a supper in the farmhouse. The work was done to what Vancouver rather sourly calls 'noisy jokes and ribaldry', but it was done without wages. When the grain harvest was in, much of the threshing was done by flail, with the barn doors open to create a through draught for winnowing. Threshing machines may have spread rapidly but there were only twenty in Suffolk in 1803, in a county of 800,000 acres.

It is customary to lament the passing of the traditional rural society of eighteenth-century Britain, and nostalgia for the old ways was given moving expression in the poetry of John Clare at the time. Certainly much that was of value has been lost. The orchards of Worcestershire, although many of their trees were old, overladen with moss and mistletoe and their branches hopelessly entangled, were none the less stocked in 1813 with local varieties – Stire, Hagloe Crab, Old Redstreak, Woodcock, Dymmock Red – varieties evolved long before Mr Richard Cox, in about 1830, had finished his work on his Orange Pippin, an apple that would sweep all the others into oblivion.

Unlimited cider at harvest suppers could blur only for a moment the harsh realities of rural life. At Linton in Tweeddale it was reported in 1791 that the mode of living had much improved within living memory. Farmers had once eaten no flesh but what had died of itself, and their clothes had been homespun and coarse. Of Cumwhitton in Cumberland it was said in 1794 that no newspaper had entered the parish before 1792. Tea, although a luxury that was creeping in, was held in such detestation by some that they would rather cherish a serpent than admit a tea-pot. There was no golden Arcadia in eighteenth-century Britain.

21 This painting of the countryside around Dixton Manor, Gloucestershire, by an unknown early eighteenth-century artist, gives a remarkably vivid picture of the numbers of workers required, both men and women, at haymaking and harvest-time. Morris dancers can be seen in the bottom right-hand corner

4 Country houses, parks and gardens

We have been concerned in the previous two chapters with some of the factors at work in the moulding of the rural landscape of Britain during the course of the eighteenth century. Very many of these factors, especially enclosure and the replanning of farms and farmsteads, were shaped and directed by wealthy owners of country estates. Their farms and fields, turnips and sheep, chaff-cutters and steam threshing machines were, however, but one side of the estate, although perhaps the most important, since they provided the rents and profits which paid for the other, namely the mansion house, park and gardens, the pictures and books and dogs, the social standing and the political influence.

The eighteenth century saw throughout Britain a truly astonishing building and rebuilding of country houses, accompanied by the reshaping of their parks and policies. This building left no part of the country untouched, and in due course penetrated almost all ranks in society. What the great ones did lesser men imitated where they could. Few village manor houses or country parsonages escaped altogether this fever for building and gardening, whilst the symmetry of façade given to the cottages of agricultural labourers is an echo, faint and far, of that given to their new mansions by their landlords.

This building and gardening reflect closely changing tastes and fashions in literature and painting, and all four interact in a most complex and fascinating manner. Some of the leading figures in the story straddle two or three of these four interrelated arts, and many were close friends. In the first part of the eighteenth century Alexander Pope was the key figure, as poet, gardener and the friend and correspondent of the Earl of Burlington, William Kent, Lord Cobham, Lord Bathurst, and so on. Only at the very end of the eighteenth century does this unity start to fragment. Romanticism emphasises a more personal, emotional response to art. Architecture becomes a matter of engineering, and gardening, inundated by a flood of new plants and trees from America, South Africa and the Far East, instead of being a subject for aesthetics, becomes instead a branch of botany.

It is possible to recognise two basic themes running through the design and layout of country houses during the eighteenth century, two themes summarised in the convenient shorthand terms of classical and Gothic. The architecture and literature of Greece and Rome were considered the acme of intellectual and aesthetic achievement and were widely admired, studied and imitated. Only slowly, during the course of the eighteenth century, was the same scholarly and critical attention turned towards medieval architecture, and it is the end of the century before neo-Gothic building begins to acquire the archaeological accuracy to be found in much neo-classical building. Eventually, Gothic architecture in the nineteenth century surpassed classical in the high moral seriousness claimed for it by its practitioners.

The greatest of English architects, Sir Christopher Wren, died in 1723, at the incredibly advanced age of 91. His masterpiece, St Paul's Cathedral, was finished in 1709, by which time the almost inevitable reaction against his interpretation of classical architecture was already beginning to form. The new movement sought to return to what it considered to be the pristine purity of classical architecture, more especially as exemplified in the work of Andrea Palladio and Inigo Jones, but without fully realising just how eclectic and original these two men had been. The movement was given point, guidance and stimulus by the publication in 1715 of the first volumes of Colen Campbell's

Vitruvius Britannicus, and of Leoni's edition of Palladio's *I Quattro libri dell'architettura*. For half a century Palladianism dominated almost every aspect of building in England, and in due course it was adopted in Scotland.

The books attracted the attention and enthusiasm of Richard, third Earl of Burlington, then a young man of 21 with large estates in Yorkshire, and just returned from his first visit to Italy. He began the rebuilding of his house in Piccadilly where he found apartments for Handel for two years, employing Campbell as his architect. He returned to Italy in 1719 for six months, visiting Vicenza and Venice. He bought drawings by Palladio, and returned home in the company of William Kent, who also took up residence in Burlington House. He began alterations to his house at Chiswick at about the same time, but it was not until after a fire in 1725 that he decided to rebuild. The house that eventually emerged was modelled on, without slavishly imitating, the Villa Rotonda of Palladio, and, cool, elegant and compact, it became the exemplar for every cultured gentleman's semi-rural retreat.

Palladianism could also work on the grand scale. In 1712 Thomas Coke, then aged 15 and with an income of £10,000 a year, set out on the Grand Tour; he was away nearly six years. He met William Kent in Rome, and became acquainted with Lord Burlington shortly after his return. He began improving, enclosing and draining the bleak marshes and heaths around Holkham almost immediately, but the heavy losses he sustained when the South Sea Bubble burst prevented his starting to rebuild the house until 1734. Drawings from the 1720s made by Matthew Brettingham senior show that Coke had been thinking long about his house before building actually began, and that he designed almost all of it himself. William Kent did some work in the gardens as they were developed, and also designed the interior to the Southwest Pavilion, the first part of the house to be built. Thomas Coke died in 1759 and his splendid mansion was finished in 1764. At Holkham many of those strands which go into the making of eighteenth-century

Britain are focused on one spot: the practical problems involved in farming and the contribution that the landlord could make by providing fixed capital and encouraging innovation in husbandry techniques are united with new directions in architecture and landscape gardening, in themselves facets of change in philosophical, literary and aesthetic values and concepts, moulded and shaped by political opinion and experience.

22 A view of Burlington House, Piccadilly, in about 1698, drawn by Leonard Knyff and engraved by Johannes Kip. The gardens are formal in their layout, and the open countryside is clearly visible just beyond the gardens. There is a carrier's waggon in the bottom left-hand corner and a coach in the bottom right-hand corner. Pedestrians and vehicles are separated by a post-and-rail fence. This is the house that Lord Burlington began to re-model from 1713 onwards

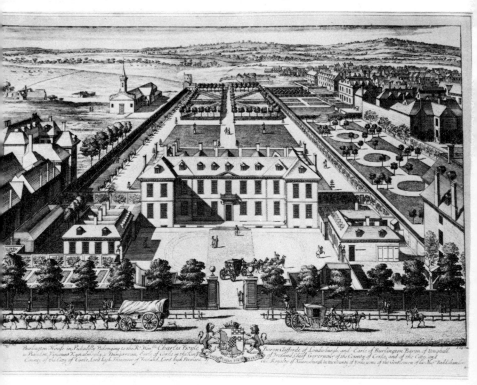

Lord Burlington and Colen Campbell were undoubtedly the most influential figures in architecture in the first half of the eighteenth century. Campbell designed the great house at Wanstead in Essex upon which were modelled even larger country houses – Wentworth Woodhouse in Yorkshire and Prior Park near Bath. He also designed smaller houses, at Stourhead in Wiltshire, Newby Park in Yorkshire, and Mereworth Castle in Kent, an almost exact replica of the Villa Rotonda. These, together with Lord Burling-

23 Holkham Hall, Norfolk – the brick-built Palladian mansion of Thomas Coke, finally completed in 1761. The grounds and the lake were laid out by Lancelot 'Capability' Brown, but the formal gardens and fountain on the left of the picture are nineteenth century. The monument in the top right-hand corner is to Thomas Coke, the agriculturalist, who died in 1842

24 An aerial view of Stourhead, Wiltshire, looking west. The mansion lies right of centre while the lake and surrounding gardens lie in the centre distance. Immediately above the island in the lake is the Pantheon. The Temple of Apollo can be seen among the trees on the left-hand margin of the lake. The church is a little below and to the left, and the medieval cross, brought from Bristol in 1765, lies in the V formed by the roads to the right of the church

ton's Chiswick House, became the models for the 'villas' of the second half of the century. Comparatively small, semi-rural and very fashionable, they rapidly lost any pretence of

25 Mereworth Castle, Kent, designed by Colen Campbell in 1723 for John Fane, later Earl of Westmorland, and modelled on Palladio's Villa Rotonda, near Vicenza

being at the centre of a rural estate, which is what the word 'villa' originally meant, and instead they became eagerly sought after by wealthy business and professional men in the suburbs of London and the large provincial towns.

Palladianism, which began as the fad of an exclusive coterie of wealthy noblemen and gentlemen, rapidly became the style against which all building was to be measured. It spread far and wide over Britain. Provincial builders and masons, on a tide of pattern books, including much cheaper editions of Palladio than that of Leoni, were provided with abundant examples of mouldings, decorations, details of the classical orders and some guidance in the handling of proportions. Occasionally a local architect, such as John Carr of York, or firm of builders such as the Bastard family of Dorset, emerged who could handle the style with individuality and distinction. Others copied or imitated what they could, often fairly successfully, sometimes rather feebly. The hundreds of small, unassuming country houses they left behind rarely fail to be visually pleasing, are frequently well-built, and never vulgar.

One of the visitors to Chiswick House shortly after it was finished was Sir John Clerk of Penicuik. He had studied at Leiden University and had himself visited Italy. In 1727, just before his visit to Chiswick, he had finished his own version of a Palladian villa at Mavisbank, which he had designed himself in conjunction with William Adam, then the leading Scottish architect and the father of Robert Adam. John Johnstone, a wright who had actually worked on the building of Mavisbank, went on in 1738 to supervise the remodelling for Sir Duncan Campbell of Lochnell House in Argyll-

26 Lochnell House, Argyllshire. The left-hand portion, including the advanced pedimented entrance section surmounted by urn-finials, was built in 1737–9. The remainder dates from between 1818 and 1820. Concealed behind this part is a late seventeenth-century kitchen and bakehouse

shire, where an oblong block of three storeys, complete with triangular pediment and elaborately carved urn-finials, brought a refracted image from sixteenth-century Italy and ancient Rome into the Highlands of Scotland.

Lord Burlington died in 1753. He was deeply in debt, the consequence not only of his building extravagances but also of the draining and improving he had carried out on his Yorkshire estates. He was the last of the first Palladians, and had seen his ideas become accepted, almost conventional, practice. He cannot fail to have been aware of the slow growth during his lifetime of other ideas, ideas that would make his own as outmoded as those he had once sought to replace, and it was one of his closest friends, Alexander Pope, who had a large share in their fostering.

Pope was also the friend of Allen, first Earl Bathurst, whose mansion at Cirencester he visited often. Lord Bathurst rebuilt the house between 1715 and 1718, probably to his own designs, but his principal interest lay in the planting of trees, and as he added more and more land to his estates so he planted more and more trees. In one of his woods he and Pope designed what was at first called the Wood House, and eventually Alfred's Hall. It was begun in 1721, but Lord Bathurst was still tinkering with it in 1732, by which time the Earl of Strafford had probably finished building his ruin, Stainborough Castle, on his estate at Wentworth in Yorkshire. These were the ancestors of a remarkable progeny, the castle follies of the second half of the eighteenth century.

Interest in medieval building had never really died out in late seventeenth-century England. This interest became increasingly more widespread as the eighteenth century wore on. In 1732 William Kent rebuilt part of the Clock Court at Hampton Court Palace in a prettily decorative imitation of Tudor Gothic, and in 1734 Nicholas Hawksmoor designed the west towers to Westminster Abbey. Gothic architecture became so popular that in 1742 Batty Langley thought it worth his while to publish a book with that title. However the real push to the growth of interest in things 'Gothick' came, as with so many of the artistic and intellectual trends of the eighteenth century, from two men with the means and the leisure to develop their ideas, or at least to indulge their fancies. Sanderson Miller was a Warwickshire gentleman who built a castle folly on Edge Hill, and followed it up with the new hall at Lacock Abbey, where 'Gothick' detail is applied with the same realism and solidity that is to be found in the sugar-icing decoration on a wedding cake. Horace Walpole took his rediscovery of the medieval past a little more seriously. His house at Strawberry Hill was added to piece-meal over the years, using rather amateurish imitations of genuine and recognisable medieval monuments. As the house grew, so its studied irregularity, in such strong contrast to the equally studied regularity of Palladianism, became very popular, and contributed significantly to the development of the idea of the Picturesque.

27 Strawberry Hill, Twickenham. Horace Walpole began improvements and additions here in the Gothic style from 1748 onwards and continued to extend it for the next thirty years. Its irregularity, as much the consequence of chance as design, made it one of the most visited houses in England

As the dominant theme of early eighteenth-century building was introduced with the publication of two books, so were the themes of the last half of the century introduced through books. In 1753 Robert Wood published *The Ruins of Palmyra*. In 1755 came *The Antiquities of Athens*, by James Stuart and Nicholas Revett. Two years later William Chambers published his *Designs of Chinese Buildings*, and in 1764 came *Ruins of the Palace of the Emperor Diocletian at Spalato* by Robert Adam. All four are important for two reasons: they show an impressive concern for historical and archaeological accuracy, and, as their titles reveal, they show an equally impressive expansion in the geographical and chronological range of the ideas and themes becoming available to builders and architects. More especially architects and their patrons became increasingly aware of Greek architecture, and this led, in the years after 1800, to the Greek Revival. The most convincing country house built in this neo-Grecian style was that designed by William Wilkins in 1804 for Henry Drummond at Grange Park, in Hampshire. Drummond spent over £30,000 on it, but sold out in 1817, and it was never finished in the way that Wilkins had envisaged.

Some of the most splendid of English country houses, such as Harewood House and Luton Hoo, owe much to the strongly personal approach to classical architecture developed during the 1760s by Robert Adam. When he died in 1792 an obituary notice could claim with some justification that he had 'produced a total change in the architecture of this country'. He did this by returning directly to the inexhaustible riches of classical architecture, much of which he knew at first hand, and yet refusing to be bound by any of the later theorists. The strict rules imposed by those who purported to be following Palladio he considered to have destroyed the flexibility and the freedom of expression which he thought to be characteristic of genuine classical building. He had a very wide architectural vocabulary, amassed during his years in Italy, and yet he very rarely reproduced exactly from his prototypes, almost always making some change, however slight. Much of his time was taken up, either by completing work which others had begun, or by remodelling the interiors of older, already existing, buildings. At Kedleston in Derbyshire he incorporated a model of the Arch of Constantine into the south front, and at Osterley Park he grafted a double portico, based on the Portico of Octavia, on to an Elizabethan building. At Syon House he lavished all his skill, his immense attention to detail, his extraordinary range of ideas, upon an incredibly richly decorated series of rooms, to the

28 Kedleston Hall, Derbyshire, looking north-west. The imposing south front, designed by Robert Adam and based upon the Arch of Constantine, is clearly visible. The parish church of Kedleston lies in the angle formed by the main block of the house and the kitchen wing

point where even the prodigiously wealthy Duke of Northumberland had at last to cry 'Enough!'

The principles and main lines of development of medieval architecture were only very slowly recovered during the eighteenth century. Much so-called 'Gothick' building continued to be a matter of detail and ornament, applied with almost no sense of period or historical accuracy to what were fundamentally classically regular buildings. At Inveraray Castle, where the Duke of Argyll began rebuilding in 1745, the central block of the castle is square and regular, the only external Gothic features being the crenellations and the pointed windows, whilst the interior decoration is

29 Inverary Castle designed by Roger Morris for the Duke of Argyll. Work on the Castle started in 1745

30 Downton Castle, Herefordshire, built by Richard Payne Knight between 1774 and 1778 as a deliberately irregular castle, and as such it was the fountain-head of the Picturesque style

almost entirely classical in style. At Wedderburn Castle in Berwickshire built between 1770 and 1775 with a west front certainly designed by Robert Adam, there is the same vast square building, the only obviously medieval elements being the battlements.

The same kind of ambiguity is to be found at Downton Castle, built between 1774 and 1778 for Richard Payne Knight. His castle, unlike that of the Duke of Argyll, was deliberately irregular, but the interior was classical in layout and decoration, complete with Greek columns and entablatures. Downton Castle set the fashion for castellated country houses for half a century. Genuine castles had to be rebuilt, as at Taymouth Castle in Perthshire where Archibald and James Elliot built another square main block, this time with a Gothic interior. Modest country houses had to be Gothicised. Scrope Bernard recast the exterior of his house at Nether Winchendon between 1798 and 1803, adding a Gothic screen and battlements, all to his own designs. Ardmaddy Castle in Argyllshire, a late medieval tower house, had a Palladian extension built in 1773. Its boat house, built in 1790, had a stone screen in Gothic.

Richard Payne Knight and his friend Uvedale Price became the chief protagonists of the Picturesque movement of the last years of the eighteenth and the first of the nineteenth century. All that was rough, irregular, uncultivated and untamed was now to be sought out for its own sake. Country cottages were discovered to be picturesque, and many comparatively small ones were built by John Nash, complete with half-timbering, thatched roofs, wrought iron balconies and verandahs, an idea that had come from India. Some were mildly Italianate, some vaguely Tudor, whilst the spiders, earwigs and sparrows encouraged by the thatch were conveniently ignored. The largest *cottage orné* must be that built at Endsleigh in Devonshire for the sixth Duke of Bedford between 1810 and 1811. This was no agricultural labourer's cottage, but an elaborate exercise in make-believe, extending to the building of a real cottage in the middle distance so that a fire could be lit in it for the scenic effect of the smoke curling up from its chimney.

The confusion which this welter of styles could induce by the end of the eighteenth century is perhaps best exemplified in Castle Goring, Sussex. Here Sir Bysshe Shelley, grandfather of the poet, completed in about 1798 a building which had a south front in brick, classical in design, with a portico and Ionic pilasters, and a Gothic north front in flint, complete with battlements, pointed windows and turrets.

The country house was not however created in isolation. It was set in its own gardens and park, and as much attention was paid to this setting as to the house itself, and changes in the style and layout of houses were mirrored in changes in their surroundings.

Gardens at the beginning of the eighteenth century were formal in plan and rigid in layout. Stephen Switzer, writing at the beginning of the century, thought that there were two kinds of formality in the gardens of his time. These he characterised, ungrammatically for the first, as 'La Grand Manier', and 'the Dutch Taste'. The model for 'La Grand

Manier' was the work of Le Nôtre in France, and more especially the immense gardens he laid out at Versailles for Louis XIV. Long straight rides, stretching through woodland as far as the eye could see, gave extensive views from one or more central points. Much use was made of water, of statuary, and of elaborately patterned parterres, which were designed to be viewed from the windows of the palace. Everything was done on the grandest scale. The garden stretched to the horizon on all sides, and the visitor could not fail to be impressed with the power and authority

31 A view of Chatsworth, drawn by Leonard Knyff and engraved by Johannes Kip, published in *Britannia Illustrata*, volume 1, which first appeared in 1707. This view is reproduced from the 1720 edition. The formal gardens are characteristic of 'La Grand Manier'

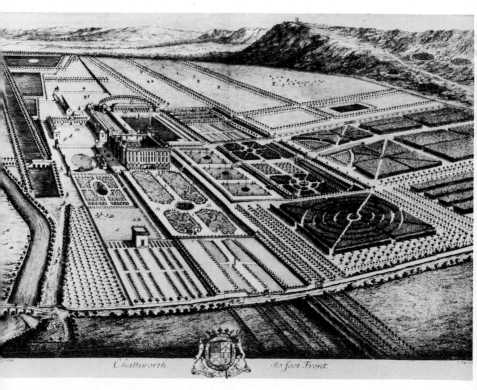

of the owner of so splendid a monument. The 'Dutch Taste' worked on a much smaller, more intimate, scale, making use of straight canals, clipped hedges and elaborate topiary work, but it was still arranged on the same rigid straight lines of 'La Grand Manier'.

Such gardens, of both kinds, were common in England at the beginning of the eighteenth century, and persisted in Scotland until well into the second half of the century. They were to be found at Longleat, at Blenheim and at Chatsworth, but although the influence of Versailles was so important, only Louis XIV could afford to work on so vast a scale.

In the first decades of the eighteenth century opinion began to move away from the formalities and the frigidities of these gardens, and turned instead to an increasingly relaxed, more informal style. Almost from the first this movement had political overtones. The formalities of Versailles were associated with the authoritarian regime of Louis XIV. Informal gardens were associated with liberty in general, and with the Whig version of it in particular.

The new gardening style as it emerged replaced the straight lines of Le Nôtre with gentle curves. Trees which had been cut and clipped into grotesque shapes were allowed to grow naturally. The straight edges of lakes and canals became sinuous. Not even the wealthiest of English noblemen could command all that his eye could see, and so the surrounding countryside was incorporated into his garden by means of the ha-ha, a concealed ditch that gave uninterrupted views out beyond the garden or estate boundary, while keeping the cattle away from the house. Charles Bridgeman was building such a ditch in the gardens at Stowe in 1719.

At the same time the elements assembled in a garden were deliberately composed into a picture, and the most widely acclaimed gardens were those in which the spectator was led on from one 'picture' to the next. An appreciation that garden design was essentially visual and that the pictures were to be articulated by movement was the contribution of William Kent. The most complete example of his work to survive today is the garden at Rousham in Oxfordshire. Here the 'circuit walk' is given variety and direction by the skilful use of flowering shrubs, water, garden buildings and statuary, with an arcade of seven arches, called the Praeneste, as the pivotal point.

The pictures composed by Kent and those who patronised or imitated him, such as the Earl of Burlington, Lord Cobham and Henry Hoare, were of an idealised landscape drawn from sources similar to those which had inspired the new style in architecture; the poetry of Virgil and Horace,

32 The lake and gardens at Stourhead in Wiltshire. The Pantheon, designed by Henry Flitcroft, was completed in about 1754. The stone bridge was built in 1762

the description of the Garden of Eden in *Paradise Lost*, whilst over all lay the warm golden light of the Roman Campagna as presented through the paintings of Claude.

The most famous of these pictorial circuit gardens is that created at Stourhead in Wiltshire by Henry Hoare in the years after 1741. He did much of the planning himself, and it is clear that the *Aeneid* was almost constantly at the front of his mind as he worked. Paths leading round the gardens are shaded with trees until a suitable vantage point is reached. Then they open out to reveal a carefully contrived scene, such as that over the lake to the Pantheon, completed in about 1754. From the portico of the Pantheon itself the view, again carefully contrived, is of the church and village of Stourton, with a medieval cross brought from Bristol especially to enhance the view (see Plate 24).

The outer circuit of the Stourhead gardens had in the eighteenth century to be made by coach. Other gardens were planned on a lesser scale. Philip Southcote bought Woburn Farm in 1735. On its 116 acres he built a ruined chapel, seats, alcoves, bridges and planted groves of trees and shrubs, creating the first *ferme ornée*. William Adam bought 28 acres of land at North Merchiston near Edinburgh in 1730. Here he laid out a formal garden with a series of radial avenues, one of which had Edinburgh Castle as its terminal point. After his death his son John progressively relaxed these formal lines, introducing irregular belts of trees and a small circular temple, creating a garden that was plain and simple to the point of being stark and uninteresting.

The changes at North Merchiston seem to have been taking place at the same time that the poet William Shenstone was making his much more famous garden at The Leasowes. Shenstone, like John Adam, had to be content to work on an altogether smaller stage than that enjoyed by Henry Hoare. Nevertheless the path that led through his garden stopped at no less than thirty-nine vantage points. Each had a seat, a view, either over some part of the garden or out over the surrounding countryside, and an inscription designed to draw the visitor's attention to an appropriate literary parallel.

At Stourhead and The Leasowes the allusions with which the gardens were loaded were primarily literary. At Stowe the gardens created by Lord Cobham were primarily political. A Temple of Virtue, designed by William Kent and based by him on Palladio's drawing of the Temple of Vesta at Tivoli, contained statues of Lycurgus, Socrates, Homer and Epaminondas. Close by was the Temple of Modern Virtue, symbolically ruined, and with a caricature of Robert Walpole. A Gothic temple, designed by James Gibbs, was completed by about 1744, and known at first as the Temple of Liberty. This too had its political overtones, since Gothic architecture was associated by Lord Cobham and his friends with the Saxons and King Alfred, who was included in the Temple of British Worthies built at Stowe in about 1735, and hence with liberty and virtue, qualities which had been subverted by the Norman Conquest, re-established by the Glorious Revolution of 1688, and were, in the 1740s, in grave danger of disappearing.

Throughout the eighteenth century immense sums of money and decades of labour were spent on moving hills, damming streams, excavating lakes and subterranean grottos, building temples and commemorative columns, and upon planting trees by the thousand. Such gardens, when they finally emerged, were both rich and sterile. They were rich in a wealth of literary, artistic, philosophical and political allusions. But their success depended upon a detailed knowledge of a shared cultural tradition. The inscription over the door of the Temple of Flora at Stourhead is taken from the *Aeneid*. It reads: *'Procul, o procul este profani'*, 'Be gone all you who are uninitiated'. Such gardens were very much for the initiated.

These gardens were also remarkably sterile. Pre-occupied with a literary and pictorial landscape created in the mind's eye, their creators almost totally ignored the landscape which lay physically before their eyes, a landscape the result of centuries of organic growth and slow change, its features created by the needs of generations of craftsmen and peasant farmers. Again and again, as these new gardens crept out over the countryside, villages and hamlets were swallowed up, their cottages levelled, their inhabitants dispossessed. At Stowe the village seems to have finally disappeared somewhere about 1730, although its church still stands, discreetly screened by trees on the south front of the great house. When Sir Gilbert Heathcote was building his great Palladian mansion at Normanton in Rutland early in the century, the village was in the way, and so it had to be demolished. The village of Edensor was moved to improve the view from Chatsworth, and the village of Henderskelf now lies under the south front of Castle Howard. The passing of villages and hamlets in this way was lamented by Goldsmith in his poem *The Deserted Village*, published in 1770. In regretting the depopulation of the countryside he inveighed against the increase of luxury, but the picture he drew of traditional English village life was no less idealised than the landscape of those who would demolish it. Although he writes in general terms it seems very likely that he had a specific place in mind, namely Nuneham Courtenay in Oxfordshire, where the village was incorporated into newly landscaped grounds about ten years before Goldsmith published his poem.

The landlord did not, however, always get his own way without a struggle. In the 1760s and 1770s Alexander, the fourth Duke of Gordon, was busily improving the policies to Gordon Castle. The formal gardens were levelled, the ornamental canals were filled in. Straight tree-lined drives were replaced by more gently curving ones. The only problem was that a flourishing town, Fochabers, had grown up little more than half a mile from the south front of the castle. In January 1776 the duke began letting out plots in a new town, laid out on a gridiron pattern a further half mile to the south, at the same time buying up plots in the old one. The inhabitants were very loath to move, and it was 1802 before the last feu in the old town had been bought up, and the grand design, maturing for so long, could at last be completed.

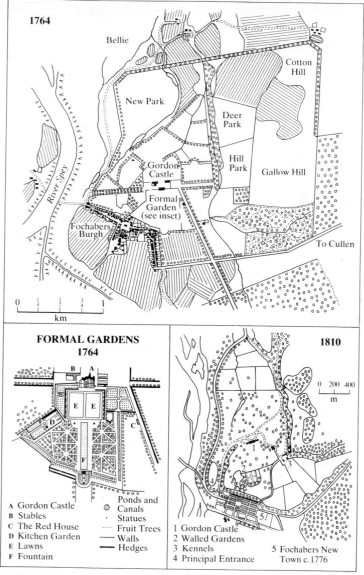

1764

Bellie

Cotton Hill

New Park

Deer Park

River Spey

Gordon Castle

Hill Park

Gallow Hill

Formal Garden (see inset)

Fochabers Burgh

To Cullen

0 ¼ ½ ¾ 1
km

FORMAL GARDENS 1764

B A

E E

D

C

F

A Gordon Castle
B Stables
C The Red House
D Kitchen Garden
E Lawns
F Fountain

⊚ Ponds and Canals
· Statues
···· Fruit Trees
── Walls
── Hedges

1810

0 200 400
m

1 Gordon Castle
2 Walled Gardens
3 Kennels
4 Principal Entrance

5 Fochabers New Town c.1776

Figure 11 The changing layout of the policies of Gordon Castle, Moray (based on original map by T. R. Slater published in *The Making of the Scottish Countryside*, edited by M. L. Parry and T. R. Slater, Croom Helm, 1980)

135

By about 1730 the new style in gardening was well-established. This does not mean of course that every formal garden had by this date been swept away. In Scotland in particular the new style scarcely established itself. Very many English gardens were crowded, indeed over-crowded, with buildings of every kind, from temples and grottos to obelisks and bridges. Buildings such as these were uncommon in Scottish gardens, and those that there were had none of the overtones, political or literary, of their English contemporaries. Taymouth Castle, the property of the Earl of Breadalbane, had an unusually large number and variety of buildings, including a Chinese bridge, and at Dunkeld there was a hermitage and a Chinese temple.

A reaction against this proliferation of garden buildings was perhaps inevitable. As early as 1744, even before they were all completed, the Duchess of Portland could complain that Stowe was overcrowded with buildings. When Sir Richard Colt Hoare returned in 1791 from his Italian journeys he took a deep interest in the gardens bequeathed to him at Stourhead by his grandfather Henry Hoare on his death in 1785, and yet, because he disapproved of nature being overwhelmed with buildings, he demolished a Gothic greenhouse, a Turkish tent and a Chinese temple.

By 1760 the greatest of all the natural, informal landscape gardeners was well established, and he very rarely used garden buildings at all. Lancelot Brown was born at Kirkharle in Northumberland in 1716. By March of 1741 he was working at Stowe. He married in November of 1744 in the parish church there, all that was left of the village, and left for good in the autumn of 1751, taking a house in Hammersmith, then a hamlet in Fulham. From then on, until his death in February of 1783, he dominated landscape gardening as no other man has done, either before or since. He is known to have been involved personally in some two hundred projects, mainly in the south and east of England, but also including Mamhead in Devon, Newton Castle in Carmarthenshire and Alnwick Castle in Northumberland. His style was widely copied and imitated by many without his skill and perception, notably by Thomas White, father and son, working unimaginatively and stolidly in Scotland between 1770 and about 1820.

'Capability' Brown's contribution to the making of the English rural landscape has become so much a part of the national consciousness of what that landscape is that it is almost impossible either to appreciate fully the extent of his achievement or to grasp that older, quite different, landscapes lie behind where he worked. Using only three elements – trees, water and grass – he succeeded in creating an illusion of eternal tranquillity, something which, on a clear summer's day in the largest of his parks, as at Burghley or Petworth, it is still possible to recapture.

His principles were comparatively simple. A park was enclosed within a belt of trees, broken here and there to allow a glimpse of a distant prospect. A lake in the middle distance was an essential part of his composition. He was often careful to conceal its ends, especially if it was formed by damming a stream. Within the park, and he was capable of working on the grandest scale, clumps and individual trees were most carefully placed on skilfully shaped mounds. He wrote himself of the need for the greatest delicacy in planting, since so much depended upon the size of the tree and the colour of its leaves to produce the effects of light and shade which he sought. He planted trees by the thousand: oak, ash, beech, chestnut, elm, lime, with some larch and Scots pine, and occasionally a cedar. He was very sparing in his use of garden buildings, but he could use them to very good effect when he wished. In 1766 he prepared a scheme to incorporate the ruins of Roche Abbey into the grounds of Sandbeck Park in Yorkshire, at about the time that William Aislabie at last succeeded in taking the ruins of Fountains Abbey into his park at Studley Royal. Gothic ruins were much sought after by this date, and to have genuine ones was an achievement indeed.

He was also an architect of real ability. He frequently designed the bridges which spanned his lakes. He designed a greenhouse and stable block in a rather pretty Gothic style for Lord Exeter at Burghley House. Claremont was built for Lord Clive to his plans. He added rooms and a portico to the west front of Broadlands in Hampshire for the second Viscount Palmerston, and designed an enchanting bridge pavilion at Scampston, Yorkshire.

In the last years of his life he was increasingly criticised, and after his death his reputation sank almost to nothing. As William Cowper wrote:

> Lo! he comes –
> The omnipotent magician, Brown, appears.
> Down falls the venerable pile, the abode
> Of our forefathers, a grave whiskered race,
> But tasteless. Springs a palace in its stead,
> But in a distant spot, where more exposed,
> It may enjoy the advantage of the north,
> And aguish east, till time shall have transformed
> Those naked acres to a sheltering grove.
> He speaks. The lake in front becomes a lawn.
> Woods vanish, hills subside, and valleys rise,

33 The lake and park at Burghley House, landscaped by Lancelot 'Capability' Brown from 1755 onwards

34 The bridge pavilion at Scampston Park in the East Riding of Yorkshire, designed and built by Lancelot 'Capability' Brown in 1773

And streams, as if created for his use,
Pursue the track of his directing wand,
Sinuous or straight, now rapid and now slow,
Now murmuring soft, now roaring in cascades,
Even as he bids.

His critics complained of the ruthlessness with which he
brushed aside old formal gardens, such as those at Burghley
House, to replace them with grass that swept right up to the
house, thus depriving it of the foreground that gave it
height and dignity. His critics also complained of the mono-
tony of his landscapes, depending so much as they did
upon line, whether a slope or the division between water
and grass, their only colour coming from the massing of

trees. By the end of the eighteenth century his landscapes were too subtle for many tastes. It was time to bring back flowers and statues.

Humphry Repton (1752–1818) set up as a landscape gardener in 1788. He moved only very gradually away from the precepts and practices of Lancelot Brown. Brown, by bringing his grass sweeping up to the very walls of a house, had effectively abolished the distinction between park and garden. Repton slowly brought it back. He re-introduced terraces, avenues, fountains and flower beds, and the flower beds become increasingly more ornate and artificial. Like Brown, he worked over large areas and also introduced changes and alterations to the houses of his patrons. Brown's landscapes can be severely simple. Those of Repton can be over-charged with detail to the point of being fussy.

The range of flowers and plants was, by the end of the eighteenth century, enormous. The pelargonium, so popular with Victorian gardeners, was introduced from South Africa in 1710. The hydrangea came from China in 1789, the chrysanthemum at about the same time. These new plants were brought to this country as part of a growing interest in botany, an interest which came to be centred on the gardens built up at Kew by Princess Augusta, the mother of George III. In 1772 Princess Augusta died, George bought the gardens, which hitherto had been leased, and sent out the first collector, Francis Masson, to the Cape of Good Hope to bring back new plants. By 1789 there were 5,535 species being cultivated in Kew Gardens.

The new plants and trees needed to be protected, both from cattle and from the weather. The garden wall was re-introduced, finally cutting off the park from the garden, and the greenhouse, aided by improvements in the manufacture of glass, rapidly became a feature in many gardens. To quote Cowper once more:

Who loves a garden, loves a greenhouse too.
Unconscious of a less propitious clime,
There blooms exotic beauty, warm and snug,
While the winds whistle and the snows descend.

At the same time gardening changed style and direction. Hitherto largely the preoccupation of a wealthy coterie, it became increasingly more popular further and further down the social scale. In addition, instead of attempting to recreate a classical, literary landscape, it became more and more concerned with the plants themselves. The new style was called Gardenesque, and is best described by the man

35 The formal gardens laid out in the 1820s and 1830s at Drummond Castle, Perthshire, for Lord Gwydyr by Lewis and George Kennedy

who invented the term, John Loudon. The characteristic feature of the Gardenesque

> is the display of the beauty of trees and other plants, individually. According to the Gardenesque School . . . all the trees and shrubs planted are arranged in regard to their kinds and dimensions. In short, the aim of the Gardenesque is to add to the acknowledged charms of the Repton School, all those which the sciences of gardening and botany, in their present advanced state, are capable of producing.

The Gardenesque school of landscape was, he thought, particularly adapted for laying out the grounds of small villas. An entirely new class of initiates was in the making.

By the time of Repton's death in 1818 the formal flower bed had been re-established as one of the central features of the garden, and the garden itself had become once again separated from the park. Formal flower beds were now set in ostensibly Italianate settings, with clipped hedges, statues, straight gravel walks and fountains. In the 1820s an immense formal garden of this kind was laid out at Drummond Castle, Perthshire, for Lord Gwydyr. In his library at the time was a copy of John James's translation, published in 1712, of A. J. Dezallier d'Argenville's *La Théorie et la practique du jardinage*, the apotheosis of the grand manner of Le Nôtre. The wheel had come full circle.

5 The urban landscape

The line from the most isolated farmstead to the largest conurbation is an unbroken continuum which historians divide up quite arbitrarily into hamlets, villages, towns and cities. The terms themselves admit of no clear cut or satisfactory definitions, and certainly the dividing lines between them are almost impossible to draw at all consistently. Mere size is no guide, and the legal status of a borough has been conferred on settlements quite haphazardly. Function is perhaps a better guide. In a village the majority of the inhabitants were primarily engaged in agriculture, or were dependents of those who were. In a town a significant proportion of the inhabitants were engaged for the larger part of their working lives in trades and occupations which were not directly connected with agriculture. This means that they had to look to shops and markets for the supply of their foodstuffs and necessities rather than to their own land holdings. Perhaps a third is the minimum proportion of such people required for a village to become a town.

The problem of the distinction between village and town is particularly important for a number of reasons. First of all, British towns in the eighteenth century were very much smaller than they are today. This means that places which on mere numbers of inhabitants would today be considered villages were, in the eighteenth century, by reason of their function, entitled to be called towns. Thus in Buckinghamshire, for example, there was at the beginning of the eighteenth century no place with more than 2,000 inhabitants, and yet Olney, Newport Pagnell, Buckingham, Stony Stratford, Marlow, High Wycombe, Amersham, Beaconsfield and so on were truly towns in that each had a handful of professional men such as lawyers and physicians, a number of shopkeepers and innkeepers, as well as craftsmen such as tailors and shoemakers.

This pattern of small towns is repeated all over Britain. After London, which has always been *sui generis*, the largest town in England was Norwich, with about 30,000 inhabitants. The smallest market town in England at the end of the eighteenth century was said to be Bootle in Cumberland. It was described as a neat little town, with only one public house and very few shops, but these were sufficient to raise it, however marginally, from being a village into being a town. The small size of towns meant that the span between Norwich and Bootle was not so great as that between Birmingham and Sandbach today. Towns were not swallowed up by huge neighbours. Very many more places qualified as important, in eighteenth century terms – as centres of services, trade and fashion – than do so today. Harleston in Norfolk had 1,344 inhabitants in 1789. They included thirty-eight husbandmen and twelve farmers. There were also twenty-six spinners, five blacksmiths, six bakers and eight tailors. In addition there were three attorneys, three surgeons, and one or two each of watchmaker, draper, breeches-maker, mason, brick-maker, midwife, milkwoman, bookseller, milliner, wheelwright and mole-catcher, in addition to the rector and his curate. Towns like this were distinctive, living communities, perhaps self-centred and introvert, but quite unlike present-day dormitory towns. Their sense of importance was of course enhanced by the difficulties of travel.

Secondly the small size of towns meant that the country was never far away. Fields and farms, the smell of new-mown hay, or of a farmyard midden, were the common experience of most townsmen. As late as 1800 there were cornfields within a quarter of a mile of Liverpool Town Hall. Many townsmen had a close personal tie with the land since many towns still had their common fields and meadows. Burgesses combined shoemaking or shopkeeping with the cultivation of their strips in the open fields. The common fields of Stamford, some 1,700 acres of arable, meadow and pasture, were not finally enclosed until 1875. The majority of tenants were not farmers but Stamford tradesmen and craftsmen. It was 1927 before the rated inhabitants of High Wycombe lost the right to depasture cows on Rye Mead. Up to that date the cows would return home each evening up the High Street, turning off when they reached their own byres, to be milked, bedded down for the night, and milked again the next morning before returning to their pastures.

To the small size of eighteenth-century towns and their much closer, more intimate relationship with the country, must be added an internal structure quite unlike that of a twentieth-century town. The centres of towns today are characterised by shops, offices, banks, cinemas, commercial properties of every kind. In the evenings, apart from those in search of entertainment, the centres of towns are almost deserted. Those who work there during the day have gone back to their suburban homes, a round journey of perhaps a hundred miles. The development of the central business district is a nineteenth-century phenomenon, and in many towns the last residents in central streets disappeared only in the years after 1945.

The internal structure of the eighteenth-century town was quite unlike this. The centre of the town was densely inhabited. The separation of work from home had scarcely begun. Workshops, warehouses and offices were integral parts of the domestic establishments of rich and poor alike. Prosperous merchants and professional people lived right in the centre of their towns, and well-to-do shopkeepers lived over and behind their shops. In January of 1798 the dwelling house and premises of Mr Peter Bicknell, linen-draper, of 149 Cheapside, London, were advertised for sale in *The Times*. The property comprised a suite of elegant and commodious shops with modern sashed fronts. The house contained eight bed chambers, with dressing rooms and closets, a handsome drawing room and dining parlour, a good kitchen, two staircases and roomy cellarage. On the same page were also advertised a very convenient house with two counting houses and exceeding good wine vaults in an airy and cheerful part of Bishopsgate, and a house and workshop in Goodmans Fields, Mansell Street, built of brick, with forges and foundry and a small dwelling house adjoining.

There was at the same time much greater social heterogeneity in the composition of communities in the sense that the poor were not yet relegated to slums and the rich had not yet migrated to the suburbs. Residential location was not yet an important status indicator since eighteenth-century society provided so many others. These developments were, however, beginning to take place in London and the other large provincial towns, where fashionable quarters were being developed, a trend that becomes increasingly noticeable during the course of the century.

Thus the social structure of British towns in the eighteenth century differed markedly from that of towns at the end of the twentieth century. The physical structure also differed. Streets were often badly paved, and were almost entirely lacking in drains, whilst post and rail fences separated foot travellers from vehicles (see Plate 22). Domestic refuse of every kind was allowed to pile up outside houses, becoming increasingly noisome as each week passed. It was quite usual for town refuse to be sold as manure to neighbouring farmers. Large quantities were taken by barge into the countryside from Great Yarmouth at the end of the century, and in Sampford Hundred in Suffolk the inhabitants bought large quantities of 'town manures' which had come from London to Manningtree, paying 10s. for a 5-horse load at the quayside.

It was often difficult for strangers to find their way about because streets were frequently without name boards, and houses were rarely numbered before the end of the eighteenth century. The streets of Southampton, for example, were named and the houses numbered following a Paving Act of 1770. The streets were also badly lit at night, but this is something which changed dramatically in the first decades

146

of the nineteenth century. In 1805 William Murdoch succeeded in lighting a Salford cotton mill using gas. By 1807 the offices of the Manchester Cleansing and Lighting Commissioners were being lit by gas. In 1812 the London Gas Light and Coke Company was established, laying gas mains in Pall Mall for house lighting. Street lighting by means of gas spread very rapidly, first of all to the large cities and then to the smaller towns, so that by 1826 very few towns with more than 10,000 inhabitants were without gas street lighting. Macclesfield in Cheshire had some gas lighting in 1815, Southampton in 1820. The gas works at Black Rock near Brighton were built in 1818–19.

Eighteenth-century towns had a greater physical individuality than do towns of the late twentieth century. Local building materials were still widely used, and this is something which gives to those towns where the hand of the nineteenth and twentieth centuries lies comparatively lightly – Stamford, for example, or Bradford-upon-Avon or Edinburgh Old Town – an inescapable aura of organic unity with their environment.

Nevertheless the physical structure of towns was changing, and in some towns this rate of change was already accelerating and would continue to do so throughout the nineteenth and twentieth centuries so that in cities like Birmingham and Sheffield there is almost nothing left from the eighteenth century, let alone from their Tudor, Stuart or medieval past. There are a number of reasons for this. First of all very few towns escaped a serious fire during the eighteenth century. Fires were common occurrences in towns, and the Great Fire of London is but the most famous example. There was a fire at Blandford Forum in Dorset in 1713, and another in 1731 which destroyed almost all of the centre of the town. William and John Bastard, local builders, then rebuilt the church, the town hall and the houses round the market-place. Fires in closely packed communities of timber-framed and thatched buildings spread very rapidly, doing considerable damage. Rebuilding by the end of the seventeenth century was often in brick and tile, by which time those artistic and architectural influences which we have seen at work in country houses and mansions were also to be found in towns. New buildings were put up in the new fashions, and old ones were refaced. The eighteenth century saw some towns grow very rapidly in size, a growth based either upon manufacture, as at Birmingham, or trade, as at Bristol, or fashion, as at Bath. As the numbers of their inhabitants grew so such towns spread further and further out into the countryside as building land became available, whilst the gardens, courts and yards in the existing built-up

36 Barn Hill, Stamford – an almost unchanged eighteenth-century town-scape

areas were progressively filled in with cottages, warehouses and workshops.

Just as the traditional fabric of the rural landscape of Britain was changing at an accelerating pace during the course of the eighteenth century so too was the traditional fabric of urban Britain changing, although the pace of change seems to have been much faster in towns than in the countryside, more especially in those towns which were experiencing the first stages of industrialisation. It seems to be axiomatic that industrialisation is also accompanied by urbanisation, such urbanisation being based upon immigration into towns rather than upon their natural increase. The industrial and commercial growth of towns like Glasgow and Nottingham, St Helens and Swansea, was accompanied by a rapid growth in their population. The people had to be accommodated somewhere. The consequence was a series of booms and slumps in building and construction work, culminating, in the years between 1783 and 1793, in the biggest building boom of the century. Few towns anywhere in Britain escaped entirely. In some, like Birmingham and Manchester, the housing stock was doubled. A thousand new houses were built in Bath between 1788 and 1793. The actual process of building and development was complex, protracted, and in many respects each town has its own unique history, the only common factor being a total lack of overall centralised control, something which may have prevented the worst of the Nottingham back-to-back houses, but which would almost certainly have perpetrated horrors almost as bad.

If we are to look at this process of urban change at anything beyond the level of vague generalisation then we must study a specific example. London in 1700 was by far the largest city in Britain, with a population of perhaps 675,000. By 1831 its population was 1,474,069. Its sheer size means that somewhere within it is to be found almost every facet of the urban experience of eighteenth-century Britain. London is at once a centre of political authority, an industrial and commercial city, and a fashionable resort. Within

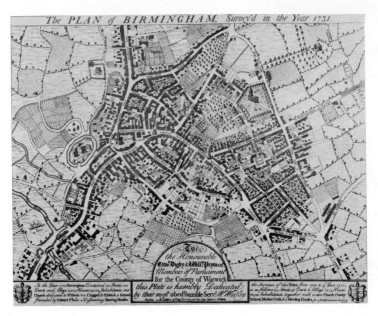

37 Westley's map of Birmingham, made in 1731, when the population of the town must have been 18,254, and not the 8,254 given in the bottom right-hand corner. Compare with Plate 38 (note the north lies in the bottom right-hand corner in this map)

London itself the development of the Grosvenor Estate, which is particularly well-documented and has been closely studied, may serve as an epitome of what was happening.

The Great Fire of London of 1666 was of central importance in the shaping of London over the next 150 years. The designs of Sir Christopher Wren for a completely replanned city were ignored, and the rebuilding after the Great Fire largely followed the old streets and lanes and the old property boundaries. The importance of the Fire lay elsewhere: first the Act for Rebuilding, passed in 1667, standardised house building in a number of ways by laying down structural requirements which it was hoped would prevent any future fires from spreading without check. Further acts of 1707 and 1709, and even of 1774, extended and developed

150

these requirements. Thus the haunting spectre of fire had a profound influence over the way in which houses were designed and built in eighteenth-century London. This fear of fire was not unjustified. Scarcely a year went by without a fire in some part of London: Lady Molesworth's house at 49 Upper Brook Street was burned down in 1763; houses in the Little Piazza, Covent Garden, were destroyed by fire in 1769; Vanbrugh's theatre in the Haymarket was burned out in 1789. The list is endless.

Secondly the Great Fire compelled large numbers of

38 Hanson's map of Birmingham, made in 1785, when the population was 52,250. There has been much expansion to the north-west of St Philip's church since 1731, and more streets are under construction. Extensive building has also taken place south-west of New Street

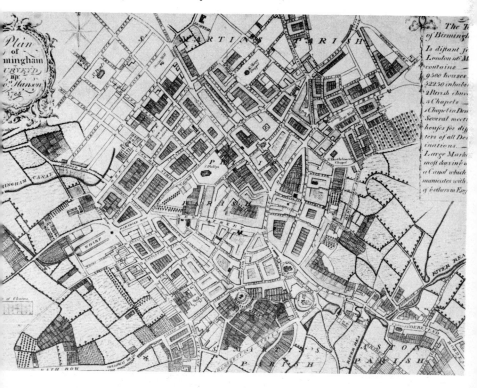

people to find new houses, especially to the west of the old city, a movement which had long been going on under the pull of the magnet of the Court in and about Westminster. The Great Fire hastened the process.

In 1677 Sir Thomas Grosvenor, a Cheshire gentleman, married Mary Davies, the twelve-year-old daughter and heiress of Alexander Davies, a wealthy London scrivener who had died in the year of her birth. Her dowry included about 500 acres of land, largely meadow and pasture, lying to the west of the built-up area of London, with one portion, called the Hundred Acres, lying to the south of what is now Oxford Street and east of Hyde Park. Sir Thomas died in 1700, leaving three sons, all of whom eventually succeeded to his title and his estates. The complexities of the family

Figure 12 The growth of London

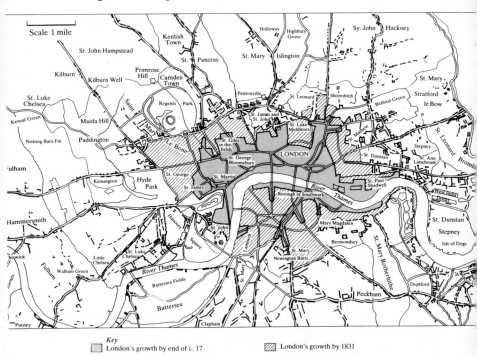

settlements, and the fact that Mary was declared insane in 1705 so that her interests from that date until her death were administered by the Court of Chancery, meant that it was necessary to obtain a private act of parliament before building leases could be granted. These acts were obtained in 1711 and in 1726. When Dame Mary Grosvenor died in 1730 Sir Richard Grosvenor was at last able to break the settlement and hold his estate in freehold.

In 1720 the Hundred Acres site was laid out on a lavish scale, with Grosvenor Square as the centrepiece, covering an area of 8 acres. There were to be two main east to west streets, Grosvenor Street and Brook Street, each 60 feet wide. The actual work of laying out the estate was done by Thomas Barlow, surveyor to Sir Richard, and one of the leading London builders of the time. His plan did little more than provide the skeleton framework of streets and squares. There was remarkably little control over the plans, elevations or designs of the actual buildings. It was well over fifty years before building was finally completed, by which time some of the earliest leases were already beginning to fall in and some rebuilding could be undertaken.

Once the ground plan of the estate had been determined it was left to individual builders to take out leases and erect such buildings as they could afford or were prepared to speculate upon being able to sell. During the half century or so in which the estate was being built almost a hundred building leases were granted, covering areas ranging from single house sites to large areas of several acres. Individual leases show considerable diversity of terms and conditions, but generally the builder was required to erect a good and substantial brick dwelling, to follow a common building line, to put up iron railings at the front, and wooden posts in the street, to complete the paving, and to make stables and other service buildings as low as possible. There is remarkably little on the type and quality of building materials, the height of the buildings or of individual storeys, and no requirement as to the amount of money that should be spent. Some houses in Brook Street were required to be 'large', some in Grosvenor Square itself were to be at least 30 feet wide by 30 feet deep.

Nearly 300 people are known to have worked on building the estate during the first fifty years, but only a handful of these can be called architects, of whom the best known is Colen Campbell. He certainly took a lease on two adjoining house plots in Brook Street, on which he built the house in which he died in 1729. Any further connection with the design of the estate is uncertain. In any case he is quite untypical of those who actually carried out the building. This was done by people like John Simmons, Edward Shepherd and Benjamin Timbrell, master builders working on a large scale, together with scores of other bricklayers, masons and carpenters who built one or two houses at a time.

Much building was done by what has been called 'a remarkably efficient system of barter', in which the carefully costed work of one type of craftsman on one building was traded off against similarly costed work by another type of craftsman on another building. In this way building could go ahead with surprising speed and with surprisingly little ready money changing hands. When cash was required it was often obtained on mortgage. One of the most important mortgagees for the building of the estate was Sir Richard Grosvenor himself, but much capital also came from tradesmen working or living in and about Westminster, people such as apothecaries, fishmongers, a gingerbread-maker, a brewer, timber merchants, a peruke-maker, a coachman, several clergymen, attorneys and scriveners, and the Earl of Uxbridge.

If he were fortunate the builder himself might be able to sell the house before or during building. He might alternatively sublet it, or, in one extreme case, raffle it, in the same way as the Adam brothers had to hold a lottery to get themselves out of the financial mess that the building of the Adelphi scheme had landed them in. Builders themselves often worked on very narrow margins, and if there was any serious delay in selling or subletting then they could find themselves in difficulties, and on occasion bankrupt – a fate which overtook somethi' ig like one in eight of all those who worked on the estate between 1720 and 1775. The highest price paid for a new house was £7,500, for no. 19 Grosvenor Square, paid in 1730 for a house with 60 feet frontage. At the other extreme no. 11 North Audley Street was bought in 1737 for only £180.

The enormous span from the £7,500 for the house in Grosvenor Square to the £180 for the house in North Audley Street serves to emphasise one of the most important features of the development of the estate, and this is its considerable social heterogeneity, something which is reflected in the size of the houses and the width of the streets. Only in Grosvenor Square itself was there anything approaching strict social segregation. Some houses, especially in Grosvenor Square, were very large indeed. In other streets, Mount Row, for example, small houses were subdivided from the first, and a number of courts and passages were built. Brown's Court, built by John Brown, bricklayer, between 1730 and 1739, contained nine tiny two-storeyed houses along a 10-feet wide court entered through even narrower arched passage ways. Each house was one room deep with a yard behind, the rooms themselves no more than 13 feet square. This court was by no means unique, and that part of the estate which lay immediately to the south of Oxford Street was by the early nineteenth century an area of poverty and misery quite the equal of anything to be found in Manchester or Nottingham at the same time.

Grosvenor Square itself was from the first one of the most fashionable residential squares in London, and it retained that character for almost two centuries. But outside the square tradesmen were to be found almost everywhere, and in some quarters of the estate they formed the overwhelming majority of the inhabitants. Even in Grosvenor and Upper Grosvenor Streets, Brook and Upper Brook Streets, almost as fashionable as Grosvenor Square itself, tradesmen were to be found. Benjamin Timbrell, one of the foremost master builders in London, lived at no. 12 Upper Grosvenor

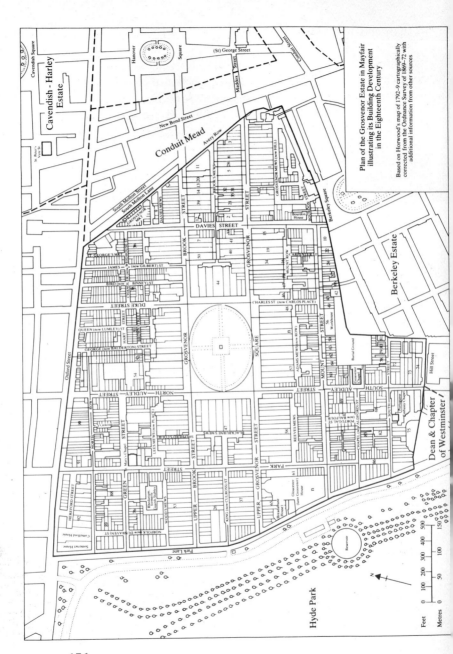

Plan of the Grosvenor Estate in Mayfair
illustrating its Building Development
in the Eighteenth Century

Based on Horwood's map of 1792–9 cartographically
corrected from the Ordnance Survey of 1869–72 with
additional information from other sources

Cavendish - Harley
Estate

Cavendish Square

St Peter's
Vere St

Hanover
Square

(St) George Street

Conduit Street

Maddox Street

New Bond Street

Conduit Mead

Avery Row

South Molton Street

South Molton Lane

GROSVENOR HILL

DAVIES STREET

BROOK STREET

GROSVENOR STREET

GROSVENOR MEWS (now HILL)

Berkeley Square

Bourdon
House

Berkeley Estate

ST GEORGE'S MEWS

JAMES (now GILBERT) ST

BIRD (now BINNEY) ST

DUKE STREET

CHARLES ST (now CARLOS PLACE)

MOUNT ROW

QUEEN (now LUMLEY) ST

HART STREET

GEORGE (now BALDERTON) STREET

GROSVENOR SQUARE

MOUNT STREET

Workhouse

Oxford Street

NORTH AUDLEY STREET

ADAMS MEWS (now ROW)

Burial Ground

Grosvenor
Chapel

Hill Street

Mary's Chapel

BROOK STREET

BLACKBURNE'S MEWS

SOUTH AUDLEY STREET

PORTUGAL ST
(now BALFOUR)

CHAPEL (now ALDFORD) ST

Portuguese
Embassy Chapel

Dean & Chapter
of Westminster

LEES MEWS (now PLACE)

WOODS MEWS

GREEN STREET

REEVES MEWS

PARK STREET

UPPER BROOK STREET

UPPER GROSVENOR STREET

KING (now CULROSS) ST

HEREFORD STREET

NORFOLK (now DUNRAVEN) ST

Camelford House

Gloucester
(late Grosvenor)
House

Gloucester
Row

Breadalbane
House

Somerset House

Park Lane

Hyde Park

Reservoir

N

Feet   0   100   200   300   400   500
Metres 0   50   100   150

No.	Date	Name(s)
1	8 Aug. 1720	Thomas Barlow, carpenter
2	2 Sept. 1720	John Deane, painter
3	Do.	William Barlow senior, bricklayer
4	Do.	Robert Hearne, joiner (not carried out. replaced by no. 35)
5	Do.	Thomas Ripley, carpenter
6	Do.	Mathew Tomlinson, carpenter (assigned to Benjamin Timbrell, carpenter)
6a	Do.	Robert Scott, carpenter
7	24 Nov. 1720	Francis Bailey, carpenter
8	Do.	Do. (not carried out. replaced by no. 53)
9	3 Dec. 1720	Robert Pollard, yeoman, and Henry Avery, bricklayer
10	12 Dec. 1720	Francis Commins, mason
11	Do.	Thomas Phillips, carpenter
12	Do.	John Barnes, bricklayer
13	17 Dec. 1720	George Pearce, plumber
14	Do.	Joseph Osborne, ironmonger (assigned to Edward Shepherd, plasterer)
15	Do.	William Waddell, plumber (assigned to Thomas Barlow, carpenter)
16	Do.	Henry Huddle, carpenter
17	Do.	John Pritchard, gentleman
18	20 Dec. 1720	Stephen Whitaker, brickmaker (assigned to William and Benjamin Benson, esquires)
19	21 Dec. 1720	Benjamin Timbrell, carpenter
20	Do.	David Audsley, plasterer
21	4 Jan. 1720/1	George Chamberlen, carpenter, and George Wyatt, bricklayer
22	5 Jan. 1720/1	William Watkinson, bricklayer (assigned to Thomas Elkins, bricklayer)
23	17 Jan. 1720/1	Thomas Barlow, carpenter
24	20 Jan. 1720/1	John Owen, carpenter (assigned to Samuel Phillips, carpenter)
25	11 March 1720/1	William Barlow junior, bricklayer (not carried out, replaced by no. 36)
26	11 May 1721	Stephen Whitaker, brickmaker
27	14 July 1721	Joseph Watts, esquire (not carried out, replaced in part by nos. 61 and 65)
28	11 Jan. 1722/3	John Jenner, bricklayer
29	18 April 1723	Do.
30	10 May 1723	George Chamberlen, carpenter
31	22 June 1723	John Laforey, esquire
32	20 July 1723	Benjamin Whetton, bricklayer
33	19 July 1723	Francis Commins, mason
34	9 Aug. 1723	Robert Hearne, joiner
35	Do.	Samuel Phillips, joiner
36	7 Nov. 1723	Edward Shepherd, plasterer
37	25 April 1724	Robert Andrews, gentleman
38	27 April 1724	Augustin Woollaston, esquire
39	25 May 1724	George Pearce, plumber
40	10 July 1724	Richard Lissiman, mason
41	24 July 1724	Robert Scott, carpenter
42	Do.	John Elkins, bricklayer
43	4 Nov. 1724	Charles Vale, brewer
44	24 Nov. 1724	John Simmons, carpenter
45	22 Jan. 1724/5	John Jenner, bricklayer
46	28 Jan. 1724/5	Do.
47	6 Feb. 1724/5	Thomas Ripley, esquire (assigned to Robert Scott, carpenter, and Robert Andrews, gentleman)
48	6 March 1724/5	Thomas Cook and Caleb Waterfield, carpenters
49	Do.	Benjamin Whetton, bricklayer (assigned to William Newball, bricklayer)
50	Do.	Francis Bailey, carpenter
51	Do.	Augustin Woollaston, esquire
52	Do.	Do.
53	Do.	Do. (assigned to Robert Andrews, gentleman)
54	Do	Edward Shepherd, gentleman
55	6 March 1724/5	Thomas Barlow, carpenter, and Robert Andrews, gentleman
56	24 April 1725	Henry Elkins, bricklayer, and Francis Dudley, joiner
57	29 April 1725	Robert Grosvenor, esquire
58	18 Nov. 1725	Richard Andrews, gentleman
59	18 June 1726	William Rogers, carpenter
60	18 Aug. 1726	John Ellis, joiner
61	5 June 1727	Thomas Goff, blacksmith (assigned to Robert Grosvenor, esquire)
62	29 Aug. 1727	Peter Vandercom, mason (assigned to William Rogers, carpenter)
63	12 April 1728	William Rogers, carpenter
64	Do.	Philip Chandler, bricklayer
65	Do.	Richard Lissiman, mason
66	23 April 1729	Thomas Scott, poulterer (assigned to Joseph Kendall, gentleman)
67	6 April 1730	Benjamin Timbrell, carpenter, Robert Scott, carpenter, William Barlow senior, bricklayer, and Robert Andrews, gentleman
68	Do.	Do.
69	Do.	Do.
70	Do.	Do.
71	Do.	Do.
72	1 Feb. 1735/6	Roger Blagrave, carpenter
73	24 May 1736	William Singleton, plasterer
74	Do.	John Eds, carpenter
75	24 May 1736	Edward Shepherd, esquire
76	Do.	Roger Morris, carpenter of H. M. Ordnance
77	2 July 1736	John Doley, carpenter (not carried out, replaced by no. 90)
78	19 Feb. 1736/7	Edward Scott, bricklayer
79	Do.	Charles Durham, bricklayer
80	5 March 1736/7	William Harrod, gentleman
81	Do.	Roger Blagrave, carpenter
82	Do.	Benjamin Timbrell, carpenter, Robert Scott, carpenter, William Barlow senior, bricklayer, and Robert Andrews, gentleman
83	Do.	Richard Teage, victualler
84	Do.	Benjamin Timbrell, carpenter, Robert Scott, carpenter, William Barlow senior, bricklayer, and Robert Andrews, gentleman
85	2 June 1739	John Eds, carpenter
86	17 Sept. 1739	Roger Blagrave, carpenter
87	Do.	Thomas Skeat, bricklayer, and Richard Teage, carpenter
88	9 June 1750	John Spencer, carpenter
89	14 May 1757	Do.
90	1 Aug. 1764	Do.
91	20 June 1765	Do.
92	Do.	John Phillips, carpenter
n		No building agreement found

Figure 13 The Grosvenor Estate, London (redrawn from a plan in *Survey of London*, vol. XXXIX The Grosvenor Estate in Mayfair Part I)

Street. There was an apothecary and a shoemaker on the north side of Brook Street. In the lesser streets – Mount Street, Davies Street, North and South Audley Streets – tradesmen formed well over half of the population. When a detailed survey of householders was made in 1789–90 it listed 1,526, of whom 55 per cent were engaged in trade, and some 120 different occupations were listed, including victuallers – there were seventy-five public houses in the estate in 1793 – butchers, chandlers, grocers and greengrocers, bakers, cheesemongers, dairymen, including a cow-keeper, fishmongers and a muffin-maker, chimney sweeps, stationers, watch-makers and a piano-maker. Some of these tradesmen, especially the tailors, milliners, glovemakers, perfumers, peruke-makers, upholsterers and cabinet-makers, provided for the needs and tastes of their rich, titled and fashionable neighbours. In St James's Square, equally as aristocratic as Grosvenor Square – there were six dukes living there in 1721 – the firm of Josiah Wedgwood had its showrooms at no. 8 between 1797 and 1829 expressly for that reason.

During the half-century that work was in progress, bricklayers, masons and carpenters formed a permanent element on the estate. Almost as numerous were those concerned with the indispensable horses and carriages: there were coachmen, saddlers, farriers, smiths, wheelwrights, stable keepers, even a riding academy. Other trades were almost industrial – brewers, pewterers, brasiers, soap makers. Some leases attempted to exclude the more noxious trades, such as butchers, tallow chandlers, brewers, distillers and blacksmiths, by demanding an extra rent, £30 in main streets, £10 in lesser ones, but there appears to have been no consistent policy: the lists of trades varied, and the additional rent, certainly in the lesser streets, looks more like a licence to continue than a deterrent.

Before the end of the century the practice of letting furnished lodgings had become well-established, especially among upholsterers and cabinet-makers, although it was not unknown for private owners also on occasion to let their houses whilst they themselves were in the country. Lord North, the prime minister, used regularly to let his house at no. 50 Grosvenor Square. The demand for furnished lodgings led eventually to the establishment of several private hotels, especially in Brook Street, and it is from two of these, Wake's Hotel, opened in 1805, and Mivart's, opened in 1813, that Claridge's Hotel is descended.

Mount Street, North and South Audley Streets were fashionable shopping centres, with cabinet-makers and upholsterers catering for the luxury end of the market. Other areas, especially that just to the south of Oxford Street, where there were several narrow streets and courts of small houses, were far less savoury, being inhabited by a raffish and drifting population, worlds apart from the *beau monde* of Grosvenor Square, a world of taverns and cheap lodging houses, and at least one house of ill-fame in Norfolk, now Dunraven, Street.

The history of the Grosvenor Estate is fascinating in itself, but it is made even more so because it serves as a microcosm of the nature and direction of urban growth and change throughout Britain in the eighteenth century. Every facet of the pattern of its development is to be found repeated, with due consideration given to local variation, in almost every town in Britain.

Sir Richard Grosvenor required a private act of parliament before he could undertake the development of his estate. In an age when probably half of England was subject to strict settlements, an age which gave punctilious attention to property rights, however remote or contingent, such preliminaries to estate development were both normal and necessary. Private acts of parliament in 1718 and 1734 were necessary before Lord Burlington could develop the area to the north of Burlington House laid out first of all as Old Burlington Street, Cork and Clifford Streets, and then New Burlington Street and Savile Row. It took a private act of 1746, authorising leases of up to 120 years, to make the Colmore estate available to accommodate the growth of Birmingham, and a further act of 1766 made the Gooch estate available. An act of 1768 facilitated the development of the Pulteney estate in Bath, and in due course two more were needed.

It was private landlords who made land available for urban expansion, whether in London, Birmingham or Manchester, in large or small quantities. The size of the pieces of land could have a profound effect upon the morphology of the emergent town. In Leeds, enclosure to the north and east of the ancient urban nucleus had produced a pattern of small fields in individual ownership. This led to a similar pattern of small-scale building when urban expansion began in the second half of the eighteenth century, and no new street was laid out in Leeds between 1634 and 1767. The pattern of ancient field boundaries could still be recognised beneath the streets, closes and terraces of Leeds until quite recently. At Brighton in the eighteenth century there were five open fields called 'tenantry laines'. The laines were divided into furlongs by means of leakways, with the actual strips, called 'paul-pieces', running at right angles. The leakways themselves ran at right angles to the hill sides. When, early in the nineteenth century, the expansion of Brighton began, these ancient patterns exercised a permanent influence on the layout of the new town. The leakways became the main streets, North Road, Gloucester Road and St James's Street, whilst the paul-pieces became side streets, such as Upper Gardner Street and High Street.

Variations in the forms of land tenure could have a significant influence upon the development of individual towns. Nottingham in the eighteenth century was surrounded on three sides by open arable fields, together with meadow and pasture, held in common by the burgesses. They guarded jealously all their rights, refusing all entreaties to enclose, until the nineteenth century was half over. As a consequence building land in the centre of the town became increasingly expensive, and more and more houses had to be crammed into less and less space, leading to the creation of some of the most appalling slums ever to be found anywhere in Britain.

In Scotland, a similar problem led to a different solution. The purchase price for a piece of land was paid in two parts: one part was a lump sum, the other part consisted of a 'feu', or rent charge, paid in perpetuity. The feu could on occasion be extinguished by the payment of a second lump sum, usually calculated at twenty-one years' purchase. The initial feu was usually set fairly high. This meant that building land was expensive to rent, and so the answer was found in the building of high rise tenement blocks. Lands south of the river Clyde, opposite to the old town of Glasgow in the barony of Gorbals were divided up and feued from 1795 onwards. The tenement blocks then created became even more notorious than the back-to-back houses of Nottingham. Feuing in Edinburgh, together with the sometimes precipitous slopes of the site, the restricted area of the royalty and the need for defence, created in Parliament Square a tenement which was reputedly the highest building in the city, with seven storeys towards Parliament Close and fifteen towards the Cowgate. Such tenements were served by a common staircase, characterised in a pamphlet published in 1752 as 'no other in effect than an upright street, constantly dark and dirty'. The dirt was unimaginable. Yaws, a disease that spreads in temperate climates only in conditions of extreme filth, was undoubtedly present in early eighteenth-century Edinburgh.

The principal role of the landlord in eighteenth-century urban development was to release land for building as and when it was required. His reward was a steady rise in his income from ground rents. The actual building was done by a host of men, and occasionally women. The business of John Simmons, the carpenter who built the east side of Grosvenor Square, was continued by his widow after his death. These men were drawn from the trades most heavily engaged, namely bricklayers, masons and carpenters. They usually worked on a very small scale, one or two properties at a time, and much work was done on a barter system. Many over-reached themselves and became bankrupt. The outbreak of war with France in 1793 brought the building boom of the previous decade to a sudden halt, with bank-ruptcies all over the country. Scores of half-finished schemes, from Bristol and Bath to London and Edinburgh, where the new university buildings designed by Robert Adam remained roofless for over twenty years, survived half-finished for decades. Many more builders lacked the capital with which to finish their projects, and saw them deteriorate. Thus Daniel Laurie bought 47 acres of land on the south bank of the Clyde in 1801–2, hoping to lay out a high-class residential district. But he was chronically short of money. When, after seventeen years, largely of inactiv-ity, the scheme was at last completed, Laurieston in fact emerged as one of the most insalubrious areas of Glasgow.

Much building was financed by channelling small savings into building societies, institutions which have their first fragile beginnings in the last quarter of the eighteenth century. Societies which actually built houses emerged in the Black Country, the earliest known being Ketley's of Birmingham in about 1775. Societies of this kind were concerned only to complete one particular scheme, after which they were wound up. Permanent societies, which lent money to their members, were formed in Lancashire and the West Riding of Yorkshire, spreading to other parts of the country after 1800.

Money also came from prosperous townsmen who were drawn into property speculation from other trades, men like Richard Paley, a soap boiler of Leeds who, in 1800, was the second largest property owner in the town and by 1803 was bankrupt, or Thomas Sambourne, a Sheffield attorney, and Charles Spackman, a wealthy coachbuilder who financed the building of Lansdown Crescent in Bath.

The Grosvenor Estate was laid out on a regular gridiron pattern of straight streets and a spacious square. A similar pattern is to be found all over Britain. In Manchester the Aytoun, Mosley and Stevenson developments followed the same gridiron pattern. In Birmingham the Old Square, east of Bull Street, was started in 1713. In Bristol Queen Square, measuring 550 feet square, was laid out between 1700 and

1727, whilst King Square, laid out by 1742, took just as long to fill up. George Square and its neighbouring rectilinear streets were laid out for wealthy Glasgow merchants between 1750 and 1775. At Aberdeen plans for a new town

39 A view of Edinburgh from the air – the main streets and other features may be identified from Figure 14

were drawn up in 1799 and with little regard for natural obstacles. George Street was driven straight across the loch, which had to be drained first, and St Catherine's Hill was levelled to allow the building of King Street. Much of the actual building was done in local granites and the name of the 'Granite City' was given to Aberdeen from this time.

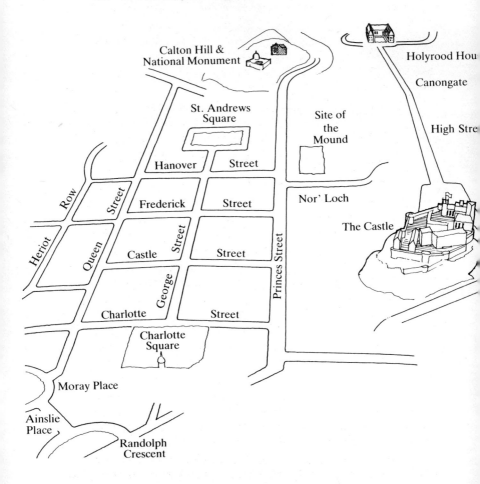

Figure 14 Edinburgh, Old and New Towns, as seen from the air. (See also Plate 39)

Edinburgh occupies a peculiarly cramped site, between the castle hill on the west and Holyrood House and its park on the east. The site was even more cramped in the eighteenth century because of the Nor'Loch on the north and another shallow lake to the south. In 1752 proposals for the improvement of the city were published. The idea was enthusiastically taken up by George Drummond, the lord provost, and it was largely owing to his efforts that it eventually came to fruition. The draining of the Nor'Loch began in 1759, and the building of the North Bridge to give access to the building land beyond began in 1765. A competition was held for designs for the new town which was to be built on this land, and James Craig's plans were accepted in July of 1767. His plan has been called 'painfully orthodox'. Rigid and unimaginative in concept though it may be, it none the less succeeds – first of all because of its splendid site, secondly because of the restrained simplicity of so many of the buildings that were erected, and thirdly because of the contribution that Robert Adam made in Charlotte Square. Craig's plan consisted of three straight streets, Prince's, George and Queen, linking, on the west, St George's Square, and on the east St Andrew's Square. As building slowly moved westwards from St Andrew's Square the town council imposed progressively stricter controls over the designs of the buildings that were put up. By the time building reached the fringes of St George's Square the plan had to be changed, largely because the town council did not at the time own the land. Agreement was reached with the owner, the Earl of Moray, in 1791, and Robert Adam was commissioned to produce Edinburgh's first scheme for uniformly designed house frontages to the four sides of the newly named Charlotte Square. The result has with justice been called 'a marvellous achievement; spacious, elegant, symmetrical without needless duplication.'

Straight streets on a gridiron pattern relieved by an occasional square, became the small change of unimaginative landlords and jobbing builders the length and breadth of Britain, from Aberdeen and Crieff to Portsea and Maryport.

165

40 Charlotte Square, Edinburgh

It was the genius of John Wood senior which introduced curves into a rectilinear world. He settled in Bath in 1727, at a time when the town was already well-established as a fashionable resort. His grandiose schemes for an almost total rebuilding of the town were rejected by the town council, and so he turned instead to the Barton estate, lying almost due north. The owners, the Gay family, granted him a series of 99-year leases, and Wood in his turn sublet plots to individual builders and masons, retaining very much stricter control over the buildings that were actually put up than was ever done on the Grosvenor Estate.

Queen Square was begun first, taking about seven years to finish. The Parades were completed in about 1749 and King's Circus was begun in 1754, the year of his death, to be completed by his son, also called John, who then went on to build the Royal Crescent, finished by about 1775, and the New Assembly Rooms. John Wood senior had an almost mystical vision of classical architecture, and saw the circle as a symbolic manifestation of the Divine perfection. These ideas are most fully developed in the King's Circus – two perfect circles one inside the other, broken into three equal segments to represent the Trinity. Here in Bath is a land-

41 Bath from the air, looking north. The principal buildings and streets may be identified from Figure 15

scape of the mind projected into the real world with the same fervour as that which created Stourhead or Castle Howard.

The astonishing achievements of the Woods, father and son, in Bath added the circus and the crescent to the vocabulary of urban property developers. The splendour of the procession from Queen Square to the Royal Crescent was matched in conception if not realisation by John Nash's plans for the development of Regent's Park in London. These included a series of terraces, of which Cumberland Terrace is the longest, a circus that was only half-finished, namely Park Crescent, linked by the grand sweep of Regent

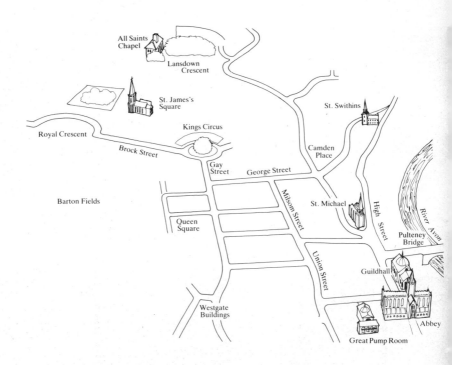

Figure 15   Bath as seen from the air. (See also Plate 41)

Street to Carlton House. By the 1820s the scheme had been expanded to take in St James's Park. A new square was laid out on the site of the Royal Mews, to be named Trafalgar Square in 1830, and Buckingham Palace was rebuilt. The whole project was enormously expensive, the rebuilding of Buckingham Palace was an architectural disaster, and so, when in 1830 George IV, who had consistently backed the scheme against all criticism, died, Nash was dismissed and no further work was undertaken.

Crescents and circuses had by this time become almost commonplace. The Crescent at Buxton was built by John

42 Cumberland Terrace, Regent's Park, London, designed by John Nash in 1827

Carr of York for the Duke of Devonshire between 1779 and 1781. The Royal Circus was built in Edinburgh between 1820 and 1823. Lewes Crescent in Kemp Town in Brighton was planned in about 1825. Atholl Place in Perth was laid out as a crescent at the very end of the eighteenth century. Control over design, layout and elevation of the buildings became stricter and stricter as landlords and their architects increasingly sought to emulate the noble monumentality that uniformity of façade had brought to the Royal Crescent in Bath. Some of the most detailed requirements were those laid down by the Earl of Moray in 1822 for his new estate in Edinburgh, to the west of Craig's New Town. Drawings and elevations by the architect, Graham Gillespie, were supplied to each builder, as well as plans for the sewers. Even the quarries for the stone were named. As a consequence Moray Place became the most splendid residential quarter in Edinburgh.

The Royal Crescent, Cumberland Terrace and Moray Place lie at one end of the spectrum of urban change in Georgian Britain. The foul courts, back-to-back houses and cellar dwellings of Nottingham and Liverpool, the indescribable tenements of Glasgow, lie at the other. The long straight rows of rather pleasantly proportioned, three-storeyed houses, with mass-produced doors, window casements and balconies that spread with breathless speed over Islington in the early nineteenth century perhaps lie somewhere in between. *The Times* of 8 September 1803 carried an advertisement for a genteel commodious house, three storeys from the basement, four rooms to a floor, with a spacious, handsome drawing room, walled pleasure garden, coach house and separate carriage entrance in Church Row, Islington, only a few doors from the Green. Suburbia was being born.

The physical expansion of towns was entirely uncontrolled in any respect. It was left to individual estate developers, large and small, to lay out streets, fix building lines, provide sewers, decide on building standards, the width of plots, the size of gardens if any, the siting of churches and markets. Much building was done on a very small scale, and masons, carpenters and bricklayers had often to build quickly and cheaply to stay in business at all. In Birmingham some 5,000 houses were built between about 1745 and 1780. The great majority had no more than two or three rooms, and sold new for less than £100. Better class schemes took years to fill up. Birmingham's only crescent, planned in 1788, was to have twenty-three houses costing £500 each. Twenty-four years later it was still only half-finished. Even when development was carried out by the town council, as in Edinburgh New Town, Bristol

43 Canonbury Square, Islington, London, built in about 1800 by Jacob Leroux

and Liverpool, there was the same lack of detailed control for much of the eighteenth century.

It is important, however, to appreciate that towns had always been insanitary, over-crowded and unhealthy. The rapid urban and industrial expansion that was taking place in Britain in the second half of the eighteenth century was occurring for the first time in human history, and an awareness of the social problems that it was creating came only when their horrors far exceeded any previous experience. There were enormous technical problems to be overcome. A number of towns had a piped water supply to some quarters early in the eighteenth century, and George Sorocold of Derby was one of the first engineers to develop a specialised knowledge of this branch of engineering. But the water came through wooden or lead pipes and was totally untreated. Not until 1817 were wooden pipes forbidden in London. Water was being purified by passing it through filter beds at the end of the eighteenth century, but it was first used in the dyeing and bleaching industries. Such treatment was not extended to public drinking water until 1804 in Paisley, and the filter beds built in Chelsea in 1827 were the first in London. Filter beds certainly purify water, but contemporaries had no idea why, because there was total ignorance of the existence of water-borne bacteria. Water closets were quite common in middle- and upper-class houses by the end of the eighteenth century, but they were almost always connected to a cesspit rather than to the sewer, and the cesspits were rarely emptied. Only long experience taught the proper gradients and shapes for sewers, and the need for firm support for the pipes. The sewers themselves discharged straight into rivers and streams. The Thames became so heavily polluted that on a number of occasions the stench from the river compelled the House of Commons to abandon its sittings. The tributaries of the Thames, such as the Fleet, were if anything even worse. The King's Circus in Bath may represent a reconstruction of the ideal classical city. Its drains were no better, and probably worse, than those of Imperial Rome.

172

No attempts were made on a national scale to improve the cleanliness of towns before the middle years of the nineteenth century. Townsmen and their visitors were none the less aware of the filth and stench, and many efforts were made on a purely local and *ad hoc* basis to make things a little better. This was done by applying to parliament for a local act to set up a body of improvement commissioners. By 1830 there were over 300 such bodies, nearly a hundred of them in London. The majority were run by groups of men, appointed for life by the act, filling vacancies by co-option. They were usually created to pave, cleanse and light the streets. Those in York could regulate hackney coaches. Those in Cheltenham pulled down the old market house, and those in Birmingham demolished many of the old buildings huddled round the Bull Ring and St Martin's church. Normally they took on the responsibility that since medieval times had lain with the individual occupier to pave and cleanse the street in front of his house, performing these tasks themselves, either by hiring labour or by contracting the work out, and levying a rate to meet the expense.

Some improvement commissioners did nothing for years together. Others could at times be fairly efficient, but even these almost always confined their attention to the central streets. Side streets, alleys, courts and lanes remained in their primordial state. Their efforts were hampered by a lack of technical knowledge, by squabbles over jurisdiction, by protracted disputes over their legal powers, and by the refusal of householders to pay for what many considered to be unnecessary improvements.

We began this chapter by stressing how small towns were for much of the eighteenth century and how imprecise and blurred was the distinction between town and country. By 1830 this rural/urban dichotomy has become much sharper in some, but by no means all, parts of Britain. There were a number of reasons for this, and we have looked at one in this chapter, including the physical expansion of towns, impelled by a swelling population based upon immigration rather than natural increase. Few towns escaped this physical growth altogether, but some grew very much more rapidly than others, and their rate of growth accelerated when steam power was eventually applied to industrial processes on a large scale, so that factories had no longer to be tied to the streams that provided their power. It is industrialisation that provides the other main reason for the sharpening of the rural/urban dichotomy, and it is to this that we must now turn.

6 The search for power

The family and household were of basic importance not only to the social organisation of eighteenth-century Britain, but also to its economic organisation. They constituted the basic unit of industrial and manufacturing enterprise no less than of husbandry and agriculture, which is why such enterprises were very small in scale. (At the beginning of the century it is likely that the largest industrial site in Britain was neither a factory nor a mine, but the Royal Navy's dockyard at Chatham, employing perhaps over a thousand men.) It was the household that was the basic unit of manufacture, with very many of the actual manufacturing processes being carried out in workshops which were physically part of the house of the craftsman or artisan who performed them.

But the craftsman did not work alone. The labour of wife and children made as important a contribution to family prosperity as that of husband. Moreover, their contribution is to be found across the entire spectrum of economic activity, including manual labour of the heaviest kind in agriculture and mining. Women and children worked in gangs in the fields at harvest time (see Plate 21), and in the Scottish Highlands it was the women who reaped the grain, gathered the potatoes and carried them in from the fields in creels on their backs. Women were at work across a wide range of metal industries, including nail, pin and file making. They worked in baking and in building, often taking over the business when their husband died. Indeed it has been suggested that the years after 1815 saw a remarkable contraction in economic opportunities for women, except in the textile factories and in domestic service. The accomplished, but essentially idle, gentlewoman in fact formed a small minority, to be found only at the very top of the social hierarchy.

Much production, whether of nails, stockings, woollen cloth or linen yarn, was carried out at home, in conditions of heat, noise and squalor that are almost impossible now to re-create. The low level of technology meant that long hours of work were necessary before even a modest reward could be earned. On the other hand the very nature of the domestic system meant that very long hours of work alternated with equally long hours of idleness, by no means all of it involuntary. The Feast of Saint Monday (whereby Monday was taken as an unofficial holiday) was widely observed and was a long time dying.

The domestic craftsman was supplied with his raw materials, and frequently also with his tools, and the finished goods were bought from him by someone who is probably best described as a dealer. Thus Peter Stubs of Warrington, who was an innkeeper, maltster and brewer as well as a file-maker, supplied Sheffield steel to individual workmen over a wide area of Lancashire and Cheshire, and sold their finished products all over Britain, America and the West Indies and many parts of Western Europe. He branched out into tools of every kind, especially those for the shoemaking trade, added the manufacture of parts for watches and clocks, horn and ivory combs, writing slates and slate pencils. Some of his workmen combined manufacture with farming and were sometimes quite prosperous. Others had only their trade, were almost always in debt and were frequently paid in goods rather than in cash. Similarly, Abraham Dent of Kirby Stephen in Westmorland was at once a shopkeeper, a wine merchant, a brewer and a dealer in knitted stockings, which he bought in tens of thousands from households all over the Pennines, households in which farming and knitting were combined, with much of the actual knitting being done between haymaking and lambing. Robert Paling, of Hoby in Leicestershire, called

176

44 Matthew Boulton's Soho factory, Handsworth Heath, Birmingham, finished by about 1765, from an engraving in James Bisset, *Magnificent and Grand National Directory*, published in 1800

himself a dyer in his will made in 1762, but he bequeathed a stocking frame, then hired out to John Taylor of Syston, stockingmaker, to his son Robert as well as a dyehouse to his son James 'as soon as he has learnt the business'.

The examples of Stubs, Paling and Dent serve to underline how blurred the distinctions were in the eighteenth century between occupations and between town and country. All three men were astute enough to recognise an opportunity, and had sufficient money to exploit it, when it came along. They were not large-scale manufacturers in the way that Matthew Boulton and Sir Ambrose Crowley were, but they belonged to the same breed, and there were very many more Stubs's, Palings and Dents than there were Boultons or Crowleys.

The normal manufacturing enterprise for much of the eighteenth century was domestic and small-scale. The jour-

177

ney to work was the exception, and buildings devoted solely to industrial and commercial purposes were unusual. This is why the large-scale enterprises which did slowly appear during the course of the eighteenth century seemed so astonishing and so extraordinary to contemporaries, whether it was Thomas Lombe's silk factory established in Derby in 1717, or Matthew Boulton's Soho factory, established just outside Birmingham in 1761 and with about 700 work people by 1776, whilst Coalbrookdale, where there were several industrial plants in close proximity to one another, was considered one of the wonders of Europe. It was the 1780s before factories of this kind became at all numerous, and even then they were largely confined to certain areas of the country. Many were at first water-powered, and so they sought out streams which were swift-flowing and unfailing. As steam power came to replace water power they migrated to the coal fields. Contemporaries writing even in the 1820s and 1830s were astonished at the new industrial landscapes around Manchester or Birmingham, but, with the benefit of hindsight, we can see that in fact at this time industrialisation had only just begun. Although few parts of the country escaped the indirect effects of industrialisation in that cheap cotton goods, pottery, nails and tinned candlesticks became readily available, many counties of Britain remained profoundly rural. In Buckinghamshire and Dorset, in Norfolk and Sussex, in Banff and Kirkcudbright, the pace of change was very slow, its impact perceptible only in isolated spots, when compared to what was going on in South Lancashire, Staffordshire, the Black Country, the Rhondda or the valley of the Clyde.

The technical and managerial problems involved in the establishment of large-scale industrial enterprises had to be recognised and resolved as they arose, since the transformation which was taking place in Britain during the course of the eighteenth century was occurring for the first time anywhere in the world, and even the most perceptive of contemporaries could have had little real appreciation of the direction in which the Prometheus they had unbound

45 A view of the now restored Old Furnace, Coalbrookdale, where in 1709 Abraham Darby first successfully used coke to smelt iron

was taking them.

If the problems involved in 'thinking big' were unforeseen and unresolved, there was yet a further constraint upon the size of industrial and commercial enterprise. The frantic speculation in the stock of the South Sea Company pushed its price from 130 in January 1720 to 1050 in the June of that year. This was accompanied by an equally frantic speculation in the shares of hundreds of joint stock companies promoted for the wildest schemes. The Bubble burst in the September; the financial crash ruined thousands. The scandal destroyed the credibility of the joint stock company as a form of business enterprise. To establish one would now require a private act of parliament, an expensive and uncertain procedure. Finance had instead to be obtained from family circles, from a timely legacy or a prudent marriage. The South Sea Bubble deprived industrialists of one tool for financing their enterprises, although in fact it seems very unlikely that this had any real inhibiting effect on the growth of industry.

The eighteenth century is the age when for the first time natural forces other than wind and water were harnessed to provide power on a large scale. The discovery of atmospheric pressure in 1643 by Evangelista Torricelli led at first to a number of displays of its power to provide a moment's diversion and astonishment to fashionable audiences. It was Savery and Newcomen who turned it from a toy to a

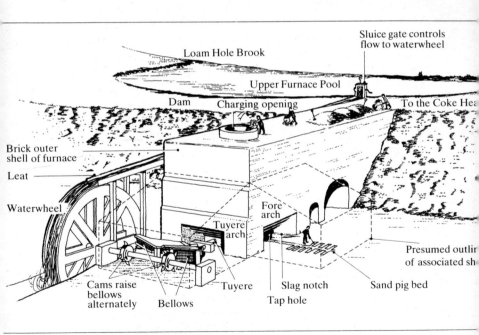

Figure 16 The Old Furnace, Coalbrookdale (redrawn from diagram in *The Coalbrookdale Museum of Iron*, Museum Guide no. 2.01)

servant of unimagined power. When refined and improved by James Watt, and then his successors after his patents expired in 1800, the steam engine provided the power base for the transformation of Britain that took place in the nineteenth century. It is impossible to overemphasise the contribution of this first taming of natural power to the economic and hence the social changes which are most conveniently summarised in the phrase 'the Industrial Revolution'. But the very significance of this contribution, coupled to the enthusiasm with which every aspect of the development of the steam engine has been studied by historians and industrial archaeologists, has perhaps tended to obscure the fact that its contribution was comparatively narrow. The dependence of society upon human and animal muscle and effort, together with the power of wind and water, for the performance of almost all of its labour had been only marginally reduced by the steam engine by the end of the Georgian period.

In the countryside horses and oxen contributed their strength to ploughing, carting and harrowing. Francis Moore's patent of 1767 for a fire engine to replace horses was premature to say the least. It was the very end of the eighteenth century before machines began to make any contribution towards threshing, reaping, chaff-cutting or the raising of water from wells. Hedging and ditching, the building of dry-stone walls in the Pennines and the Lake District and the enclosure dykes in Scotland, the levelling of runrig, the paring of moss or heath land, the digging of drains and all the other tasks of the agricultural year were performed by human labour, employing a wide range of tools showing local and regional adaptation to local and regional needs. Such work was often done by gangs of labourers. When the Earl of Strathmore was improving his Glamis estates in the 1760s and 1770s his estate surveyor, James Abercrombie, employed gangs of men, sometimes as many as eighty or ninety at a time, often Highlanders, to clear stones, drain peat mosses, build dykes, level and straighten ridge and baulk, plant trees and hedges. At the same time he could call upon the services in kind due from tenants to plough, harrow, spread manure, cut hay, bring home peat and carry coal, and take to market that part of the rent payable in kind.

Human labour was as important in manufacture and urban life as it was in the countryside. Canals and their tunnels, cuttings and embankments, were built by armies of navvies using pick, shovel, wheelbarrow and horse drawn cart. The furnaces at Coalbrookdale were charged with iron ore, coke and limestone by men trundling wheelbarrows and tipping the loads in at the top of the furnace (see Plate 45 and Fig. 16). The bellows to the furnace may have been worked by water power, but neither water wheel nor steam engine could replace the men with their wheelbarrows. Coke was first used as fuel at Coalbrookdale in 1709, but it was the 1750s before its use in iron smelting became at all widespread, and even then charcoal continued to be used until the end of the century and beyond. Charcoal could only be made by human labour, whilst coal and iron were mined in conditions of extreme danger and discomfort of the harshest kind. The drainage soughs of the Derbyshire lead mines were excavated in similar fashion. The heat and noise in which the furnace men had to work at Coalbrook-dale was probably matched only by that endured by the glassmakers of Bristol and Stourbridge in the brick cones where the glass was made. At Harwich there still survives from the former naval dockyard a crane built in 1776 which was operated by a treadmill, and there is another on the quayside at Guildford, dating from the time when the River Wey was an important 'moving highway'.

Human energy had by the beginning of the eighteenth century long been supplemented and reinforced by animal energy, whether from horses, oxen, dogs or donkeys. Horses and oxen were used in ploughing and for pulling carts, waggons, coaches, sledges and other vehicles, as well as for towing boats and barges on canals and rivers. Howeverer as the eighteenth century drew on horses in particular were used to provide the motive power for an increasingly

46 The Red House glass cone furnace at Stourbridge. The furnace was in the centre of the cone at ground level. The glass-blowers and other craftsmen had to work in the space between the furnace and the walls in conditions of intense heat. This cone was built between 1788 and 1794

wide range of machinery. This was done by means of the horse-gin (see Fig. 9). The horse trod a circular path and as he did so he pulled round with him a wheel that was geared to a driving shaft. The wheel could either be raised on a central column so that it was above the horse's head, or else it was at ground level in which case the horse had to be trained to step over the driving shaft, something which he very quickly learned to do. The wheel was frequently housed in a separate building. On occasion, however, and especially when the wheel was at ground level, there was no protective housing. The gin was outdoors, its driving shaft going into the barn by means of a hole in the wall. Gins of this kind were portable, and those owned by a tenant farmer could be taken with him on the expiration of a lease. Horse-gins are to be found all over Britain, although today it is almost always only the building that survives, the machinery having long disappeared.

Most horse-gins appear to have driven agricultural machinery. The threshing machine invented in 1786 by Andrew Meikle was at first, literally, horse-powered. But their role in industry must not be overlooked. They were employed to raise coal to the surface at the Saltom pit near Whitehaven, opened in 1729. In many Derbyshire lead mines the ore was raised to the surface by means of 'whims', the local term for a horse-gin. They continued to be used in the Derbyshire coal field until the end of the nineteenth century. The cotton mill that Samuel Unwin built at Sutton in Ashfield in about 1770 was powered by horses and oxen harnessed to rotating beams. They were eventually replaced by a water wheel, and Unwin built a windmill on top of his factory to pump back the water so that it could be used again. The first cotton spinning mill that Richard Arkwright built in Nottingham was horse-powered, and the original specification for his spinning machine shows that it was designed to be operated by horses. The gunpowder works at Waltham Abbey in Essex did not abandon horses for working the grinding mills until 1814. A horse-gin was used in a tannery in Storrington in Sussex and another in Arundel was used to crush linseed. The horse, plodding patiently round the endless circle of his gin, lives on into the age of the jet engine because, in 1783, when attempting to measure the power of his steam engine, James Watt devised a unit which he called a 'horse', namely the power to lift 33,000 pounds through 1 foot in a minute. This unit of horse-power has been used ever since, although in fact it is

47 The eighteenth-century Fenney windmill at Blackbrook near Coalville, Leicestershire. It is a tower mill with fantail and ogee roof. It now has only two sails

about 1⅓ times the power of a horse.

Windmills first appeared in Western Europe in the first half of the twelfth century, and must be ranked among the most ingenious and skilful products of the medieval carpenter. By the beginning of the eighteenth century they were common over much of England, and they were also to be found, although less frequently, in eastern lowland Scotland. The earliest type was the post mill, in which the main body, or box, of the mill, carrying the sails and containing the machinery, pivoted on an immense wooden upright post, strengthened by quarterbars and resting on crosstrees. These crosstrees sometimes lay directly on the ground, but by the eighteenth century they were frequently supported on brick or stone piers. A tailpole was necessary to turn the mill into the eye of the wind. The fantail, patented in 1746 by Edmund Lee, did this automatically. A later development was the tower mill. Here the machinery was contained in a fixed tower, and only the cap which housed the sails actually turned. A variation on the tower mill is the smock mill, an eight- or twelve-sided structure of wooden frames clad in clapper boarding.

Windmills were used principally for grinding corn into flour or meal, but they could be adapted to other purposes, including the grinding or crushing of lead ore and of flints for use in pottery manufacture, as well as being used in the fens for pumping water. They were undoubtedly an important source of power throughout the eighteenth century, and indeed continued to be so until the end of the nineteenth, but they suffer from a number of disadvantages. The wind will not always blow when it is required, nor with an appropriate strength. Considerable skill and dexterity are called for to keep the sails facing into the wind, and for windmills to be destroyed in a gale was by no means an uncommon occurrence. Nevertheless windmills were, until the beginning of the twentieth century, a common sight over lowland Britain, and few parishes in south-east England at any rate were without at least one, and two or three were not unusual.

Horse power and wind power were certainly important in eighteenth century Britain, but their limitations were marked and intractable. Of much greater importance was water power, and it is probably impossible to over-exaggerate its importance in the eighteenth century as the chief source of energy in those manufactures, iron and textiles, which lay at the heart of the Industrial Revolution.

Although by 1709 coke was used to smelt iron in the furnaces at Coalbrookdale it was water power that drove the huge bellows necessary to raise the temperatures needed. The cotton industry, the leading growth sector of the early nineteenth century and the steam powered industry *par excellence*, was still drawing at least a quarter of its energy requirements from the water wheel as late as 1830.

The water wheel had been known in Britain since Saxon times, and by the eighteenth century it had been developed and improved in a number of ways. Basically there were two methods by which water could be used to turn the wheel: by water passing underneath the wheel to give the 'undershot' mill, or by water falling on top of the wheel to give the 'overshot' mill. John Smeaton carried out a number of carefully controlled tests to discover the relative efficiency of these two kinds of water wheels, from which he concluded that the undershot mill was about 22 per cent efficient, but the overshot was about 63 per cent. These results he communicated to the Royal Society in 1759. He then went on to design and construct iron components for water wheels. He was consulting engineer to the Carron iron works near Falkirk in Scotland, and his first cast iron water wheel was in fact made for a blowing engine to a Carron furnace.

A third type of water mill was to be found in northern and western Scotland. This was the horizontal, or Norse, mill. A lade, or cut, brought water from a stream to the mill house, a small rectangular stone building. Here the water turned a wheel which lay horizontally. This drove a vertical shaft which passed through the lower millstone to turn the upper stone. Mills of this kind were often to be found strung along a suitable water course in many parts of the Scottish Highlands, and one is still maintained in working order at Dounby in the Orkney Islands.

A fourth kind of water mill, found only along the coast, is the tide mill. A dam was built to impound sea water as the tide came in. As the tide retreated the outflow of water was controlled by sluices to turn a wheel. Such mills were once not uncommon. One at Bishopstone, near Newhaven in Sussex, had a windmill on top to work the sackhoist. When extended in about 1800, it drove fifteen pairs of grindstones. There is a tidal mill still standing at Woodbridge in Suffolk.

By the beginning of the nineteenth century the water wheel had become an engine of remarkable power and efficiency. William Strutt's North Mill at Belper, built in 1803–4, was five storeys high with a schoolroom in the attic for the pauper children who lived and worked in the mill, and 127 feet long. It was powered from a single water wheel, 18 feet in diameter and 23 feet wide, a gentle giant dipping with measured tread into the Derbyshire Derwent.

So important was water power that the location of the earliest textile mills, iron furnaces and forges, and a wide range of other industrial enterprises, was dictated by the presence of suitable streams, and it was better that they should be steady and unfailing rather than swift. It was upon water power that the prosperous eighteenth-century textile industry of the Cotswolds was built, and it was upon water power that the astonishing variety of Lakeland industry was erected – iron furnaces and forges, slitting, rolling and boring mills, bobbin mills, woollen, cotton, flax and silk mills, gunpowder mills and pencil mills. The bellows to the furnaces at the Backbarrow iron works continued to be operated by water power until 1870. The first silk mill in England was that of Thomas Cotchett, built in Derby in 1702. This was followed in 1717 by Lombe's mill. Both were powered by the Derwent. By 1734 Derby had what amounted to an industrial estate: there were mills for slitting and rolling iron sheet for nail-making, for rolling copper sheets for sheathing sea-going boats, for lead smelting, as well as a number of iron foundries, and gypsum, plaster and colour works. All drew their power from the indefatigable Derbyshire Derwent.

In Scotland wind mills were relatively uncommon, and so it was upon stone rubble water mills, two or three storeys high and with an attic, often L shaped in plan and with a kiln to dry the grain before it was ground, that Scotland had to depend for its meal. The most important textile industry in the country was the manufacture of linen. Almost every branch of this except bleaching and scutching was domestic in its organisation. Scutching was carried out in water-powered lint mills, of which a fine example still remains at Inverar in Perthshire.

The first water mills were intended for the grinding of corn. By the eighteenth century it was quite usual to adapt an existing water mill to a new industrial purpose. The town

48 The central L-shaped five-storey block in this photograph is William Strutt's North Mill at Belper, Derbyshire, built in 1804. Behind it is the East Mill, built in 1912

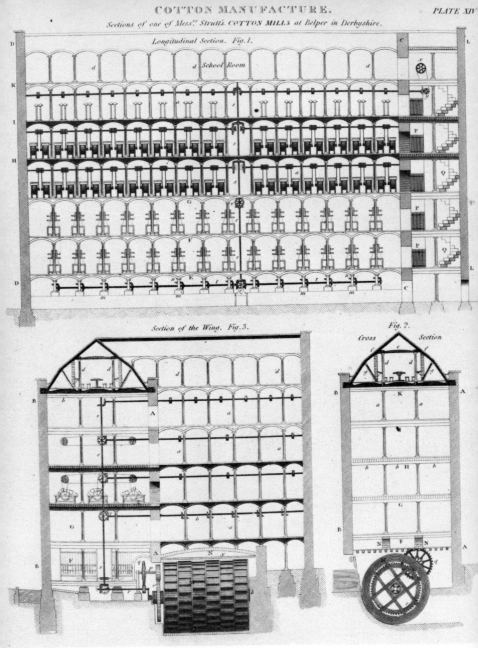

49 Sections through the North Mill at Belper from Abraham Rees, *Cyclopaedia*, published 1819–20

mill at Halstead in Essex was converted from corn grinding to silk throwing by Samuel Courtauld in 1825, and at Cheddleton in Staffordshire are two water mills, one purpose-built and the other adapted from a corn mill, for grinding flints for use in the pottery industry. Many industrial mills were built on sites which had been used for generations. Richard Arkwright built his cotton spinning mill at Cromford on the site of a corn mill, and his Masson mill, built in 1783, was on the site of a paper mill.

Streams which proved to be suitable sources of power were often lined with mills. The six miles of the Frome between Garston and Beckington were said in 1800 to have 200 mills along it, whilst the valley of the Derbyshire Derwent has with some justification been called the cradle of the Industrial Revolution. Water power is widespread, and so industry which was dependent upon water power was also widespread. A paper mill was established at Scandale Brook, Ambleside, by 1681, and there were other paper mills along the river Loose near Maidstone in Kent. At the Ashford marble works in Derbyshire the stone was cut, ground and polished by water power. A water-powered wooden screw cutting mill was at work in Hartshorne, also in Derbyshire, by 1776. Blade mills for the grinding of scythes lined the swiftly flowing streams of the Staffordshire–Worcestershire border area. There were water-driven gunpowder mills at Albury in Surrey and at Faversham in Kent. The Titchfield foundry in Hampshire, established in 1775, was where Henry Cort developed his puddling process for making iron; it drew its power from the river Meon. At Laverstoke, also in Hampshire, is the water mill where the manufacture of paper for bank notes was established in 1724. In 1753 the Newland Company, a partnership of Lancashire and Cumberland ironmasters, established the Lorn Furnace at Bonawe, on the southern shores of Loch Etive and about ten miles to the east of Oban, which did not then exist. The bellows of the furnace were operated by a water wheel, the water coming along an aqueduct for about half a mile from the river Awe. The iron ore came by a

50 A view of the Lorn iron furnace, Bonawe, from the north-west. The water wheel which drove the bellows stood behind the broken wall on the left-hand side, and the bellows in front. The loading mouth was under the roof, unlike the one at Coalbrookdale

difficult sea voyage from Lancashire. The fuel was charcoal, made in the surrounding woods. Two rows of workers' cottages, a manager's house, ore and charcoal sheds, a pay office, school, church and quay were built in this remote and isolated spot, but in spite of its isolation the enterprise was a success, not finally closing until 1874.

Water power was essential to eighteenth century Britain. For tasks beyond the power of the horse-gin and the wind-mill there was no alternative before the 1780s and it was a long time before steam power replaced it in the minds of contemporaries. Richard Arkwright, for instance, bought a Boulton and Watt steam engine for his Cromford mill in 1780, not to drive the machinery but to pump the water back over the wheel. Unfortunately water power has several disadvantages. Rivers and streams do not always yield a constant flow of water. Frosts in winter and droughts in summer could mean no water for days together. This could be overcome to some extent by building reservoirs, such as the Upper Furnace Pool at Coalbrookdale (see Fig. 16) and those at the Lorn Furnace at Bonawe. The flow of water could then be controlled by weirs and sluices. Nevertheless, in spite of considerable ingenuity, water power was not always available exactly when it was wanted. If there was a good head of water, then the mills would work for incredibly long hours, some employees sleeping in their clothes on the premises, changing only at the weekend. If the water failed, then the children who worked in the mills went out to play.

The inherent disadvantages of wind and water power had long been recognised and much attention was given during the seventeenth century to finding some more reliable alternative. Success came at the very end of the century when two separate strands of effort were brought together. The first strand was the increasing theoretical interest in atmospheric pressure and the power it could exert through a piston beneath which a vacuum had been created. The second strand was the desperate search for some practical, efficient method of pumping water out of mines. It was Thomas Savery who brought these threads together in his patent of 1698 for an engine for raising water 'by the Impellent Force of Fire'. His workshops were in Salisbury Court, between Fleet Street and St Bride's church in London, and it was here that the first steam engines were made. His engine was operated by condensing steam in a cylinder. This created a vacuum which was filled by water being sucked up into it. Steam was then used to force the water even higher and out of the cylinder, and the cycle began again. In practice he used two cylinders, which were filled and emptied of water in turn. He scarcely realised the power he had unleashed, since in fact he was using steam at high pressure, something which very quickly tested to breaking point the engineering and metal working skills of the time.

Working quite independently, Thomas Newcomen, a Dartmouth ironmonger, perfected at about the same time an engine that was far more practical than that of Savery in that it used steam at atmospheric pressure, but he found his path blocked by Savery's patent. The two men seem to have come to some kind of agreement, and in any case after Savery's death in 1715 the patent was taken over by a group of proprietors. The first Newcomen atmospheric steam engine for pumping water from a mine was erected at Dudley Castle, Worcestershire, in 1712. Its massive nodding beam projecting through the brickwork of its engine house raised 120 gallons of water every minute from a depth of 150 feet. It was grossly extravagant in its demands for coal, its thermal efficiency being about ½ per cent. Nevertheless it worked, without regard for wind, frost or drought, and for twenty-four hours a day. By the time of Newcomen's death in 1729 his engine was widely used for pumping out mines, not only in Britain but also in France, the Low Countries and Germany. The last operational beam engine, at the South Crofty mine near Camborne in Cornwall, was closed down as recently as 1955.

Newcomen's beam engine could be adapted only very clumsily to provide rotary motion. Until this problem could be overcome then the water wheel would reign supreme outside the mines. It was James Watt who provided the solution. He worked for a number of years on improving the efficiency of the Newcomen engine, taking out in 1769 his patent for a separate condenser. His first partner, John Roebuck, went bankrupt in 1773, and his rights in the patent were taken over by Matthew Boulton. In the following year Watt moved to Birmingham, and in 1775 he and Boulton obtained an extension of the patent to 1800. At about the same time John Wilkinson, the Shropshire iron-master, took out a patent for a boring machine that would cut cylinders to the new standards of precision that Watt required. The new steam engine was both more powerful and more efficient than Newcomen's, needing only a third of the coal. It proved very successful, and mine owners willingly paid the royalty of a third of the savings in the fuel costs that Boulton and Watt demanded. By 1781 a number of devices to provide rotary motion had been patented, and further refinements to increase efficiency and smoothness

Figure 17 The Newcomen steam engine (based upon an engraving by Thomas Barney made in 1719)

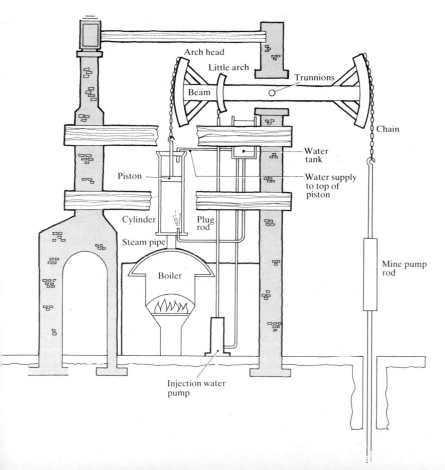

followed, although the thermal efficiency was still little more than 4 per cent. Only now did the Age of Steam really begin.

The adaptation of the steam engine to purposes other than the pumping of water from mines progressed only very slowly. In 1776 John Wilkinson used one to supply the blast for his iron furnace at Willey in Shropshire. Four years later he had four engines at work. He also employed a steam engine to drive a forge-hammer at his forge in Bradley, also in Shropshire. In 1785 Boulton and Watt built the first steam engine in a textile mill at Papplewick in Nottinghamshire. That the term 'mill' continued to be applied to textile factories long after they had given up water power is yet another indicator of the fundamental importance of this source of power in the early stages of the Industrial Revolution. From now on the use of the steam engine as the prime mover spreads rapidly. Supplies of coal became of the first importance, and so industrialists looking for sites for new factories turned to the coal fields and away from the river valleys of Derbyshire and the Cotswolds. This movement to the coal fields must not however be exaggerated. Water-powered mills were not easily abandoned – too much had been invested in them for that. It was, for example, not until the slump of 1825 that there was any real reduction in the numbers of water-powered textile mills in Gloucestershire and Wiltshire, and steam power was not introduced into the blanket mills of Witney until 1850. Water-powered mills continued to be built. The mill of Foresterhill in Meldrum was built as a water mill in about 1800, and when the Mill of Aden, Old Deer, in Aberdeenshire, was rebuilt in 1868, the water wheel was also rebuilt.

James Watt refused to entertain the idea of using steam at pressures more than a few pounds per square inch above atmospheric pressure, and so failed to appreciate the full potential of steam power. In 1820 there were only sixty steam engines in Birmingham. There were 169 by 1835 but even then they averaged only 15 horse-power each. Once his patents expired in 1800 it was open to other engineers to

196

experiment, and the most notable and most successful of these was Richard Trevithick. He built a high pressure steam engine in 1800, and the first steam locomotive in 1801. In 1802 he built at Coalbrookdale a pumping engine working at 145 pounds per square inch, using a cylinder only 7 inches in diameter, in sharp contrast to the 80-inch diameter cylinder of the South Crofty mine beam engine just mentioned. The sharp reduction in the size of engines that followed the use of steam at high pressure meant that it became practicable to think of using a steam engine to drive a vehicle. In 1804 Trevithick built a locomotive that pulled a load of 10 tons over the ten miles of cast iron rails linking the Glamorgan canal and the Pendarron iron works. A similar locomotive was built in Gateshead in 1805 for a colliery near Newcastle, and eight years later George Stephenson built his first locomotive, the *Blücher*, for the Killingworth colliery in the same coalfield. Both of Trevithick's engines were too heavy for the track then in use and were converted to stationary engines.

At this time a group of coal owners were seeking a way of transporting their coal from Darlington to the sea at Stockton-on-Tees. A canal, they concluded, would be too expensive, and so they planned a horse-drawn railway twenty-seven miles long. But Stephenson's locomotives so impressed them that, from the day of opening onwards, steam-powered locomotives were used to haul the trains over at least part of the route with, at first at any rate, a rather bizarre mixture of horse power and stationary engines taking up the rest. There was no regular passenger service. It was the coal traffic that provided the mainstay of the enterprise.

The line was a commercial success from the first, and attracted much attention. Visitors came from all over Britain, including a group of Liverpool and Manchester businessmen who went on to obtain an act of parliament in 1826 for the construction of a railway to link their two cities. They chose George Stephenson to build the first railway line in the world. When it opened on 15 September 1830 it began a new era.

Lombe's Derby silk mill was unique in its time, not least because of the large number of employees, about 300, that it brought together under one roof. In some industries, such as iron smelting and forging, glass and pottery making, shipbuilding and brewing, the concentration of workmen away from their homes was a necessity. In other industries, especially textiles, it was possible for workmen to install the comparatively simple machinery in their own homes, and domestic weaving, stocking knitting and lace-making persisted throughout the Georgian period. None the less centripetal forces were already at work, and became increasingly powerful as the eighteenth century drew on. The application of water power and then steam power to manufacturing processes, especially the spinning of cotton, became profitable only when a number of machines were harnessed to the prime mover, and the more that could be harnessed the more profitable the whole enterprise became. The result was the factory of which William Strutt's Belper North Mill, with its four floors of spinning machines all turned by one powerful, tireless water wheel, is a fine example.

There were other factors at work. The domestic system in the textile trades meant that quality control was difficult, embezzlement was common, regularity of output impossible to obtain. Technical improvements were difficult to introduce and impossible to safeguard against piratical imitators. Domestic workshops were often squalid, frequently as noisy as any factory was to become, the hours worked often as irregular and as long as those imposed by the nature of water power. Only the relentless, unsleeping steam engine brought round-the-clock working and long unbroken 12-hour shifts.

As with so many other changes in the eighteenth century, the emergence of the factory was a very slow process, and the distinction between domestic workshop and factory was for a long time very difficult to draw. In the stocking knitting towns and villages of Nottinghamshire and Leicestershire, for example, existing cottages were, during the

51 A sixteenth-century timber-framed and thatched cottage at Shepshed in Leicestershire, with wide windows inserted to give light to stocking-frame knitters

first part of the eighteenth century, being adapted, and purpose-built ones, containing living room, scullery, bedroom and workshop, were being erected to contain the knitting frames. In the last decades of the eighteenth century rows of terraced houses, back-to-back and three storeys high, were being built in Nottingham, with room for three knitting frames. In Rochdale square blocks were built containing four dwellings, each having one room on each floor, with workshops on the top floor running the full width of the block. At Mellor in Lancashire two cottages share a weaving room which is built between them. In Halifax Road, Smallbridge, near Rochdale, there is a block of five pairs of back-to-back houses, three storeys high, with workrooms on the top floor over the full extent of the building.

The concentration of knitting and lace-making frames into workshops containing more and more frames was

52 New Lanark – a view from the south, from an aquatint by J. Clark, 1825

already under way at the very beginning of the century. By 1728 a number of Nottingham framework knitters were employing poor apprentices, recruited from parish workhouses, sometimes as many as forty at a time, although the frames themselves were still hand-operated. Not only were cottages with attached workshops purpose-built, but existing buildings of every description were converted and workshops were built in the gardens and yards of existing houses. A small farm advertised for sale in Wirksworth in 1794 had a large barn 'lately converted into a cotton factory'. It was from this huddle of small, overcrowded sheds, barns, workshops and attics, whether in Birmingham or Witney, Shepshed or Trowbridge, that the idea of a purpose-built factory slowly emerged. Only in 1802, and after fourteen years in business, did Peter Stubs of Warrington build workshops of his own and bring some of his employees together under the one roof. Several small mills were built in Derby in emulation of Lombe's silk-throwing mill, and there was one of four storeys in Chesterfield by 1757. In 1760 Jedediah Strutt built a silk-throwing mill in Derby on the Markeaton brook, but it was really Richard Arkwright who was the first to exploit the opportunities that the factory offered.

Arkwright arrived in Nottingham in 1768, and moved out to Cromford to build his first water-powered cotton spinning mill in 1771. He had considerable initial success, and proceeded to build other mills, in Derbyshire, at Rocester in Staffordshire, at Keighley, and in Manchester. In 1783 he visited Scotland, where he met David Dale, a wealthy merchant banker. The two became partners and established, on the banks of the Clyde, the village of New Lanark. The first mill was in operation by 1785. Robert Owen arrived

53 An aerial view of New Lanark. The principal buildings may be identified from Figure 18

in New Lanark in 1798, and became managing partner in the following year, when he also married Dale's daughter Caroline. Owen was undoubtedly a very successful businessman. He bought out Dale in 1799 for £60,000. At the end of 1813 the capital value of the New Lanark complex was £114,000. He was also a benevolent, paternalistic and enlightened employer. He gave up employing children under 10. He built a 'New Institution' for the educational benefit of all his employees. By 1816 the village had a population of 2,297, of whom 1,700 actually worked in the mills. It became one of the showplaces of Britain, attracting visitors from all over Europe. Although the mills themselves have been extensively modernised internally, and one was destroyed by fire in 1882 and never rebuilt, much still remains, both of the mills and the cottages, from which to re-create a very good picture of what an early nineteenth-century industrial village was like.

Richard Arkwright was essentially an entrepreneur and business man. He failed, however to keep abreast of technical innovation. All of his mills, and those built by his licencees and his imitators, were rather similar in scale and design, and few were insured for much more than £4,000. By the 1790s textile mills and factories were getting larger and more expensive. The vast Dunkirk mills near Nailsworth in Gloucestershire were built in three stages between 1798 and 1827, and were powered by four water wheels. The splendid Bell mill on the Tay was completed in 1790, a six-storeyed building 90 feet long. Sir Richard Arkwright was one of the partners in the firm that built this mill. Major Cartwright's Revolution mill, built in 1788 at Retford and designed from the first to be steam-powered, was insured for £12,000, the steam engine alone costing £1,500.

Many of the first factories, especially those in the remote rural situations to which the search for water power took them, share many of the themes from classical architecture to be found in those town and country houses described in previous chapters. Venetian windows may be seen in Arkwright's Masson mill and the Stanley mill at Stroud in

Figure 18 A sketch of New Lanark as from the air. (See also Plate 53)

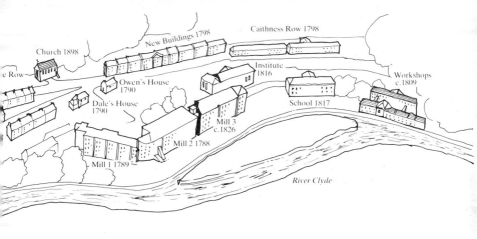

54 The Dunkirk mills at Nailsworth, Gloucestershire

Gloucestershire, built in 1813. The simple, unpretentious façade to Cressbrook mill, Miller's Dale, in Derbyshire, first built in 1779 and then rebuilt in 1815 after a fire, has a pedimented central section, neat stone quoining and a regularity of proportion that would have satisfied the aspirations of a good many gentlemen of the middle rank. As factories increased in size however and moved into the towns they became more severely utilitarian in their design and more grimly depersonalised in their appearance.

Textile factories, whether at Cromford or New Lanark, Paisley or Oldham, huge blocks perhaps 450 feet long, four, five or six storeys high, standing grim and four-square to the street, their gates disgorging hordes of gaunt, bleary-eyed women and children, are to many the epitome of the worst excesses of the Industrial Revolution and unbridled capitalism. But it is possible that their importance can be overemphasised, and the harshness of their working conditions may be overdrawn, either in contrast to an idyllic pre-industrial rural Golden Age which in fact never existed, or in comparison with standards and conventions of the late twentieth century rather than the early nineteenth. The textile industry was, after all, only one industry, although one which astonishes because of the speed at which it grew and the rapidity with which technical innovation was introduced. Its concentration into large, steam-powered factories in Lancashire, Lanarkshire or the West Riding of Yorkshire, was by no means complete, even by 1914. Many mill-owners were benevolent employers, although the late twentieth century would find the paternalism with which they treated their employees intolerably condescending. William Strutt took great pains to design mills that were light, airy, warm and as fireproof as the limits of the technology of the time would allow. The houses which had to be provided to attract employees, especially the skilled engineers upon whom so much depended, were often substantial, well-built, warm and dry, which was often more than could be said for the rural cottages from which they came. Richard Arkwright built the houses in North

55 The houses built in North Street, Cromford, Derbyshire, by Richard Arkwright between 1771 and 1776 to accommodate his workers. The wide windows under the eaves were to provide light for the framework knitters

Street, Cromford, before 1777, adding an inn, the Greyhound, in 1788 and a church in 1797. Birtwhistle Street in Gatehouse of Fleet was laid out in the late eighteenth century to house the workers, many of them English, brought to the water-powered cotton mills built by James Murray in the new town he created at the gates of his country mansion. A church and a school were added, as well as a market and four fairs. At Catrine, another Scottish industrial village founded in 1787 by Sir Claud Alexander and David Dale, cotton mills were supported by rows of two-storey rubble cottages. The Blantyre mills, established in 1785, where David Livingstone worked as a boy, also have their rows of cottages.

Housing had also to be provided for workers in the iron industry. We have looked already at that provided at the

Lorn Furnace. Both of the major ironmasters in Merthyr Tydfil, William Crawshay and John Guest, built some cottages. Many more were the work of small-scale building speculators. No one paid any attention to drainage, sewage disposal or the proper layout of streets and squares. The wounds then inflicted, both on the landscape and in the hearts and minds of men, have still not yet healed.

The water wheel was the prime mover of eighteenth-century industrial Britain. It had been used for centuries, both for grinding corn and for other industrial purposes. Water-powered textile mills in Gloucestershire and iron furnaces in the Lake District were nothing new. What was new was the increasing scale upon which water power was being exploited during the course of the century, a scale which the Dunkirk mills at Nailsworth may be said to exemplify. It was the 1780s before a reliable alternative was successfully developed, but the steam engine replaced the water wheel only very slowly.

The increasing scale upon which water power was utilised, and then its gradual replacement by steam power, wrought the most profound changes throughout the entire fabric of eighteenth-century Britain. The domestic basis of manufacture was slowly broken down as more and more machinery was concentrated under one roof, although it had by no means entirely disappeared by 1830. Mechanisation came first to the spinning of cotton. The resulting bottleneck in weaving brought a period of unparalleled prosperity to the domestic handloom weaver and it was the 1820s before this began to be seriously threatened.

As manufacture ceased to be domestic in its organisation so the structure of the family and household was changed. Apprentices disappeared, and servants became exclusively domestic in their functions and a symbol of middle-class prosperity rather than assistants in small-scale manufacturing processes. The demand for female labour in the cotton mills brought considerable change to family structure. It became quite common for an elderly relative to be taken into the family to act as a child-minder whilst the mother went out to work. The kinship network still remained important since much recruiting for the factories was done on this basis. How far these changes had penetrated either into or beyond the Lancashire cotton towns by 1830 are questions to which at present there can be no certain answers.

Machinery may have been taken out of the home, but those who worked in the new factories had to be housed close by because their only means of reaching the factory was by walking. Workers' housing in semi-rural surroundings was fairly satisfactory, at least to contemporaries, largely because there was little overcrowding. It was only when factories began to be built in close proximity in towns and on the coal fields that rows upon rows of mean streets and courts appeared, creating conditions of gross overcrowding which were exacerbated by the total lack of sanitation engineering from which all suffered to a greater or lesser extent. It is the 1790s before conditions became so bad that they begin to impinge upon the consciousness of contemporaries and then only in the most rapidly growing industrial towns. The benefits brought by the successes of the search for power were dearly bought.

7 Transport

The pattern of fields and farms, country mansions, wind-mills, villages and towns which lay across the landscape of eighteenth-century Britain was integrated by a dense net-work of roads and lanes and navigable rivers, and served by a myriad of tiny coastal ships which operated from one small port to the next. Along this network moved an infinite array of men, women and children, on foot, on horseback, in coaches and waggons, on barges and ships, carrying with them their goods and merchandise, the latest fashions, gossip and newspapers, visiting friends and relatives, sear-ching for work, avoiding creditors, bringing new ideas which, in however attenuated and distorted a form, would eventually reach the most isolated hamlet and the remotest farmstead.

The transport system of eighteenth-century Britain was slow, cumbersome, expensive, unreliable and uneven. In-deed to call it a system at all is to suggest that it possessed uniformity, cohesion and central direction, whereas these were the very things which it lacked. The coming of the railway in 1830 brought a smoothness, efficiency and speed to transport which make it almost impossible for genera-tions living in a post-railway age to appreciate what has gone before. Road maintenance fell entirely on the indi-vidual parish, supervised by county justices of the peace. Any improvements, whether to roads, rivers, ports or har-bours, were carried out at a purely local level. A number of writers and commentators envisaged a national network of navigable waterways. John Taylor, writing in 1641, advo-cated a canal joining the Stroud and Churn brooks, a canal

208

which would have linked the Severn and the Thames, and Francis Matthew in 1655 suggested a canal to join the Thames to the Bristol Avon. But the times were not right. The mechanisms for assembling the investment required for such ventures were as yet in their infancy. Engineering knowledge, even rule of thumb, pragmatic, knowledge, was rudimentary, and the notion that it was the duty of government to provide social overhead capital and infrastructure of this kind was far in the future. Nevertheless the schemes of Taylor, Matthew, Yarranton, Defoe and others are symptomatic of the pressures which were mounting in very many parts of Britain as changes in farming practices and manufacturing processes, interacting with the demands for foodstuffs, coal and manufactured goods from the steadily growing numbers of townspeople, created increasing quantities of grain, dairy produce, textiles, nails, bottles, chains, knives, stockings, lace, jugs, plates, eggs and turkeys, to be fetched and carried from one part of the country to the other. Bottlenecks in transport became increasingly frustrating and increasingly costly to all concerned. Each one, in the absence of central government direction, had to be overcome individually, and each individual solution produced a new set of stresses and strains. The process was cumulative and self-reinforcing.

The capacity of the roads of Britain was already under considerable stress well before the opening years of the eighteenth century. In 1555 a statute had entrusted the repair of roads to the parishes through which they passed. For remote rural parishes this system may have worked reasonably well, but for parishes around London and the growing manufacturing towns such as Manchester, Halifax and Leeds, the traffic on the major roads imposed an intolerable burden. Those Hertfordshire parishes through which the Great North Road passed found it impossible to cope with the immense traffic along the road. Their attempts to keep the road in repair were rendered futile, by the absence locally in these heavy clayland parishes of suitable repair material such as gravel, and the failure of the

56 The turnpike toll gate just outside Great Missenden in Buckinghamshire

system of annually appointed surveyors of highways to provide for the accumulation of practical experience of road repair. In winter the road was almost impassable because of the mud; horses and coaches became hopelessly stuck. In summer it was almost impassable because the sun baked the ruts hard, and horses broke their legs, coaches their wheels and axles. Breaking point in this particular bottleneck came in the parish of Stanton, Hertfordshire. The inhabitants of this parish were presented before the Hertfordshire justices of the peace for failing to keep the road in repair more times than any other parish. In 1660 they appealed to parliament for assistance, and again in 1663. This second petition was joined by parishes in Cambridgeshire and in Huntingdonshire, and culminated in the first turnpike act in June 1663. Toll gates were to be erected at Wadesmill, Caxton and Stilton. County surveyors were appointed and it was their responsibility to keep the road in repair, using the receipts from the tolls in addition to the ancient statute labour and, if necessary, a parish rate, all under the supervision of the county justices. The act was to last for eleven years, and thirty-two years passed before a second turnpike act was passed. Several were passed in the years between 1695 and 1706 following a rather similar pattern. The really important development came in the act of 1706 which provided for the turnpiking of the road from Fonthill in Bedfordshire to Stony Stratford in Buckinghamshire. This road was placed under the control of thirty-two trustees with power to administer the road and provide for its repair quite independently of the county justices. This act provided the model for all subsequent turnpike acts until they were finally allowed to lapse after 1864. Turnpike trustees were empowered to erect tollgates and collect tolls, to appoint surveyors and collectors, to demand statutory labour from the parishes through which their road ran, and to carry out any necessary repair works. They could also raise capital by mortgaging their tolls, and fill vacancies among their own ranks.

Turnpike acts were usually sought by local people who could see the profit and advantage of repairing and improving a particular stretch of road. A meeting of interested persons would lead to the drafting of a petition, and then its presentation to parliament. Its passage through into law was not always a foregone conclusion. Those with vested interests in the old ways did not always welcome the new. Many thought the tolls an unjustifiable burden upon road users. The proprietors of the Aire and Calder Navigation opposed the turnpiking of the Selby to Leeds and Leeds to Tadcaster roads because they feared the effects the new roads might have upon their own revenues. Opposition was not confined to counter-petitions in parliament. Tollgates were pulled down and collectors were assaulted. In 1727 rioters pulled down the gate at Marshfield on the Studley to Toghill road in Gloucestershire no less than six times in the one year.

In spite of opposition increasing numbers of acts passed through parliament during the course of the eighteenth

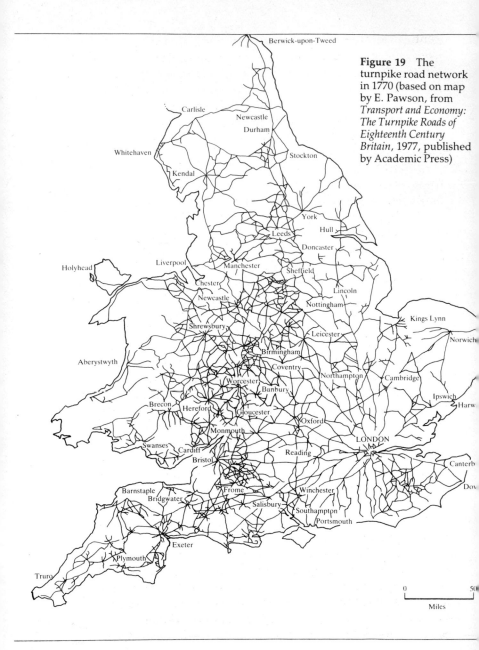

Figure 19 The turnpike road network in 1770 (based on map by E. Pawson, from *Transport and Economy: The Turnpike Roads of Eighteenth Century Britain*, 1977, published by Academic Press)

0   50
Miles

212

century. By 1750 the turnpiking of the major roads out of London was almost complete. The longest section on the Great North Road unturnpiked by that date was the thirty-five miles from Little Drayton to Doncaster. On the road through Leicester to Manchester only the stretch between Hartington and Buxton remained without a turnpike trust, whilst the roads to Bath and Bristol and to Portsmouth and Harwich, were completely turnpiked.

In the 1720s 'town-centred' trusts developed, with trustees responsible for a whole group of roads leading into a particular town. This happened for Bristol, Warminster, Worcester, Tewkesbury, Hereford and Bridgwater, for example, all save Warminster being in the region of the Severn valley, then the busiest waterway in the kingdom. In the 1750s similar trusts were established for the prosperous textile towns of Frome, Trowbridge and Melksham. In the twenty years between 1751 and 1772 no less than 389 acts of parliament were passed to establish turnpike trusts, well over a third of the 912 passed between 1663 and 1839, an outburst of investment at once the cause of, and caused by, the marked surge forward at this time in economic activity, with growing industrial and commercial investment, agricultural improvement, urbanisation and the beginnings of large-scale canal building. A map of the network of turnpike roads in existence by 1770 reflects remarkably accurately just where this industrial and commercial growth was most heavily concentrated, namely in a great swathe of western and north western England, sweeping from Frome to Leeds. By the 1830s there were 1,100 turnpike trusts covering 22,000 miles of road.

How far the turnpike trustees actually succeeded in improving the quality of the roads under their care is a different matter. Certainly they had greater financial resources than the parishes, and they were able to employ salaried surveyors and hire labour in place of the unwilling statute labourers. But their administration was often lax, jobbery was common, and there was little real improvement in the knowledge of the principles of sound road construction.

Roads were often carelessly made and poorly drained. When the Prescot to Liverpool road was turnpiked in 1726 the cart causeway was made so narrow that carriages could not pass one another. Transport costs of materials were high, and there was much reliance upon local materials. Flint was widely used in the Chilterns, for example, but it was often not broken up into sufficiently small pieces. Only when the Buckingham branch of the Grand Junction Canal was completed could stone from Hartshill be used on the roads of north Buckinghamshire.

It was not before the early years of the nineteenth century, when McAdam and Telford came to the fore, that there was any real advance in road repair methods. McAdam became general surveyor to the Bristol turnpike trust in 1816, and only then did he have the opportunity to try out in practice his theories on road repair. They proved remarkably successful, and within three years he and his sons were acting as advisors to thirty-four trusts. His roads were undoubtedly well-made, but much of his fame was also due to the skill with which he publicised his methods and their successes.

Thomas Telford began his career in Shropshire, becoming county surveyor in 1786. Between 1802 and 1828 he was surveyor to the Commissioners of Highland Roads, and it was here that he made his reputation, building not only roads, but also canals, bridges, harbour installations and churches, as well as laying out new towns (see Plate 62). In 1815 he was appointed surveyor to the newly created Holyhead Road Commission. His methods of road construction were much better than those of McAdam, but they were much more expensive. He took much greater care over providing solid, well-drained foundations to his roads, and he also paid far more attention to widening and straightening roads, and reducing the gradients on hills.

The real improvements in road construction and engineering may not have come before the days of McAdam and Telford, but the turnpike trustees and their surveyors did nevertheless make many small-scale improvements that

57 A milestone erected by the turnpike trustees on the Wendover to Buckingham road

must have contributed much to making travel safer, more comfortable and more speedy. The trustees could widen and straighten roads, and these powers were used extensively. At Padbury in Buckinghamshire the trustees for the Wendover to Buckingham road built a bridge where there had been only a ford, and re-aligned the road, which was to be made of good clean gravel, 15 inches thick and 18 feet wide. In 1720 turnpike trustees were required to measure and signpost their roads, and this alone must have saved

215

countless hours of wasted time, eased the strain on weary travellers and their horses, and saved much in the way of broken or lost merchandise. Milestones were often made of iron as well as stone, and many are still to be seen, sometimes carefully restored, sometimes half-hidden in the grass.

The roads were used by an enormous variety of travellers and conveyances. Through the turnpike gate at Lathbury on the Newport Pagnell to Northampton road there passed in a single year, 1799–1800, no less than 89,000 sheep, 3,000 coaches and 2,000 chaises. The act for the rebuilding of the bridges over the Ouse at Newport Pagnell in 1814 gives some impression of this variety. Coaches drawn by four horses were to pay 1s. 6d., those drawn by two or three were to pay a shilling, and those drawn by one were to pay 6d. Waggons drawn by four or more horses were to pay 3½d. a horse. If there were only two or three horses then the charge was 4d. a horse, and one horse paid 6d. Unladen horses were to be charged 1½d. Cattle were to be charged 4d. the score, calves, pigs, sheeps and lambs were to pay 5d. the score, and the charges were doubled on Sundays.

The slowest of these conveyances were the waggons of the common carriers. Common carriers were working between Oxford and London in 1390, and by the beginning of the eighteenth century there was a well-developed network of carriers serving most parts of the country, with many operating over long distances, especially to London. This network expanded and developed during the course of the century, being materially assisted in this respect by the parallel expansion of the turnpike roads. Costs were high, but for many destinations it was quicker to use the carrier than to send goods by sea. Thus the journey by carrier in the 1770s from London to Southampton took about 60 hours, with two overnight stops on the road. The sea voyage on the other hand could take a week, depending upon winds, tides and currents. The charges which the carriers could make were required by acts of parliament passed in 1692 and 1748 to be regulated by the justices of the peace. The charges

216

drawn up by the justices frequently show that carriage in wintertime was more expensive than during the summer, and that higher prices were often charged for light but bulky goods. That the carrier network was reliable and efficient is clear from the business records of Abraham Dent, shopkeeper of Kirby Stephen. In his shop he and his father sold tea, sugar, flour, braid, ribbons, tapes, buttons, over forty kinds of cloth, paper, pencils, books, magazines, gunpowder and patent medicine. He drew his goods from suppliers in Kendal, Cockermouth, Liverpool, Manchester, Lancaster, Barnard Castle, Newcastle and London. The journey to London took about a fortnight, but goods rarely went astray.

The waggons themselves were often huge, with four wheels, the widths of which were frequently specified by act of parliament in the pious hope that wide wheels would act as a roller for the badly constructed road surfaces. The waggons were covered with a tilt or tarpaulin and were drawn by as many as eight horses. Trundling along at little more than a walking pace they provided an indispensable link in the transport network, joining together towns and villages in a way that no waterway could ever do.

Long distance carrying was often in the hands of large firms. In 1808 it was stated that Mr Russell of Exeter was one of the most considerable carriers in the kingdom. He employed 224 horses. His waggons, when new, weighed nearly 2 tons and cost above 100 guineas each. It was in just such a waggon, owned by Messrs Brown and Co., that in 1825 John Constable loaded two of his paintings, views of Hampstead. They were destined for Mr Francis Darby of Coalbrookdale. They left from the Green Man and Stile Inn, Oxford Street, London, addressed to the Jerningham Arms, Shifnal. The journey took three days. When the Reverend Thomas Metcalf, rector of Kirkby Overblow, ordered dwarf apple trees, a Roman nectarine, a magdalen peach, jasmine, lilac and apricot trees from the Telford firm of nurserymen in York, they were sent to him by the Skipton carrier, and we saw in Chapter Three how the English

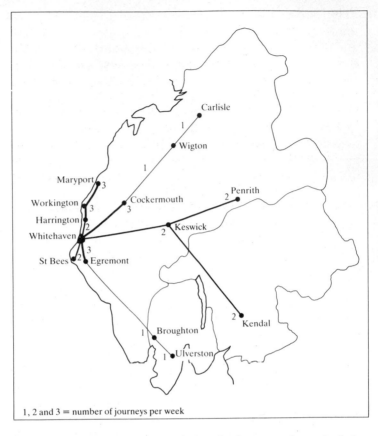

Figure 20 shows labels on the map:

Carlisle

Wigton

1

1

Maryport 3

Workington 3   Cockermouth

Harrington   3

Whitehaven 2   2 Penrith

Keswick

St Bees 2   3   2

Egremont

2 Kendal

1   Broughton

1 Ulverston

1, 2 and 3 = number of journeys per week

Figure 20 The carrier network from Whitehaven at the end of the eighteenth century

ploughs which Thomas Winter thought the most suitable for conditions at Monymusk would make the first stage of their long journey from Stow on the Wold by means of the carrier who travelled regularly between Winchcomb and London.

The carriers and their waggons were a lifeline. But they were also slow, and best suited to carrying heavy merchandise that would not perish, as well as an occasional passenger, as Hetty Sorrel discovered on her journey to Windsor.

Peter Stubs of Warrington bought the steel rods from which his files were made in Sheffield, and they came to Warrington by carrier's waggon, and it was by carrier's waggon that the finished files were sent to customers all over the country. For those passengers who could afford it, and for small, valuable packages, the stage coach was a better means of conveyance. Stage coach routes were well-established by the end of the seventeenth century, and continued to proliferate throughout the eighteenth. The network of routes could expand and contract quite rapidly as individual coachowners sought to establish what they hoped would be profitable routes, or withdrew from those where they were clearly losing money. The establishment of turnpike roads benefited stage coaches and the times for journeys were steadily reduced. In 1754 the journey from London to Manchester took four and a half days. It was down to three days in 1770, and under 24 hours by 1825.

The Golden Age of coaching was crammed into the fifty years from about 1780 until the railways began to make their impact in the 1830s. Intense competition provided a network of routes and services. The Leeds to Newcastle route in the 1830s was served by three coaches a day. The coach called *The Times* started early in the morning, going via Thirsk and Stockton-on-Tees, where there were connections for Sunderland. The *Telegraph* started at about 10 am, going via Leeming Lane, whilst the *Hero*, a night coach, left at 6.30 pm, travelling through Thirsk and Darlington. At the same time no less than eight coaches a day left Leeds for Sheffield, of which two then went on to Birmingham and three to London, which was reached in 24 hours. In addition, there were thirteen coaches a day between Leeds and Wakefield, and thirteen between Leeds and Manchester, seven going via Huddersfield and six through Halifax. Coaching traffic of this density brought prosperity to many who lived along the most frequented routes providing travellers with food, lodging and changes of horses. Modern Slough owes its origins to the traffic along the Bath road. By 1830 between sixty and eighty coaches a day were passing along the road. It was the second stage out of London for the change of horses, and inns like the Three Tuns and the White Hart prospered accordingly. Coach builders also prospered, and were occasionally fortunate enough to adapt to changing circumstances. John Clark, stagecoach master of Cheshunt in Hertfordshire died in 1727 leaving personal possessions worth £311 15s. They included twelve coach horses worth £96, and five coaches and a chaise worth £66 10s. Joseph Salmon, coach builder, was established in Newport Pagnell by 1820. The firm turned to making motor cars just before 1914, and was taken over by Aston Martin in 1955.

It is likely that there was a slow and uneven improvement in road transport in England during the course of the eighteenth century, so that by the end of the century a remarkably efficient and reliable transport network covered many parts of the country, with waggons and stage coaches complementing one another in the services they provided. But it was the end of the century before the system matured and even then it was subject to delays caused by bad weather, poor road surfaces, accidents and hazards of every kind. It was reported in 1808, for example, that obstructions on roads were caused by public houses and inns placing their water troughs close to the road. This meant that waggons and carriages stopped in the middle of the road to water their horses, thus preventing other vehicles from passing. In September of 1803 *The Times* reported that a long coach had overturned near Chertsey, almost all of the inside passengers being badly hurt. Over the porch of the church at Colney near Norwich is a memorial stone to John Fox, described as a worthy and useful member of society and an honest and industrious labourer. On 20 December 1806, in the seventy-ninth year of his age, he was unfortunately killed, 'having been thrust down and trampled on by the Horses of a Waggon'. The architect James Wyatt was killed in a coach accident in 1813.

Waggons and coaches bound together much of Lowland Britain. There were, however, many parts of the country which were inaccessible to wheeled traffic, and some merchandise which was unsuited to it. The potters of Burslem and Tunstall sent their wares by packhorse to Willington on the Trent. By 1740 200 horses a week were making the thirty

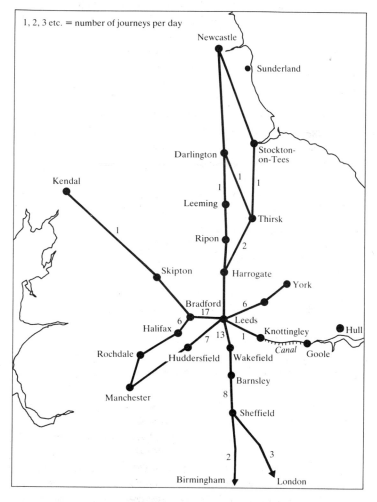

Figure 21 The coaching network from Leeds in about 1830 (based on map in *Journal of Transport History*, vol. 4, 1959–60, Leicester University Press)

58　The packhorse bridge at Hayfield, Derbyshire

mile journey. Here the pots and dishes were loaded on to barges for the voyage down the Trent and out into the Humber and then down the coast to London. Breakages would have reached an intolerable level had the carrier's waggon been used. Packhorse trains were extensively used in the Lake District, and in Derbyshire strings of packhorses carried the lead from the mines and smelting furnaces to Bawtry, where it was transferred to barges on the Idle, a tributary of the Trent. Some of the bridges specially built for the horses to use when crossing mountain streams are still to be seen. In some districts sledges were used. It was said of Cumrew in Cumberland in 1794 that peat was brought down by sledge from the mountains, where wheeled carriages could not go. There is evidence to show that pack horses were still being used to carry iron from Dowlais to

Cardiff as late as the 1790s. Pack horses were not to be found only in mountainous districts. The clays of Sussex were notoriously difficult to cross, and produce from the Sussex Weald was brought during the winter to Dorking market by pack horse.

Roads in Scotland were infinitely worse than those in

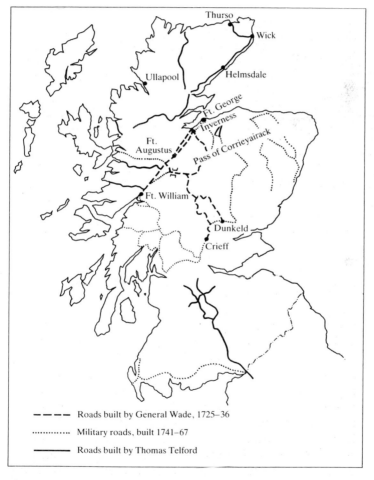

Figure 22   Road building in the Highlands of Scotland

England, and improvement came much more slowly. The system of statute labour introduced in 1669 proved even more difficult to enforce than in England. At the beginning of the eighteenth century very few roads anywhere had a made surface, and there were no roads at all west of the Great Glen. There was no cart in Selkirk before 1725, and even then the carrier between that town and Edinburgh took a fortnight over the forty mile round trip. There was no cart in Campbeltown before 1756, and no wheeled vehicle on Tiree before 1771. After the 1715 rising General Wade directed a programme of road building in the Highlands. Between 1725 and 1736 he built 242 miles of road, including one along the Great Glen, linking Fort William, Fort Augustus and Inverness, and another from Fort Augustus south to Crieff, including the dizzy ascent over the Pass of Corrieyairack, a route now largely abandoned. These roads were essentially military in their purpose, their gradients often being too steep for commercial purposes. He also built a number of bridges, including the splendid one at Aberfeldy, with a central arch of 60-feet span.

The road building programme was renewed in 1741, and pushed on with greater vigour after the 1745 rebellion, a period which also saw the building of the military road from Carlisle to Newcastle upon Tyne. After 1784 the roads were gradually turned over to civil purposes. In 1803 the Commissioners for Highland Roads and Bridges were established, and Telford became their surveyor and engineer. He extended the network of roads north of the Great Glen, building the first road from Inverness to Wick and Thurso as well as a number of roads in the islands. Altogether he was responsible for over 920 miles of roads and 1,117 bridges. One of these bridges, Craigellachie Bridge, Aberlour, built between 1812 and 1815, was a cast-iron suspension bridge. It was cast at Ruabon in North Wales. That the castings could be transported such a distance is a measure of the improvements Telford brought into the Scottish Highlands. Once the roads and bridges were built then the whole process of communication was speeded up. A coach service from Perth to Inverness was established in 1806, a journey of two days. By 1847 there was a daily service each way, by which date a London Sunday newspaper could be in Skye by the following Thursday.

The main efforts of Telford were directed to roads in the Scottish Highlands. Improvement in lowland roads came very slowly and with none of the engineering skill and central control commanded by Telford. A turnpike act was passed for Midlothian in 1714, but the next in Scotland was not until 1751. Some 350 acts then followed up until 1844, although none affected roads in the Highlands. The practice developed in Scotland of obtaining an act to cover all the principal roads in a county rather than separate stretches of road. Thus there was an act in 1767 for the Ayrshire roads and another in 1772 for those in Lanarkshire. Road building authorised under these acts often took a very long time to finish, but the state of the roads in some parts of the country, such as Ayrshire, did gradually improve. In 1754 one coach a month ran between Edinburgh and London, taking twelve to fourteen days over the journey. By 1783 there were fifteen a week, and the journey time was down to four days.

Turnpike roads were even later coming to Wales than they were to Scotland, and there was the same practice of obtaining an act for a county rather than a named road. An act of 1764 provided for Glamorganshire roads, including the main east to west coast road between Cardiff and Swansea and beyond. The act named over 300 trustees, who were divided into five groups to manage the five sections of the road. From Tongwynlais, on this road, the road north to Merthyr Tydfil was turnpiked in 1771. In 1789 a South Wales Association for the Improvement of Roads was founded. Its very existence, and the criticisms that it made, show just how limited road improvement was in South Wales, even at the very end of the eighteenth century, when packhorses were still being widely used in the Rhondda valley and to transport coal into Cardiff. In North Wales the roads were turnpiked as extensions from those in Cheshire and by 1776 a coach service was running between London and Holyhead.

Long before the end of the eighteenth century a variety of efforts had been made to break through the restraints imposed by poor road communications by turning instead to water transport. Attempts to improve rivers and make them navigable have a long history, and by the end of the seventeenth century waterways like the Severn, Thames and Trent played a vital role in the economic life of the nation. The transport of heavy, bulky goods such as coal, bricks, building stone, sand, grain, butter, cheese, wool – the list could be almost indefinitely extended – was, and still is, much cheaper by water than by road. When the Reverend William Cole moved from Bletchley to Cambridge in 1767 he sent his household goods by water. Four waggon loads of goods were safely loaded on board two lighters at Bedford to make their way along the Great Ouse and the Cam to Cambridge, a voyage that would have taken three days or more.

But travel by river could be as hazardous as travel by road. The rivers themselves were sometimes frozen in winter, and ran so shallow in the summer as to make them impassable. Shoals, rapids and shifting sand banks were other natural obstacles. To these were to be added the man-made ones of bridges, fish and mill weirs and dams. Millers, concerned only with securing a sufficient head of water, would dam a river by means of a single lock. Boats would often have to wait for days before the miller would open the central gates. The resulting 'flash' of water swept boats downstream with considerable force and not infrequently they overturned, passengers were drowned and cargoes lost. Boats going upstream had to be hauled up against the current by means of winches. Flash locks were dangerous, and very wasteful of water. The pound lock with two gates was in use on the Exeter Canal before the end of the sixteenth century, but its use on rivers spread only very slowly.

The barriers to the easier and more profitable movement

226

of merchandise presented by these dangers and difficulties became increasingly apparent in the years after the Restoration, and increasingly resented by those who had to overcome them. Groups of merchants and industrialists faced with a local bottleneck came together in locally based associations to obtain an act of parliament that would give them the powers to remove the worst hazards and embark upon the difficult and costly business of improving a stretch of river. One of the most important of these river improvement schemes was that for the Aire from Leeds and the Calder, from Wakefield, to Weeland. Up to this date Knottingley had been the head of navigation up the Aire from the Humber, and it was an important trans-shipment point for river traffic on the Humber-Ouse-Trent network and for coastal traffic to the Humber and hence all along the eastern seaboard as far south as Rochester, and even to the Low Countries. In spite of considerable opposition from those merchants and traders who used the Ouse and who thought their interests threatened by the new development, eighteen undertakers were empowered by an act passed in April of 1699 to cleanse, enlarge and straighten the course of the river, to make cuts through adjoining land, lay out towing paths and build locks. Nearly the whole of the money required was subscribed by Leeds and Wakefield merchants, who could see the benefits which would accrue from the more certain and rapid movement of their woollen textiles and coal down river, with timber, wool, iron bar from Sweden, groceries and wines from London, fuller's earth from Kent, coming up in exchange. The undertakers very quickly set about their task, building locks at Knottingley Mills and at Castleford, and warehouses in Leeds before 1699 was out. It is no exaggeration to say that this was one of the most important river improvement schemes ever devised, and for much of the eighteenth century it was the main highway for the rapidly expanding industries of the West Riding. By the middle years of the century waggon ways were being built from coal mines down to the river. The Middleton waggon way, for example, was authorised

59 *Barge building near Flatford Mill,* painted by John Constable in about 1815

in 1758, Charles Branding, the Middleton coal mine owner, undertaking to supply Leeds with 23,000 tons of coal a year once the waggon way was built. Such waggon ways, both here and in the Northeastern coal field, built first of all with wooden rails and then with iron ones, were similar to those upon which Trevithick and Stephenson experimented with steam locomotives early in the nineteenth century.

Traffic along rivers, whether improved or not, was by means of barges. A contract made in 1700 by the Aire and

Calder Navigation called for a boat 44 feet long, 13 feet wide and 2½ feet deep. It was to have a cabin for four men, and to carry 15 or 16 tons weight in 17 inches of water. It was to be made for £35. Yards for the building of boats and barges of this kind were to be found along every important navigable river in eighteenth-century Britain, and on many minor ones too. Gainsborough, for example, on the river Trent, was accessible to sea-going ships, and was an important ship and barge building centre, whilst many of the barges engaged in the coal trade on the Trent were, at the end of the eighteenth century, built by the Barnsdale family at Trent Lock near Nottingham, and at Newark. These coal barges were 80 feet long and 14 feet wide. They were horse-drawn, but were provided with sails for use when winds and currents permitted, the grateful horse then being carried on board.

When Charles Weston, barge builder of Pangbourne in Berkshire died in 1719, the probate inventory of his personal possessions gives us a fascinating glimpse into his boat building yard. He was in partnership, although how many partners there were is not stated. He had an upper and lower sawhouse, and a boathouse. There were 7,466 feet of planking, 60 feet of elm boards, four barrels of tar, sixty loads of oak timber valued at £108, and a new boat, valued at £116. His house was comfortably furnished, with a clock on the stairs, a looking glass in the chamber over the kitchen and brass candlesticks in his parlour. He was worth £341 all together.

In the last quarter of the eighteenth century, after much bitter criticism and growing dissatisfaction with the state of the river, the undertakers of the Aire and Calder Navigation Company spent considerable sums on further improvements, including the building of the Haddlesey to Selby canal to cut out some of the worst meanders in the river. This brought boom conditions to Selby, the trans-shipment point from canal barge to coastal ships. Receipts from tolls doubled in the 1790s, reaching £126,000 in 1800, and the trade in coal reached 300,000 tons a year. By this time the river itself was hopelessly overcrowded with traffic, and the undertakers were once again being criticised for the natural deficiencies of the river – shoals, low water and tortuous loops. In 1819 they applied to parliament for an act to enable them to build a canal, eighteen miles long, from Ferrybridge to an almost deserted spot on the Lower Ouse called Goole. Here, in an area where the careful warping of the flood waters of the Ouse, Trent and Don had deposited a rich silt which formed the basis of intensive cultivation of vegetables and root crops, especially potatoes, was a mill, three inns and a handful of cottages, in all a population in 1821 of 450 persons.

The undertakers bought sufficient land to lay out a new port and town. A barge dock, a wet dock for ships, a four-storey warehouse and a bonding warehouse were built. A main street, called Aire Street, was laid out, and the company built sewers, gasworks, hospital, schools and a market, and provided the site for a church. Much of the building was done in locally made bricks, and the undertakers exercised close control over standards and materials. They established a Building Committee which granted 99-year building leases and 157 houses were built between 1826 and 1829. The canal and the new port were immediately successful, and by 1841 Goole had a population of 3,629.

However, the success of the canal merely served to underline the inadequacies of the river above Ferrybridge. A further act of parliament was obtained in 1828 and over the next fifteen years the company spent over £½ million in making it possible for ships of 100 tons to reach Leeds and Wakefield. By this time, however, the Leeds to Selby railway line had been open nearly ten years, and a new chapter in the history of the company had begun.

There were limitations to what improvements to natural rivers could achieve, and the story of the Aire and Calder Navigation Company shows eighteenth-century engineers bumping up against these limitations again and again. Cuts were already being made on improved rivers to by-pass some of the more tortuous bends, and, with continental examples before them, it would not be long before someone would abandon all connection with a natural waterway and strike out boldly across country with an entirely artificial waterway. Apart from the Exeter Canal, built in 1564, the earliest canal in the British Isles was that built in the 1730s to link Lough Neagh to Newry in order that coal from the Tyrone coalfield could more easily be carried to Dublin. From 1736 the work was under the direction of Thomas Steers, engineer of the new dock at Liverpool which had been authorised by parliament in 1710. The Newry canal, just under eighteen miles long with 15 locks, was no mean achievement, and this in spite of the faults in its construction which very quickly revealed themselves.

Thomas Steers died in 1750, to be succeeded as dockmaster at Liverpool by his deputy, Henry Berry. By this time the problems of bringing coal into Liverpool from the pits about ten miles away were becoming acute. The turnpiking of the road to Prescot, and then to St Helens and Ashton-in-Makerfield, made little real contribution. Mining itself was also becoming increasingly expensive. By 1753 pits at Prescot were 280 feet deep. When the proprietors of the pit nearest to Liverpool put up their pithead prices by a fifth in order to meet the costs of installing a pumping engine, a radical solution to the problem had to be found. In June 1754 Liverpool Corporation ordered a survey to be made of the Sankey brook. Their petition to parliament was unopposed, and the act became law in March of 1755, whereupon Henry Berry was given leave of absence for two days a week to superintend the works.

The act provided for the making navigable of the Sankey brook, a meandering trickle of water that could never have been made navigable, and Berry must have realised this. He, and certainly the leader of the promoters, John Ashton, almost certainly intended from the first to build an artificial waterway. It seems most likely that the petition for the act was a subterfuge to ensure that it would pass speedily through parliament, since a plan for a canal from Salford to Wigan had been rejected in the previous session and a

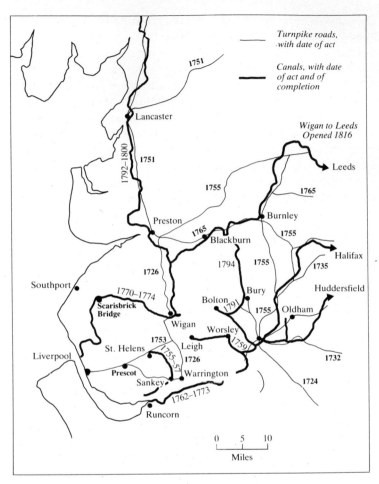

Figure 23 Canals and turnpike roads in Lancashire

proposal for an entirely artificial canal would certainly have been very controversial.

Nothing is known of the actual building of the canal, but in November of 1757 the *Liverpool Chronicle* could announce that the Sankey brook navigation was open. The first stretch of the canal ran from Sankey Bridges northwards for about seven miles to the collieries at Haydock and Parr. In 1762 it was extended south from Sankey Brook to the Mersey, by which time it had also been extended further north to other collieries near St Helens.

The Sankey Brook Navigation was an outstanding success in every way, providing the crucial stimulus for the industrial development of the South Lancashire coalfield and the rise of St Helens, but its success has been overshadowed in the popular imagination by the astonishing engineering achievements of the Duke of Bridgewater's canal, and especially the aqueduct over the Irwell.

The third Duke of Bridgewater owned an extensive estate, including coal mines, at Worsley, about ten miles from Manchester. The transport of coal from his pits in to Manchester was difficult and costly, transport costs more than doubling the pithead price of coal by the time it reached Manchester. To cut these costs would undoubtedly lead to a corresponding increase in the sale of a commodity for which the demand was so elastic. In 1759 the duke obtained an act of parliament authorising him to construct a canal from Worsley to Salford, and in 1760 a second act empowered him to extend the canal over the river Irwell into Manchester itself. The first cargo of coal was brought in a horse-drawn barge over the Barton aqueduct on 17 July 1761. At Worsley itself a canal basin was built at the foot of a sandstone cliff, and tunnels ran from it directly into the mines, so that coal could be loaded straight into the barges.

The boldness and originality with which the Worsley canal was designed and executed aroused both scepticism and admiration among contemporaries as the duke's engineer, James Brindley, pushed on with the work.

The success of the Worsley canal, a success to be measured not only in economic terms by the quantities of coal carried and the reductions in its price, but also in the release of imagination at the successful surmounting of apparently insurmountable engineering problems, led to the planning of a far more ambitious project. Schemes to link the main rivers of the country by means of canals go back to the sixteenth century, but now, by one of those happy concatenations of history the man, the opportunity and the technology came together. On the same day, 14 May, of the same year, 1766, parliament passed acts authorising the building of a canal to link the Trent and the Mersey and to build a canal from this new waterway at Great Haywood in Staffordshire to join the Severn at what was to become Stourport, where an entirely new town was to be created. Both companies of promoters employed James Brindley as their engineer. On the Staffordshire and Worcestershire canal, completed in 1772, the year of his death, he built forty-three locks and four aqueducts. On the Trent and Mersey, finished in 1777, he built seventy-five locks and the Harecastle tunnel, 2,880 yards long.

After the first outburst of canal building, terminating in the act for the Chester canal of 1772, there was a long period of inactivity, the consequence of the outbreak of the American War of Independence. With the restoration of peace in 1783, a dramatic upsurge of activity brought renewed pressure upon the communications network and early in the 1790s a period of feverish enthusiasm for the promotion and building of canals that has with justice been called the 'Canal Mania'. In the years from 1791 to 1794, forty-four canal acts were passed, with an authorised capital of £6,661,700, and these were only the ones that received parliamentary approval amidst a frenzy of madcap schemes as speculators bought and sold shares, lured on by the prosperity of the first canals. Many of these schemes were wildly improbable, and a number of those that were sanctioned in fact turned out to be failures. The Herefordshire and Gloucestershire canal took from 1791 to 1845 to reach Hereford from Gloucester. That from Salisbury to Southampton was abandoned unfinished. Yet others did make a valuable contribution to further industrial expansion. The Barnsley canal, for example, provided an important outlet for West Riding coal and manufactured goods, with grain, foodstuffs, timber and building materials as the return cargoes.

Something of the frenzy of these years can be gathered

234

from the history of the plans to link Chester to the Severn via Wrexham. When subscriptions were opened in 1792 £1 million was promised in an afternoon. The act was passed in 1793. Thomas Telford was appointed engineer. There was much changing of lines, with the result that the aqueducts at Chirk and Pontcysyllte ended up on branch lines, which, it was hoped, would exploit the coal mines at Ruabon. The link from Chester to the Mersey was completed early in 1796, the canal coming out to the Mersey at a spot entirely without habitation in 1795. A small inn was completed in 1801 on the ground between the locks and the upper basin, and there was a lock-keeper's cottage further to the south-east. From these inauspicious beginnings Ellesmere Port was to develop. Passenger traffic grew rapidly along this canal, with in due course a steam packet boat to take passengers on to Liverpool from Ellesmere Port. For a time bathing in the Mersey was fashionable, and the spot became a resort in miniature, but it was 1835, when the canal to Middlewich was finally completed, joining up with the Birmingham to Liverpool canal at Hurleston, that the growth of Ellesmere Port really began.

One of the very few canals promoted by government was the Caledonian Canal from the Moray Firth near Inverness along Glen Mor to Fort William. Telford reported in 1802 on the feasibility of the project, and an act was passed in the following year. Parliamentary commissioners were appointed and Telford was yet again the engineer. It took twenty years to build, costing over £900,000, nearly three times the original estimate, and nearly three times the time estimated. It was never fully completed. There are long sections without towing paths, and the Great Glen, acting like a funnel, created adverse wind conditions that could hold ships up for weeks on end. Some rebuilding took place between 1842 and 1847 but it never became a commercial success. It was used to some extent during both world wars, but is now almost entirely given over to pleasure craft.

It is scarcely possible to exaggerate the contribution of canals to the making of Britain in the years between 1760 and 1830. The effects of their coming touched almost every aspect of the national life, and very few parts of the country could have escaped their influence entirely. The conveyance of merchandise of every kind became easier, cheaper and more convenient in ways which it is almost impossible for a generation brought up on the motor car to appreciate. The prices of basic raw materials such as coal, timber, iron, wool and cotton tumbled dramatically. Building materials, whether bricks, sand or slate, became cheap and accessible. It was the beginning of the end of the vernacular tradition in building. The needs of agriculture, whether for manure or lime or for access to markets for grain, cheese and butter, were more adequately satisfied wherever the canal penetrated. Passengers were conveyed, often by an integrated system involving stage coaches and packet boats. By 1830 a stage coach was running from Leeds to Knottingley, and from there passengers were taken by fast packet boat, pulled by horses, along the canal to Goole. Local and regional shortages of goods and materials of every kind could now be more speedily overcome, and with coal and grain or sand went men, women and children, with new ideas, attitudes and aptitudes.

The enclosure of open fields and the bringing of large tracts of waste and common under cultivation may have been spatially more extensive, but the new aqueducts, tunnels, cuttings and embankments were visually more dramatic, providing the largest secular man-made structures yet seen in the landscape. The soaring arches of Pontcysyllte are, even at the end of the twentieth century, a splendid monument to the vision, daring and ingenuity, not only of its engineer, Thomas Telford, but also of those who laboured to build it under his direction.

The canals brought at least five entirely new towns into existence – Runcorn, Goole, Grangemouth, Ellesmere Port and Stourport – and almost everywhere they went they brought new building and development, sometimes on a modest scale, sometimes bringing striking prosperity to old established towns. At Shardlow in Derbyshire, for ex-

60 The Pontcysyllte aqueduct, carrying the Llangollen branch of the Ellesmere canal 121 feet above the river Dee, designed and built by Thomas Telford and opened in 1805

ample, where the Trent and Mersey canal joins the Trent, a complex of wharves, warehouses and lock-keeper's cottages grew up. A canal from Tetney Haven, on the southern shores of the Humber estuary, to Louth was opened in 1770, providing transport for the rising wheat production on the Lincolnshire wolds as the waste, commons and sheep walks of the hills were enclosed and laid down to arable. The warehouses at the canal basin, and the elaborately Italianate corn exchange of 1853 and the town hall of 1854 are silent witness to the prosperity that the canal helped to bring and for long sustained. At Blisworth in Northamptonshire, at the northern end of the Blisworth tunnel on the Grand Junction canal, a number of rather gaunt factories are still to be seen on the banks of the canal, reminders of the magnetic attraction of the canal itself.

The completion of the Blisworth tunnel in 1805 on the Grand Junction canal meant that the four principal estuaries of England – the Humber, the Thames, the Severn and the Mersey – were now for the first time linked by an inland waterway, whilst the two principal Scottish firths, the Clyde and the Forth, had been joined by a canal completed in 1790. Almost all river improvement and canal building over the past century and more had in fact been seeking, however indirectly, an outlet to the sea, since the sea itself formed the last element in the communications network of eighteenth-century Britain. Coastal shipping, working through small ships in and out of the dozens of ports and harbours that lined the coasts of Britain, provided an invaluable outlet for local produce, together with the means by which foreign merchandise could be distributed from the larger ports. Thus Arthur Young noted that Mr Overman of Burnham in Norfolk had a small ship which he used to send his grain to London, and to bring back rapecake for his cattle, and not only from London but also from Hull and from Holland.

Not only Burnham but also Wells-next-the-Sea, Blakeney and Cley-next-the-Sea in Norfolk, Southwold, Walberswick, Orford and Woodbridge in Suffolk, Watchet and Minehead in Somerset, Ulverston and Millom in the Lake District, Glencaple, Palnackie, Gatehouse-of-Fleet, Kippford and Carsethorne along the Solway Firth, and many more, were once ports with a brisk trade in grain, coal, stone or dairy produce, depending upon local and regional resources. The small size of ships meant that towns like Knottingley, Gainsborough, Wisbech and Spalding were inland ports, and the merchants of Dumfries and Lancaster traded directly with America and the West Indies.

The quickening pace of life in the eighteenth century meant that it became necessary to improve port and harbour facilities. Ports for much of the eighteenth century were open: open on the one side to the rise and fall of the tide, so

238

61 In the bottom left-hand quarter of this aerial photograph are the St Katherine's Docks. In fitting two docks into a very cramped and awkwardly shaped site Telford produced one of his most ingenious designs. The docks were finished in 1828

that ships settled on the mud when the tide was out, and open on the landward side to thieves, who often worked on a large scale. A dock, where sufficient depth of water was maintained by enclosing gates and walls, was built in Liverpool between 1710 and 1715, and a similar one was built on the Surrey bank of the Thames about ten years earlier. It was 1801 before an enclosed dock was built on the north bank, when the London Dock was begun. The West India Dock was started in 1802, and the East India Dock in 1808. One of Telford's most accomplished achievements, the St Katherine's Dock, was completed in 1828. Docks of this kind combined deep water berths for ships, long rows of warehouses, and high surrounding walls to keep out thieves. Even today these buildings impress with the air of confident self-assurance with which they were conceived and built. Their plain, austere lines only very occasionally make any concession to a more gracious spirit, as with the classical, pedimented portico over the office entry to the West India Dock.

Similar docks were built in all the major ports of Britain, including Hull, Bristol and Glasgow. Smaller ports were improved by building quays, piers, warehouses and breakwaters, as at Ramsgate, for example. In some cases entirely new ports were built, especially for the export of coal. This happened at Maryport in Cumberland, where Humphrey Senhouse built a new town and harbour in the years after 1749. Ardrossan was planned by Peter Nicholson in 1806 for the Earl of Eglinton, and Troon was laid out in 1808 for the Marquess of Titchfield. All three were built in order to provide outlets for the coal pits which were being opened up in the neighbourhood. They must be seen as an appropriate response within local conditions to the same problems of marketing and distribution that faced the Duke of Bridgewater at Worsley.

The most sustained and extensive programme of harbour and port improvement came in Scotland. A number were built by improving landlords, as at Invergordon in the early eighteenth century, or at Cromarty in about 1785, but it was the untiring Thomas Telford who made the greatest contribution. At Ullapool and Tobermoray he planned and built entirely new towns for the British Fisheries Society, which had been founded in 1786 to encourage fishing from the coasts of Highland Scotland as one answer to the problems

62 Ullapool, Ross and Cromarty, laid out by Thomas Telford for the British Fisheries Society

created by rapid population growth in north-west Scotland. Whilst working for the Commissioners for Highland Roads and Bridges he built the harbours at Portree, Kirkwall, Wick, Portmahomack and Helmsdale, to name but a few. At Wick he laid out a new suburb, Pultneytown, in 1813. Telford's contribution to the moulding of the fabric of Britain in the first quarter of the nineteenth century must be unique in its range, scope and quality.

Improvements in ports and harbours were matched by improvements in navigational and safety aids for ships. John Smeaton built the third lighthouse on the Eddystone Rock in 1759. The system of interlocking stones which he had to employ because it was impossible to transport blocks of stone large enough to withstand the Atlantic waves made it one of the engineering feats of the age. It had to be replaced in 1882, but it was re-erected on Plymouth Hoe. In

241

1786 the Board of Trustees of Northern Lighthouses was established, and beginning with Kinnaird Head in 1787, it provided lighthouses all round the coasts of Scotland, including the Mull of Kintyre in 1788, the Pentland Skerries in 1794 and Cape Wrath in 1828. Its chief engineer was Robert Stevenson (1772–1850), the grandfather of the author of *Treasure Island*. At the age of 19 he was in charge of the building of the lighthouse at Wee Cumbrae, and he went on to build the one on the Bell Rock in the Firth of Forth. He invented flashing and rotating lights for lighthouses as well as a lantern for lightships. In his omnivorous appetite for practical knowledge and his unflagging devotion to work he is in the same class, although perhaps not of the same stature, as Telford. The coastal waters of Scotland were certainly much safer at the end of his life than they were at its beginning.

Attempts to apply steam power to water transport go back at least to 1789, the year in which Symington tried out a steam paddle boat on the Firth-Clyde canal. There were further trials with the *Charlotte Dundas* in 1801–3, but they were abandoned because it was feared that the wash from the boat would cause excessive damage to the canal banks. In 1812 Henry Bell built the *Comet*, a steamer with side paddle wheels, and for some time this provided a regular service on the Clyde between Glasgow and Helensburgh. From about 1818 steam boats were being increasingly used on inland waterways. In 1820 for example the *Stirling Castle* began a service along the Caledonian Canal from Inverness to Fort Augustus, and this was extended as far as Glasgow when the canal was completed. But in 1830 these developments were still of only marginal significance. Transport in Britain in 1830 was at once more reliable and more speedy than it had been in 1700, but it still depended almost as much as it had ever done upon the stamina and strength of horses and upon the vagaries of winds and tides. The real impact of the application of steam transport came only after 1830, the year which saw the opening of the first passenger carrying steam locomotive railway between Liverpool and Manchester.

242

8 The secularisation of the landscape

The fabric of eighteenth-century Britain is composed of three elements. The first of these is the topography of the country – the pattern of its soils, rocks, hills, valleys, streams, coastline and islands. We looked briefly at this in the first chapter, and it has run like the ground bass in a passacaglia through the succeeding chapters, which have been concerned with the second theme. This second theme is concerned with the people who have had to make a living from and under this topography, and the external, physical expression of the way in which they have done so, namely their fields and farms, mansions and cottages, towns, villages, workshops and factories. There is, however, a third element running through this exploration of the fabric of eighteenth-century Britain. Fields, farms and buildings are much more than bricks, stones and hedgerows. They are the embodiment of a way of life and a mode of thought. This third theme may perhaps be called the 'moral atmosphere' of eighteenth-century Britain: the nexus of ideas, ideals and attitudes of mind that form what may be called a fourth dimension to the landscape. Maps and documents and surviving artefacts enable us to re-create at least part of the physical fabric of the eighteenth century with some measure of accuracy. It is the reconstruction of this moral atmosphere that is at once the most elusive, the most fascinating and the most difficult part of the historian's task, since he has to clear away, at least mentally, the accretions in today's landscape of two centuries of unparalleled change, as well as the attitudes in his own mind that these two centuries have interposed.

This moral atmosphere changes over time, so that relics from the past become stranded, left behind like seashells when the tide has gone out. These relics very frequently had, for those men and women who actually planned, built or adapted them, a meaning which is quite unlike that which men and women of the late twentieth century would give to them. There is an ever-present danger of our projecting back into the past the ideas and standards of the late twentieth century. Much eighteenth-century art and literature seems to speak directly to us, from one human heart to another across time, and so it comes as a real shock when we perceive that men and women of the eighteenth century held ideas and opinions, habits of thought and standards of conduct, which are quite antipathetic to our own.

The changes which took place during the course of the eighteenth century in the ways in which men perceived their environment, in the moral atmosphere which envelops it, can perhaps be seen as the secularisation of the landscape. For the overwhelming majority of men throughout the period covered by this book the world was theocentric, although often in very crude terms. Only at the very end of our period is it possible to discern at all clearly 'the melancholy long withdrawing roar' of the Sea of Faith, as men's effort, skill and imagination flowed into new channels of thought given outward expression in the aqueduct at Pontcysyllte. 'Secularisation' carries with it no overtones of nostalgia for a lost Golden Age. Instead it describes an objective process; the beginning of the end for a world of traditional modes of thought and customary obligations.

Perhaps the single most important facet of this process of the secularisation of the fabric of eighteenth-century Britain is the long, slow decline in the importance of the church. The church has always been seen as a bastion of the established social order, and much of the history of the sixteenth and seventeenth centuries in Britain is taken up with attempts on the part of the state to enforce religious conformity as a safeguard against social collapse. The first breach came in 1689 when the Toleration Act permitted some groups of dissenters to worship in their own churches. This had an unexpected consequence. Other people also began to stay away from church. At the same time the worldliness of the established Church of England, its preoccupation with tithes, the scramble for preferment and the disrepute that the wretched poverty of so many livings brought to the unfortunate clergymen who had to officiate in them, meant that the esteem given to the established church as a whole sank to a low ebb in the first half of the eighteenth century.

This decline in the standing of the church is matched by a decline in church building, and much of what did take place required an act of parliament. In 1711, during a brief period of Tory rule, an act was passed levying a duty on coal, the proceeds of which were to be applied to the building of fifty new churches in and about London. In fact only twelve completely new ones were built, but the commissioners did have the grace to pay to Sir Christopher Wren the arrears of salary due to him as surveyor of St Paul's which the Whigs had meanly withheld. Nicholas Hawksmoor was architect to the commissioners under the act, and he designed six churches for them. James Gibbs was also employed for the two years between 1713 and 1715, during which time he designed the church of St Mary le Strand. He was followed by John James, who built the church of St George's, Hanover Square, finished in 1726.

Application to parliament either to build a new church or to rebuild an existing one became quite common. This is because the Church of England had become so deeply embedded in the luxuriant jungle of property rights that characterises the eighteenth century that only parliament could adjudicate on the conflicting claims to tithes, glebe, fees, dilapidations, and so on, that any attempt to change any part of its fabric or its organisation inevitably provoked. Thus in 1720 James Gibbs was chosen architect by the commissioners appointed under a private act of parliament to rebuild the church of St Martin-in-the Fields in London. Similar acts were passed for St Giles-in-the-Field in 1717, and for St Olave Southwark in 1737. In 1708 another act

63 The church of St George's, Hanover Square, London, built between 1721 and 1724 to designs by John James as part of the development of the Hanover Square estate planned by the Earl of Scarborough

created a new parish in Birmingham. Twenty commissioners were appointed and they chose Thomas Archer to design their new church of St Philip, finally completed in 1725. In 1790 the inhabitants of Banbury obtained an act of parliament for the rebuilding of their church, and the inhabitants of Oldham obtained a similar act for their church in 1824.

Other church building or rebuilding took place as part of the landscaping of the grounds of country mansions. The church of St Mary Magdalen at Stapleford in Leicestershire was built in 1783 for the Earl of Harborough and stands in the grounds of his country mansion in just the same way as that at Gayhurst begun in 1723, and that at Overstone in Northamptonshire, where the parsonage was sold and pulled down in 1799, the old church demolished in 1803 and a new one, built just within the park, consecrated in 1807.

The decline in attendance at churches of the Church of England seems to have continued without interruption until about 1830. Nevertheless there was no decline or diminution in the claims that were made on its behalf, either to the deference of every member of society or to instruct every member of society. The parson was seen as the father of all the inhabitants of his parish – guiding, admonishing and mediating – supported in all that he did by the local squire. By the last quarter of the eighteenth century this dream of a rural theocracy was in many parishes the length and breadth of Britain little better than a caricature of the real situation. In 1812 there were over a thousand parishes in England with no resident Anglican clergyman. And yet the organisation, ritual and rights of the established church penetrated so deeply into every fibre of the political and social life of the country, reinforcing the entire social order, that any suggestion for its reform was viewed by its more conservative defenders as little better than a compound of treason and blasphemy. None the less it was becoming apparent even to its most loyal supporters that it must make at least some attempt to reach the inhabitants of the most rapidly expanding centres of population, where numbers were far beyond the capacity of the old parochial system, or else it must be prepared to see them slip into Methodism, indifference or atheism. In 1816 Parliament passed the Fen Chapel Act, providing for the building of chapels in the villages being established in the newly drained Lincolnshire fens. Plain brick churches appeared in Midville in 1819, in Frithville in 1821, and the church at Eastville was consecrated in 1840.

A much more ambitious attempt to improve church accommodation was made in 1818, when parliament created the Church Building Commission, providing £1 million to be spent on new churches. The need was obvious, and had been recognised for at least twenty years before the act was passed. In 1816 it was reported that in Leeds there was church accommodation for 3,400, whereas the population

64 Frithville church, built in 1821 after the draining of the fens to the north of Boston, Lincolnshire

was 67,000, and in Birmingham, for a population of 185,000 there was church seating for 24,000. Over the next fifteen years the commissioners spent some £6 million, but their efforts were in many ways only partially successful. The churches they built are for the greater part undistinguished architecturally, and Pugin's strictures – he found them miserable, absurd and paltry – are not entirely undeserved. What is even more important, however, is that this building programme failed to halt the decline in attendance. There was some justification for the stand made by the Manchester vestry meeting in 1820 when, learning that Manchester was to have three or four churches from the commission, it refused to provide funds for the purchase of the sites on the grounds that the proposed churches were unnecessary.

The Church Building Commissioners were also empowered to create new parishes, but the legislation was so complex and so timid that the commissioners, themselves a deeply conservative body, were unable to cut through the tangle of vested interests of incumbents and patrons and made almost no change in an area of church administration where change had become imperative.

However, the Church of England remained throughout the eighteenth century the guardian of traditional social values and attitudes, more especially those which served to perpetuate the political and social dominance of the landed aristocracy. The problems which it seems so reluctantly to have faced were forced upon its attention by the changes which industrialisation was bringing. New men, who had made their money in new ways, increasingly resented the air of easy superiority of the landed gentry and their clerical allies. The traditional paternalism of rural parochial life meant nothing to factory workers in Oldham, dockers in Liverpool or coal miners in Durham. This weakening in the traditional status of the established church finds its visual reflection in the comparative absence from the landscape of churches of eighteenth-century build.

The enclosure movement which gathered momentum in the latter half of the eighteenth century in some ways contributed to this weakening. The insistence of the Church of England upon its tithes was undoubtedly widely resented in eighteenth-century England. Clergymen often found themselves entangled in legal proceedings in order to enforce their rights, usually in the Courts of Exchequer or Chancery, notorious for their delays and their costs, and the quickest way to sour relationships between a parson and his congregation. A dispute over tithes in Kendal lasted for nineteen years until eventually it was resolved by that panacea of the eighteenth century, a private act of parliament. Individual enclosure acts usually provided for the commutation of tithes hitherto paid in kind, either by imposing a rent charge based upon a seven-year average of the price of grain, or else by making an allocation of land to the incumbent or tithe owner, who were not necessarily the same person. These allocations were often very generous indeed, something like a fifth of the arable land being enclosed and an eighth of the meadow and pasture. In addition the incumbent had his fencing costs paid by the other parishioners. Enclosure thus made a prosperous landowner out of a country clergyman, something which finds its tangible echo in the rebuilding of parsonages in the last years of the eighteenth century, serving at the same time to alienate him still further from the great majority of his parishioners.

There is yet a further facet to this decline in the influence of the established church. The values, both spiritual and cultural, which it embodied were those of a small minority of the population, a minority with the wealth and the leisure to buy books and pictures, to go on the Grand Tour, to acquire the languages, Greek, Latin and Hebrew, which lay at the foundation of this culture, to rebuild their houses and lay out their parks and gardens. The eighteenth century was intensely proud of its intellectual achievement and of its cultural heritage, but the extent to which a knowledge of the writings of Pope, Johnson and Gibbon, the gardens of Lancelot Brown or the furnishings of Robert Adam penetrated beyond the leisured classes can only be a matter of

65 An engraving of Birmingham Town Hall, made in 1834 by L. Tallis, soon after the building was finished

conjecture, in spite of clear evidence of rising standards of literacy, a growth in book publishing and selling, and the spread of newspapers. It became common practice to visit country houses in the second half of the eighteenth century. Guides to the gardens at Stowe were published from 1756 onwards, and Earl Temple built an inn to accommodate the visitors, but admission would have been confined to those whose dress, speech and carriages indicated that they did not come from the labouring classes. In 1830 the Birmingham Improvement Commissioners announced a competition for a design for a new town hall. What finally emerged from the builders' scaffolding was a Corinthian temple closely modelled on one in the Forum at Rome. Similarly, St Pancras New Church, built, like so much else during the

Georgian years, after the passing in 1816 of a private act of parliament, is strongly influenced by the Erechtheum, the temple lying to the north of the Parthenon on the Acropolis. Classical, and hence pagan, themes are common-place in eighteenth-century churches, illustrating the essential unity of lay and clerical culture. How far the artisans, craftsmen and labourers of St Pancras and Birmingham shared in them is entirely a different matter.

It seems very likely that the formal traditional culture of the eighteenth century was the preserve of a minority. We should not allow its brilliance to conceal the vice, brutality and crude superstition to be found among all ranks of society. The cultural traditions of the majority of the inhabitants of Britain are far less well recorded. There were at best only tolerated, usually frowned upon and occasionally forbidden by the state and its established church. The church nevertheless provided a structural framework for many popular traditional activities since they often revolved round its most solemn festivals. Christmas, Easter and Whitsun have always provided the opportunity, or the excuse, for popular celebrations. The drunkenness, ribaldry and sexual licence which seem to have accompanied them as a matter of course are one reason for the ambivalent attitude which the church has taken towards the feasting and dancing which went on.

Local celebrations of Christmas varied considerably from one part of the country to the next, and frequently went on until Twelfth Day. Scotland was by no means the only part of Britain to give more attention to New Year than to Christmas itself. There was often ceremonial dancing and mumming, with processions round the village demanding contributions from every household, to be spent on eating and drinking at the end of the day. Easter was often marked by football, cricket, bell-ringing, cock-fighting and other sports. In many parishes it was customary for children to beg for eggs from their neighbours. In Anglesey they took wooden clappers with them to accompany the doggerel verse in which they made their demands. Before the Reformation Whitsun had been one of the customary seasons for parish 'ales', when the churchwardens brewed and sold vast quantities of beer, the proceeds going towards the maintenance of the fabric of the church. The Protestant reformers were firmly opposed to church ales because of the drunkenness and promiscuity which surrounded them, but they continued in many rural districts until the early years of the nineteenth century.

The rhythms of the agricultural year were also marked by festivities and celebrations. Plough Monday fell on the first Monday after Twelfth Day, and was traditionally the time when the agricultural year began once more. The day was a holiday marked by a procession in which farm labourers dragged a plough round the village, again demanding

66 Plough Monday celebrations from G. Walker, *The Costume of York-shire*, 1814

contributions from all the households, the money raised to be spent on feasting and drinking in the evening. As with the collections made at Christmas, refusal to contribute was almost unthinkable and would certainly have invited hostility and contempt in the coming year.

Sheep-shearing, haymaking and the completion of the harvest were also marked by festivities. It was traditional for the farmer or landlord to provide a harvest supper for all who had worked in the fields to bring in the grain. The corn harvest was perhaps the climax of the agricultural year, but sheep-shearing and haymaking were also sufficiently important to deserve the wearing of ribbons, and eating and drinking on a grand scale. Very different in style and purpose were the sheep-shearings organised by some of the great improving landlords, such as the Duke of Bedford and Thomas Coke. Coke made his annual sheep-shearings an opportunity to publicise his achievements as an agricultural improver, and for more than twenty years the Holkham sheep-shearings were attended by landlords and farmers from all over Britain anxious to discover what was new in sheep breeding, to compete for cups and trophies, to see and be seen, and to take part in the immense dinners offered on each of the three or four days of the event. Similarly, rent-days were also expected to culminate in a dinner provided by the landlord, accompanied by much drinking, toasts, speeches and, for the evening, the loosening of traditional social restraints between the landlord and his tenants.

With other local and parish festivals the association of the church was far more tenuous. In many parts of southern and eastern England village feasts, also known as the wake or the revel, were held until well into the nineteenth century. The Northamptonshire historian John Bridges records that early in the eighteenth century, of the 290 parishes he visited, no less than 198 had an annual feast. The majority were held either in the late spring and early summer, or else at the end of summer, many being held on the Sunday nearest the feast day of the saint to whom the parish church

254

was dedicated. These feasts were characterised by eating and drinking, wrestling, boxing, chasing a greased pig, bull-baiting, cock-fighting, music and dancing, all serving to reinforce ties of good neighbourliness in the parish. Such feasts have sometimes given their names to the field or open space in which they were held. A 'Revel Meadow' is marked on the 1820 enclosure map of Oakley in Buckinghamshire and when the Revel Mead in Bicester was mown it too was considered an occasion for celebration.

May Day was marked by young people going into the woods to break off branches from trees and bring back a maypole, which was then dressed with garlands and flowers. Dancing, music, eating and drinking then followed. May Day was always criticised because of the sexual laxity which accompanied it. In many villages this festival became confused with Oak Apple Day, 29 May, the date of the Restoration of Charles II in 1660, and also his birthday. The other quasi-political festival of the year was Guy Fawkes Day, the occasion for bonfires and fireworks.

In this way the calendar was marked off, with very wide local and regional variations, throughout much of Britain. But many of the sports and games which were played on these festival days were also played on other occasions.

Football has been played since medieval times, and was popular and widespread throughout eighteenth-century England. It was frequently played on Shrove Tuesday, and these holiday matches had their own special rituals and customs, as well as serving to reinforce a sense of neighbourliness and acting as a safety valve for inter-community hostility. It was common for several hundred players to take part, and on occasion the goals were a mile or more apart. Such games often went on until darkness fell, and bruises, black eyes and broken limbs were commonplace. The large crowds and the violence were regarded with apprehension by the authorities, not without cause, since football games on this scale were on occasion diverted to other ends, as in the fens, where from time to time the players turned instead to destroying the new enclosures, which were intensely unpopular. Unlike a number of other sports, football remained largely without formal regulation for much of the eighteenth century and it was 1863 before the Football Association was founded.

Cricket, like football, is medieval in origin, and by the early years of the eighteenth century was being played over much of southern England. Cricket grounds were laid out, of which one of the best known was the Artillery Ground in Finsbury, where on 18 June 1744 a Kent v. All England match took place. Thomas Lord established a private cricket ground in Dorset Square in London, where the Marylebone Cricket Club, founded in 1787, made its headquarters. Lord moved to the present site of Lord's cricket ground in 1813, taking with him his turf from Dorset Square, which had already survived one move. The Marylebone Cricket Club quickly acquired a considerable reputation and became the regulating body for English cricket generally. Cricket

67 A watercolour drawing by Paul and Thomas Sandby of a race meeting on Ascot Heath, *c.* 1760

matches were often attended by large, noisy and quarrelsome crowds, and heavy betting took place.

Horse-racing was also very popular and widespread and, like cricket, it attracted huge crowds drawn from all levels of society. It appealed to the landed aristocracy for two reasons. First of all Charles II was very fond of it and it was Queen Anne who opened the racing at Ascot, and such royal approval was more than sufficient to make it acceptable. Secondly only the aristocracy could afford the expense involved in breeding and rearing race-horses. John Cheney published the first *Racing Calendar* in 1727, and *The General Stud Book* made its appearance at the end of the century. The Jockey Club was founded in 1750, meeting first of all in the Star and Garter Coffee House in Pall Mall. Shortly afterwards, Richard Tattersall, a horse dealer and auctioneer, provided it with accommodation in his premises at Hyde Park Corner. By 1762 there were seventy-six race-courses up and down the country. John Carr of York built the Grandstand at Knavesmire race-course, York, in 1754, and the first Grandstand at Doncaster race-course in 1776, in time for the first running of the St Leger. In about 1770 Lord Derby built himself a country house called The Oaks, a little to the south of Carshalton in Surrey. His house gave its name to the race first run on the Epsom Downs, about five miles away to the south-west in 1779, and the Derby itself was first run in the following year.

It was James VI of Scotland who brought golf with him into England, where he played it on Blackheath, just to the south of Greenwich. As with cricket and horse-racing, it is the eighteenth century which sees golf acquire its rules and its institutions. In 1744 the Company of Gentlemen Golfers of Leith, its title is significant, applied to Edinburgh town council for a trophy to play for over the five holes of their course. From this grew the Honourable Company of Edinburgh Golfers, which had drawn up a code of play by 1751. In 1754 a similar club was in existence in St Andrews, a club which was the ancestor of the Royal and Ancient. It was only because the course at St Andrews settled down to eighteen holes that this number became accepted as the standard 'round'. The earliest English golf club was founded, appropriately, at Blackheath in 1766.

Cricket, horse-racing and golf became popular and widespread during the eighteenth century, and acquired the basis of their present-day rules and organisations. Much of this is due to the fact that they were as popular with the leisured and landed classes as with the populace, and any impression that may have been given earlier that country gentlemen of the eighteenth century were interested only in books, pictures, classical architecture and gardening should quickly be forgotten. It was the gentry who made these pastimes acceptable, provided the patronage which enabled them to become established, and defended them from those who objected on religious or moral grounds to all forms of diversion or recreation. If the gentry did not participate, or withdrew their patronage, then a particular popular sport could not long survive the censure of the earnest reformers of the last years of the eighteenth century. Cock-throwing had largely disappeared by the end of the century. A long campaign in the first part of the nineteenth century, of which the founding of the Society for the Prevention of Cruelty to Animals in 1824 was a part, culminated in 1835 in the passing of the Cruelty to Animals Act. This effectively put an end to animal baiting, although cock-fighting continued, ever more surreptitiously, until the end of the century and beyond, and bull-baiting into the 1840s. Bull-running, on rather similar lines to that practised in some towns in southern France and Spain today, was suppressed in Tutbury in 1778, but the more famous Stamford bull-running on 13 November of each year persisted until 1839. Sports of this kind have left behind them almost no visual monuments at all. There are no grandstands for bull-baiting, or Royal and Ancient for cock-throwing, although there is still to be seen in the village green at Stainton in Furness the outlines in the grass of the circular cock-fighting pit.

There were other factors at work making for the slow

dissolution of traditional popular culture. Many village feasts and festivals required an open space. The enclosure movement of the last half of the eighteenth century saw many of these disappear, together with the field-names which recorded them. There was, for example, a 'Pleystow', meaning 'sport place', in Thornborough in the fourteenth century. It can still be recognised as a name on an early seventeenth century map but it cannot be traced after the enclosure of the village. The consequences following upon the loss of these open spaces were recognised only very slowly. The General Enclosure Act of 1845 did something to protect village greens, and suggested that provision should be made in future for playing fields. It was too little and too late. Also many traditional festivals were essentially rural in their ambience. The urbanisation of the last years of the eighteenth century destroyed their relevance and many were quietly forgotten.

The final factor is more difficult to state briefly. The more extreme Protestant reformers had always been strongly opposed to all forms of sport and recreation, condemning them because they encouraged idleness and sensuality. The Restoration put an end to their power to prohibit village feasts, games, dancing and the rest, and there was a general reaction against their severity. Gradually, however, in the second half of the eighteenth century, the tolerant, earthy paternalism that had characterised much of the social relationships of rural England and which is reflected in many of these traditional pastimes, came to be regarded as old-fashioned. The rough, often boorish, manners of many country gentlemen were gradually softened. There was a slow revival of stricter attitudes towards games and pastimes and at the same time social distances within society were widening. Agricultural labourers ceased to live-in, and harvest suppers were gradually discontinued. Idleness was more and more regarded as morally indefensible, an attitude that struck across all classes as Evangelicalism and Methodism grew increasingly powerful in the early years of the nineteenth century. In many ways traditional pastimes were most severely condemned by those who were most deeply involved in them, since Primitive Methodists in particular were drawn from the artisan classes and they laid the greatest stress upon personal piety. Strict Sabbatarianism was part of this movement, and by 1830 the pressures which it could exert were enormous. The long night of the Victorian Sunday had begun.

The triumph of the new spirit of the last decades of the eighteenth century was by no means complete, even by the middle years of the nineteenth century. Very many traditional beliefs and patterns of life continued, and remained almost untouched at least until 1914, especially in rural districts. Corn-dollies, for example, fashioned from the last sheaf of corn to be cut at harvest-time, tied with red thread or ribbon to ward off witches, and carefully preserved until next summer, were still being made for their original serious purpose of ensuring a good harvest next year until this century, and belief in charms, incantations and horoscopes is still very strong even today.

The collapse of traditional culture in this way is one facet of that secularisation of the fabric of eighteenth-century Britain which becomes steadily more pronounced in the last decades of the century. To speak of secularisation is not to deny the significance of religious belief, opinion and practice throughout this period, but it is to suggest that this significance was in itself changing, and it is not too much of an exaggeration to point to the Toleration Act of 1689 as the starting point for this change. The formal practice of Anglicanism may have declined throughout the century, but from about 1740 there is a revival in Nonconformity. In that year there were only 448 registered places of worship for dissenters of all denominations, temporary and permanent. By the end of the century there were 4,200 and by 1830 over 10,400.

The toleration brought by the act of 1689 was only grudgingly granted, and so early dissenting chapels tend to be quiet and self-effacing structures. They certainly did not want to draw unwelcome attention to themselves. The last serious riots against dissenters took place in Birmingham in 1791 when the Unitarians were singled out by the mob for its attentions because of their radical views, and it was long after 1830 before the thinly veiled hostility between Anglicans and dissenters showed any signs of abating. Quaker meeting houses in particular have always been of the plainest construction.

By the end of the eighteenth century some chapels of other denominations are on occasion quite large, and display some interest in current architectural tastes. At Penrith, for example, the Methodist chapel of 1815 has a pediment and Tuscan columns, as does the Providence chapel built in 1828 at Cranbrook in Kent, whilst the Wesleyan chapel built in Toxteth in 1827 has Greek Doric columns.

The Toleration Act did not extend to Roman Catholics, and in theory, although not always in practice, they were subject to considerable legal and political disabilities. In 1778 an act was passed freeing Catholic priests from liability to imprisonment, and allowing Catholics to buy and inherit land. The act was very unpopular throughout Britain. Proposals to extend it to Scotland led to rioting in Edinburgh and Glasgow, and in June 1780 to one of the worst outbreaks of mob violence in English history, the Gordon Riots. Order was restored only on the personal intervention of George III himself. A further measure of relief came in 1791, when Catholics were given complete freedom of worship and education, and this was extended to Scotland in 1793. From this time onwards those Roman Catholic chapels already in existence, which had been allowed to continue by the indifference, or the connivance, of neighbours, could be openly recognised, and new ones could be built. One of the earliest anywhere is that at Tynet in Morayshire built in 1755. At East Lulworth in Dorset, in the grounds of Lulworth Castle, is a Roman Catholic chapel built in 1786-7. It is said that George III would allow it to be built only on condition that it did not look like a church. After 1791 Roman Catholic churches appear quite quickly. One was built in Mulberry Street, Manchester, in 1794, and one at

Standishgate, Wigan, in 1818, and another in the same street in the following year, complete with Ionic columns. This second, St John, also has a particularly fine interior.

Churches are among the most ancient buildings in the landscape and they have always been one of the most obvious examples of the physical manifestation of men's ideals and beliefs. They continue to fulfil this function in the fabric of eighteenth-century Britain. The changes in their architectural style reflect the same changes in taste and artistic practices that we saw at work in country houses in chapter four. The proliferation in the number of bodies and sects for whose devotional purposes new churches were built is an echo of the mounting attack on the monopolistic position of the established church and a sign of the development of a pluralistic society in which a widening range of beliefs, opinions and practices would find acceptance. The Toleration Act was the first breach in the monopoly. The measures of Catholic relief of 1778 and 1791 are further cracks. The repeal of the Test and Corporation Acts in 1828 and the Roman Catholic Relief Act of 1829 see it burst wide open, and the pace of secularisation accelerates.

Churches are the best example of traditional buildings where alterations and adaptations reflect changing ideas. Similar changes are to be found in other kinds of buildings, including schools, almshouses, town halls, hospitals and military fortifications. All have long histories and all show the same principles at work.

Schools were being founded, built, rebuilt and added to throughout Britain in the eighteenth century. One of the most splendid of medieval schools is the King's College of Our Lady of Eton by Windsor, founded by Henry VI in 1440, and provided by him with a fine range of brick buildings. A brewhouse was added in 1714 and a library in the years between 1725 and 1729. During the century individual masters built boarding houses for some of the pupils – Godolphin House in 1722, Carter House in 1737, Keate House in about 1785, and others. A school and almshouses were founded in Sevenoaks in 1432. When they were rebuilt

68 The Royal High School, Edinburgh, built between 1826 and 1829 on the south side of Calton Hill

between 1724 and 1732, the designs were provided by Lord Burlington, and published in 1727 by William Kent. Some of the architecturally most distinguished school buildings were put up in Scotland at the beginning of the nineteenth century. Montrose Academy was built in 1815, Dollar Academy in 1818, and the Royal High School, Edinburgh, 'the noblest monument of the Scottish Greek Revival', was built at a cost of £24,200 on the south side of Calton Hill between 1826 and 1829. Building of this kind may be contrasted with the simple two-storey block of Skipwith Old School, built in 1714, and the first home of the Royal Military College, founded in 1799 in a large early eighteenth-century house in Marlow which it occupied until the move to Sandhurst in 1811.

Military fortification and building shows the same kind of adaptation. The reluctant acceptance of the standing army as a permanent institution of British society led in 1719 to the building of the first purpose-built accommodation for its troops at Berwick-upon-Tweed. Other barracks were built at York in 1795. A very extensive range was built in 1803 at Weedon in Northamptonshire. They were built as far from the coast as possible, and were intended to provide a refuge for George III in case the threatened invasion from France ever materialised. They had their own canal wharf, separated from the main line of the canal, the Grand Junction, by means of a gatehouse and portcullis. Further evidence of the measures taken in face of the threat from France can be seen in the martello towers that are strung along the shores of the south eastern coastline, and the Royal Military Canal, sweeping in a great arc behind Romney Marshes from Hythe to Rye. Eighteenth-century military fortification as such can best be seen in Scotland: Fort William was built in 1690; Fort Augustus, built between 1729 and 1742, was captured by the Jacobites in 1745 after a direct hit blew up the magazine. The original Fort George, at Inverness, was destroyed in 1746. A new one, on Ardersier Point, was finished by 1763. It remains the most complete of these Scottish fortresses.

69   The military canal basin at Weedon Bec, Northamptonshire, begun in 1803

It would be impossible as well as tedious to list all of the traditional types of buildings that were rebuilt or refaced, altered or adapted or built in new guises during the course of the eighteenth century. That there are so many is an indication both of the power and the strength of traditional modes of thought and also of the extended and gradual nature of the processes of change. Nevertheless new kinds of buildings do emerge during the course of the century, representing yet further aspects of the process of secularisation.

Although theatres existed in late sixteenth and seventeenth century London and companies of players performed in the courtyards of provincial inns, it is the eighteenth century before purpose-built provincial theatres make their appearance. York had one by 1736. A disused silk mill at Southampton was converted into a theatre in 1766. There was one in Birmingham by 1780, and Newcastle-upon-Tyne had its first Theatre Royal in 1788. The now demolished theatre in Roper Street, Whitehaven, was built in 1769. There was a theatre at Tunbridge Wells in 1801 and one at Bury St Edmunds in 1819. Even straight-laced Edinburgh began to unbend a little. There was a small theatre in Old Playhouse Close, off the Canongate, in the early decades of the century, although it could only survive by pretending to be a concert hall, the play being performed in the interval of the concert. A new theatre was opened in 1769 in Shakespeare Square, a corner formed by North Bridge Street and Prince's Street. Edinburgh also possesses one of the most delightful of all these eighteenth-century places of entertainment: a socially very exclusive Musical Society was founded in 1728 and St Cecilia's Hall, completed in 1762 and paid for entirely by contributions from members, still survives and has recently been restored. The Society held its concerts here until it was wound up in 1801.

Theatres are one facet of the growing importance of towns during the century as centres for social, cultural and intellectual activities, from the most fashionably frivolous to the most strenuous, high-minded and serious. Fashionable

70 Fort George, Inverness

social activities required assembly rooms, for balls, card
parties and other entertainments. The first assembly rooms
at Bath were built in 1708, the New Assembly Rooms in
1769–1771. Those at York were built in 1730 to designs by
Lord Burlington. Whitehaven had assembly rooms in 1736,
Newcastle-upon-Tyne in 1776, Kendal in 1825, Hull in 1830,
whilst the Library and Card Assembly was built at
Weymouth in about 1800, where the Esplanade dates from
the 1780s. The Portico Library was founded in Manchester
in 1802. The Wellington Rooms in Liverpool were built
between 1815 and 1816 to serve as assembly rooms, and it is
the Liverpool Unitarian banker, William Roscoe, who may
serve as the epitome of the cultural achievement of provincial city life at the beginning of the nineteenth century.
There was a run on his bank in 1816. It had to suspend
payment and eventually he himself was made bankrupt,
but his financial misfortunes do not detract from his intellectual successes. His biographies of Lorenzo the Magnificent

and Pope Leo X achieved a European reputation, being translated into French, German and Italian.

To these libraries, assembly rooms and theatres, dissenting and Roman Catholic chapels, race-course grandstands, schools and barracks there need to be added, in order to complete the picture of the extent to which the fabric of Britain had been secularised by 1830, the mills, factories, aqueducts and new, planned farmsteads described in previous chapters. The extent and direction of this secularisation may be summed up by comparing just two, very disparate, buildings. As early as 1817 suggestions were

71 The unfinished National Monument, built on Calton Hill, Edinburgh, between 1826 and 1829

72 The Saltisford gas works, Warwick, built in 1822

made in Edinburgh for the erection of a National Monument in honour of the dead of the Napoleonic Wars. A committee was established and an appeal made for funds. These came in so slowly that it was 1823 before C. R. Cockerell was appointed architect. Building began in 1826, came to a stop in 1829 and has never re-started. The money had run out. The half-finished building forms a splendid climax to Calton Hill, but its significance extends beyond this. It was intended to be a reconstruction of the Parthenon, a classical, and hence pagan, temple. Thus it is a measure of the extent to which the formal, established church had been compelled to slacken its grip on the world.

The other building is much more humble and prosaic, but just as significant. The gas works at Warwick was built in 1822. It was sited near the canal basin so that coal needed for conversion into gas could be brought in by barge. It is composed of a small single-storey central block and two wings, each of two storeys, each wing terminating in a gas holder. The gas holders themselves are encased in brick, with blind first-floor windows, and ground-floor windows of delicate Gothic tracery. It was a type of building that was entirely new and it owed its existence to recent scientific and engineering advances. It was fed by the canal, in itself a further example of such advances, and it meant that the streets of Warwick could now be adequately lit at night, something which appropriately named improvement commissioners had been trying to do in towns the length and breadth of the country for the past fifty years.

There was much enthusiasm in the second half of the eighteenth century for engines and engineering, scientific and technical developments and agricultural improvement, and we have seen something of their impact in previous chapters. Literary and philosophical societies were formed in many provincial towns to disseminate information on these improvements. One was founded in Manchester in 1781, another in Birmingham in 1800 and another in Newcastle-upon-Tyne in 1822. The Royal Institution was founded in London in 1806, and the lectures of Dalton, Davy and Faraday attracted large audiences. The late eighteenth-century reports of the Board of Agriculture are full of details of experiments with new crops and husbandry practices. The report for Lancashire, for example, goes into great detail about trials of different kinds of manures. The possibilities for the improvement of the human condition seemed at the time to be limitless, and to material improvement should be added moral and social improvement when the French Revolution first broke out in 1789. William Godwin's pronouncement that the road to the improvement of mankind is in the utmost degree simple is to be read in the light of this air of eager expectancy that was so widespread in the last two decades of the eighteenth century.

The hopes were dashed, first by the turn of events in France, more especially after 1798, and second as the conditions which the Spirit of Improvement actually created in factories and towns became more widely known. Mary Shelley's *Frankenstein*, the monster created by science which turns to destroy its creator, was published in 1818. Warwick Gas Works is no Frankenstein but it does serve as a symbol of the practical achievement of the Spirit of Improvement and of its contribution to the secularisation of Britain.

9 Britain in 1830

We began this book on 18 September 1714 with Georg Ludwig, elector of Brunswick-Lüneburg, stepping ashore at Greenwich to take up his inheritance. We can end it on 26 June 1830, the day on which his great-great-grandson George IV died. It is almost as difficult to break out of the seamless web of history as it is to break into it, but in some ways 1830 forms a more convenient and satisfactory finishing point than does 1714 a starting point, since two events in the remaining six months of the year after the death of George IV point quite clearly to the end of one era and the beginning of another.

The first of these events was precipitated by the general election which then as a matter of constitutional law had to follow upon the demise of the monarch. The election seriously undermined the strength in the House of Commons of the Tory government led by the Duke of Wellington. Tories and Whigs alike recognised that parliamentary reform could not be long delayed. Wellington resigned as prime minister on 16 November 1830, and was succeeded by Earl Grey. The reform of parliament now became the central issue of domestic politics until the Great Reform Bill passed into law in June 1832. Wellington's resignation may be said to mark the beginning of the end for the traditional distribution of power in Britain.

The second event of 1830 is the opening on 15 September of the Liverpool to Manchester railway. It is impossible to overestimate the impact of the coming of the railways upon every strand and fibre in the fabric of nineteenth-century Britain. Railway cuttings and embankments, tunnels,

73 A photograph taken in 1902 of the Liverpool Road railway station, Manchester, built in 1830 of brick stuccoed with 'Roman cement'. The three-storey brick building on the left was the superintendent's house, and had been built by 1825. Next comes the first-class passengers' entrance. This has an urn over the doorway. Next to the right is the second-class passengers' entrance, and then the entrance to the carriers' office. Even further to the right is a block of shops built in 1831 for leasing

bridges, viaducts and stations make their own dramatic impact upon the landscape, but in addition the railways themselves become the means by which the pace of change accelerates throughout every aspect of the national life, rural, urban, industrial, demographic and social.

George IV himself was at once extravagant, clever, selfish, heartless and unreliable. His interest in political affairs went little beyond intrigue. His private life made him intensely unpopular. At the same time he was genuinely interested in the arts, music and architecture. He took an

74 The Royal Pavilion at Brighton as completed by John Nash for the Prince Regent between 1815 and 1822

active part in the founding of the Royal Society of Literature. In 1823 he gave George III's library to the nation and it was housed in the British Museum in specially built accommodation. His father gave him Carlton House on his 21st birthday in 1783. He immediately engaged Henry Holland to rebuild and refurnish it. When John Nash outlined his plans for the development of Regent's Park and Regent Street, Carlton House was seen as the grand climax of the whole scheme, but it was demolished in 1827, by which time George was engrossed in the remodelling of Windsor Castle, where he spent most of his time after his accession. He made his first visit to Brighton in 1783. Three or four years later he leased from Thomas Kemp a farmhouse on the Steine. This was rebuilt by Henry Holland as a marine pavilion, and a riding house and stables were added between 1804 and 1808. Nothing further was done for some time until in 1815 John Nash began to reshape the entire building in a glorious medley of Gothic and what passed for Indian architectural themes. The interior was correspondingly lavish. This work was finished in 1822, after which, characteristically, George IV never returned to Brighton. In the following year the son of his former landlord, Thomas Kemp junior, began to lay out Kemp Town, to the east of the old centre of Brighton, a new town with terraces, crescents and a reading room. By 1821 Brighton was the fastest growing town in England.

Brighton is virtually the creation of George IV, and so he deserves a brief mention in a book concerned with the making of Britain before 1830. In 1744 it was a fishing village of about 450 houses, many of which were huddled almost on the seashore. During the course of the eighteenth century this 'lower' town was destroyed by storms and coastal erosion. It is probably true to say that it was coastal erosion of this nature, together with coastal deposition, both working upon a small, entirely local scale, which brought about the most extensive purely natural changes in the topography of Britain during the course of the eighteenth century.

If natural change had been almost imperceptible, man-made change in the surface of Britain had been extensive and far-reaching. By 1830 the enclosure movement was in its last stages. Open fields cultivated in strips were now the exception rather than the rule. They had been replaced by rectangular closes divided off by neat rows of hawthorn shrubs. Straight roads, clearly separated from the fields, had taken the place of the unkempt and ill-defined ways that had straggled between the furlongs of the open fields. Many thousands of acres of waste, moorland, marsh and common had been brought under cultivation. In the wolds of Lincolnshire and the East Riding of Yorkshire miles of rabbit warren and sheep walk had been transformed into large arable fields which, if they were properly cultivated, would yield rich harvests of grain.

This transformation of the rural landscape was not, however, everywhere complete by 1830. Two of the five largest enclosures of waste that we mentioned in chapter three, Whittlesey Mere and Dent in Sedbergh, in fact belong to the 1840s, and other large areas of common and waste still remained unenclosed. Whaddon Chase was enclosed in 1841, and the 4,000 acres of Hainault Forest in Essex had to wait until 1851 for enclosure.

Nor did enclosure by itself necessarily bring with it any widespread or uniform improvements in husbandry. Some of the most spectacular changes in agricultural practices had taken place in areas of comparatively light and infertile soils, in western Norfolk, in Lincolnshire and in the chalk-lands of southeastern England. In many districts the heavy claylands of midland England were still very poorly culti-vated because they were difficult to drain. No marked improvement was possible until the technical problems surrounding the laying of field drains had been successfully overcome, and it was 1845 when Thomas Scragg was awarded the Royal Agricultural Society's prize for the best machine for making cylindrical tile pipes.

A similar transformation of the rural landscape had taken place in Scotland. Scottish agriculture in 1714 was for the most part backward and primitive. By 1830 it had in many respects overtaken that in England, and the rich fields and farms of the Lothians were considered to be among the best in Britain. The ancient runrig had been enclosed and much had been levelled. Trees had been planted on a large scale and many districts of Scotland, both Highland and Low-land, were as well-wooded as any part of England. The loosely organised fermtouns had largely disappeared, to be replaced either by substantial but isolated farmhouses, or else by planned villages composed of two or three streets of stone cottages. The cottages were often single-storeyed, with inadequate drainage, but whatever their defects in the eyes of a late twentieth-century observer they were a great improvement upon the cabins which they had replaced.

Change had been even more dramatic in the Scottish

75 This aerial photograph of North Berwick Tor (613 feet high) illustrates the improved landscape of the Lothians, with its pattern of large rectangular fields. It may conveniently be compared with Plates 8 and 12, since Haddington lies about seven miles away to the south-west

Highlands. Here a rising population was by the end of the eighteenth century supported on three things: the kelp industry, potato growing and cattle. Kelp, obtained by burning seaweed, was almost the only source of sodium carbonate, used in the manufacture of glass and soap, during the Napoleonic Wars. Along the coasts of the Scottish Highlands and the western islands whole communities became totally dependent upon kelp burning for their livelihood. Prices soared, reaching £20 a ton by 1810. When

276

peace was restored in 1815 foreign supplies, particularly from Spain, were once again available, and the price began to fall. In 1825 the manufacture of Leblanc alkali began in Glasgow and the bottom fell out of the kelp market. By 1830 the industry was almost dead except in the furthest islands, and it had gone from there by 1850.

The cultivation of the potato spread very rapidly in the decades after 1760 and in many districts it became the mainstay of the population, especially when the grain harvest (which meant oats) failed, as it did in 1782–3. When the potato itself failed in the 1840s the results were catastrophic.

The third prop of the traditional Highland economy was the export of black cattle to Lowland Scotland and to England. Prices here began to fall steeply after 1815. The rearing of cattle became less and less profitable and their place was slowly taken up by sheep. Sheep farming was best carried on in large farms, which swallowed up fermtoun, infield, outfield, shieling and common moor alike. It was expensive, requiring considerable capital investment before it would show any profit, and so it was from the first in the hands of wealthy farmers from the Lowlands, who brought with them their own breeds of sheep, Lintons and Cheviots. An entirely new, commercial farming came into head-on collision with a traditional way of life based upon subsistence farming. 1792 was the Year of the Sheep, when the men of Ross-shire tried to drive out all the new sheep from their lands, but to no avail.

Many landlords in the Highlands were acutely aware of the problems that rising population was causing, and yet the old traditional attitudes, which regarded a large tenantry with favour, died very slowly, whilst the tenants themselves were passionately attached to their plots of land, which subdivision among members of a family was making smaller and smaller. Only after 1815 was emigration actively encouraged, although it had been going on for many years. Some Highlanders moved into Lowland Scotland; many more went to North America. By 1827 petitions from Highlanders to the Colonial Office for assisted passages to Canada and grants of land and of money and tools to maintain them once they were there reveal the extent of the distress. In January 1827 550 people from the western Highlands who had suffered from the introduction of the sheep system petitioned for assistance to emigrate to North America. In March of the same year a landowner in Coll applied on behalf of several thousand souls in the Hebrides for aid towards emigration. He himself had sent out 300 from one of his own islands and could now spare a further 1,500 from his estates. Another petition in April of 1827 was from 1,600 persons on Mull and Benbecula. These were by no means the only petitions for assistance to emigrate received at this time, a period of severe trade depression and unemployment, but they are symptomatic of conditions in the Highlands.

Yet the landlords themselves faced very real problems. Several did what they could to encourage new sources of livelihood, especially fishing and linen spinning, but the more optimistic plans of the latter part of the eighteenth century melted away before the harsh realities of the Highland environment. It was slowly recognised that emigration was the only solution and many landlords themselves sold up and moved away. Others carried out large-scale 'improvements' which often served only to exacerbate the problems. The notorious Sutherland clearances were part of a well-meaning attempt to improve the estate for the benefit of all concerned. The years between 1808 and 1821 saw the eviction of between 5,000 and 10,000 people from their traditional farms to make way for large-scale sheep farms. It was hoped to move the inhabitants to fishing villages on the coast where there would be better prospects for them, and large sums of money were spent on building the town and port of Helmsdale as a fishing port, but without success. Especially scandalous was the burning of Strathnaver in 1814 by Patrick Sellar, factor to the Countess of Sutherland. His ruthless firing of the houses of the inhabitants led to the deaths of at least two elderly people, for which he was tried and acquitted, a decision which popular sentiment has

278

refused to accept.

The creation of large sheep farms led to the destruction of traditional fermtouns. At Bourblaige in Ardnamurchan, for example, are the roofless walls of about thirty buildings of a deserted township, including dwelling houses, byres and barns. The township had about 553 acres of land, of which 93 acres were arable. It was described in about 1806 as being 'oppress'd with too many tenants'. By 1829 it had been amalgamated with a neighbouring farm to form one large grazing farm held by a single tenant. A similar ruined township is to be found at Inivea, overlooking Calgary Bay,

76 The deserted township of Inivea, Mull, with Calgary Bay in the background

in the island of Mull. Here something over twenty buildings can be recognised, including barns which have their winnowing doors in the centre of the side walls and at right-angles to the prevailing wind to allow a through draught. This township was probably deserted shortly after 1817. Emigrants who sailed from this bay to North America gave its name to Calgary in Canada.

If the landscape of rural Britain changed dramatically during the eighteenth century then the urban landscape changed even more dramatically. The change was prompted by several factors whose inter-relationships are immensely complex and admit of no simple separation. The population of the country was growing during the second half of the eighteenth century and the growth was particularly rapid during the early decades of the nineteenth. The largest intercensal percentage increase ever recorded occurred in the years between 1811 and 1821, when the population increased by a little under 18 per cent. This increase is found the length and breadth of the country, both in towns and in the countryside. Even the population of Sutherland increased by 7 per cent between 1821 and 1831. But the real increases are to be found in the towns, especially the manufacturing ones, and this increase is due to a large extent to immigration, since living conditions in towns were so bad that their natural increase would scarcely have served to maintain their numbers let alone produce any significant increase. Immigrants came into the towns from the countryside, a movement which at first slows down the rate of increase in rural districts, and then leads by mid-century to a fall in the rural population, so that by 1851 many villages in the south and east of England, rural Wales and Highland Scotland, were smaller than they had been thirty years previously.

A census of the population of Britain was taken for the first time in 1801, and there has been one every ten years since, except in 1941. This means that in 1801 we have the first reasonably accurate figures for the population of Britain.

Table 1   The population of Britain, 1801–31

	1801	1811	1821	1831
England	8,331,434	9,551,888	11,261,437	13,089,338
Wales	541,546	611,788	717,438	805,236
Scotland	1,599,068	1,805,688	2,093,456	2,365,807

Over the country as a whole the population has increased from about 6¼ million in 1700 to a little under 10½ million in 1801, an increase of about 60 per cent. Table 2 shows that, in proportion, some towns especially the manufacturing ones, had grown much more rapidly. Birmingham and Glasgow had multiplied six times, Manchester ten times, between 1700 and 1801, and the years between 1801 and 1831 show almost no signs of any slackening in the rate of growth.

Table 2   The population of certain towns in Britain, 1801–31

	1801	1811	1821	1831
London	864,845	1,009,546	1,225,694	1,474,069
Edinburgh	82,560	102,987	138,235	162,403
Manchester and Salford	94,876	115,874	161,635	237,832
Glasgow	77,385	100,749	147,043	202,426
Birmingham	73,670	85,753	106,721	142,251
Liverpool	79,722	100,240	131,801	189,244
Bristol	63,645	76,433	87,779	103,886
Cardiff	1,870	2,457	3,521	6,187
Swansea	6,099	8,005	10,007	13,256
Merthyr Tydfil (parish)	7,705	11,104	17,404	22,083

It is possible to be mesmerised by rows of figures of this kind, but they do give in broad terms a measure of the physical expansion of the built-up portion of the British landscape, and give some precision to that growth of towns which we looked at in chapter 5. It is, however, an abstract, impersonal measurement. Only by the comparison of old maps and the careful exploration on foot of towns as they survive today is it possible to clothe these figures in reality.

Towns must of necessity grow outwards from their ancient centres and although the rate and direction of this growth can be most uneven it is possible, by a detailed examination of changing building styles and materials, to plot the successive additions, and this in spite of the fact that in towns such as Coventry and Plymouth much of the evidence has been destroyed by bombing during the Second World War and by subsequent redevelopment.

This physical growth of towns is one of the factors at work in sharpening the division between town and country, something which becomes steadily more marked in the early decades of the nineteenth century. But even the most rapidly expanding manufacturing town could still show considerable evidence of the rural foundations which had nourished it for so long. It was said of Oldham in 1825, for example, that it was acquiring cotton spinning mills more rapidly than anywhere else in Lancashire; but it was still no more than a township and a parochial chapelry, with neither water works nor gas works, town hall, effective police force or regular market. Its population in 1821 was 21,662. Sixty years previously there had not been a cotton spinning mill in the chapelry. By 1825 there were sixty-three, all of them steam-powered, attracted to the town by the plentiful supplies of coal. A directory of that date lists 116 cotton spinners and manufacturers, and twenty-one machine makers. But there were also four basket and skip makers, two coopers, four corn factors, four curriers and leather sellers, four saddlers, fourteen blacksmiths and farriers, twenty five boot makers and shoemakers as well as eighty-six shopkeepers, and the traditional trade of Oldham, the making of hats, was represented by twenty-six hat manufacturers. It is this close juxtaposition of old and new which gives this particular period of British history its distinctive character.

Other towns, and large ones, reveal, even in 1831, almost no sign of industrialisation. The 1831 census gives details of the occupations in York. The population of the city was 26,260. Of this total, only 222 men over 20 years of age were recorded as being employed in manufacture, and most of those were engaged in making linen. The census then goes on to give details of the occupations of a further 3,548 men over 20 who were engaged in trade and handicrafts. The occupations listed, 122 of them, contain nothing that could not have been found in the city a hundred years earlier. The most numerous occupations were shoemaker (448), tailor (224) and carpenter (190). Others included coopers, curriers, saddlers, lace dealers, bricklayers and an artificial flower maker. The Industrial Revolution had scarcely reached York in 1831.

We saw earlier in this chapter that Brighton was the fastest growing town in England in the second decade of the nineteenth century. It is all too easy to overlook the rapid expansion that was going on in the early nineteenth century in spa and seaside towns. It was George III who made sea-bathing in general, and Weymouth in particular, fashionable, so that by the end of the eighteenth century those who could afford to do so were seeking out stretches of coastline that could offer safe sea-bathing, and obliging landlords were providing accommodation of every kind for the visitors. Torquay, for example, had a population of 838 in 1801, and consisted of little more than a row of houses and an inn and a new pier, but the local landowner, Sir Lawrence Palk, had laid out a number of plots and further building was already taking place. By 1831 the population of the whole of the parish of Torbay had reached 3,582.

In the middle years of the eighteenth century the district of South-hawes, in the parish of North Meols, contained no more than a few cottages on the Lancashire coast. In 1792 the local landlord, Mr Sutton, built a hotel, the Royal. After a slow start the spot became increasingly popular. He gave it the name of Southport, and by 1825 there was a village of one main street, 88 yards wide, composed of handsome brick houses with large front gardens. Two back streets were rapidly developing and there were in all about 200 houses and cottages, of which at least half had been built within the last four years. Two more hotels had been built, and there was a wide range of respectable boarding and lodging houses. There was a theatre, a newsroom and library, a billiards room and an assembly room. A church was built in 1820, an Independent chapel in 1823 and a Methodist chapel in 1824. Visitors during the season could come from Liverpool and Manchester by stage-coach, although it was cheaper to come along the Leeds to Liverpool canal by packet boat as far as Scarisbrick Bridge, some five miles away, where they would be met by carriages and conveyed into the village.

York and Brighton, Torquay and Southport, were as much a part of the urban landscape of early nineteenth-century Britain as was Oldham. Gritty manufacturing town, suave seaside resort and traditional regional centre were facets of an urban structure in which individual towns still exhibited a quite remarkable character of their own, whilst the snippets of information about their separate histories which there has been room to quote illustrate many of the broader themes discussed in previous chapters.

If the rural and urban landscapes of Britain in 1830 had changed dramatically since 1714, then in comparison the institutions guiding the relationships between the men and women who inhabited these landscapes had changed remarkably little. The formal structures of political power in Britain showed almost no signs of change between 1714 and 1830, although it was becoming very clear to many people that change was both long overdue and very necessary.

Parliament in 1830 was in almost exactly the same condition that it was in 1714. A minute change had in fact taken place in the composition of the House of Commons in that the rotten borough of Grampound in Cornwall was disfranchised in 1821. It was proposed at the time to give its two seats to Leeds, but this was considered too radical and so they went to Yorkshire instead. Bills were introduced in 1827 and 1828 to disfranchise East Retford and Penrhyn, two remarkably corrupt boroughs, but without success.

There had if anything been more change in the House of Lords than in the Commons by 1830. In 1782 it was finally established that Scottish peers ennobled after the Act of Union could themselves sit in the House of Lords as well as vote for the sixteen representative peers. More significant, however, was the large number of peerages created after 1760. Between 1760 and 1784 forty-three were created. During his first long ministry, from 1784 to 1801, the younger William Pitt created a further ninety-five, sixteen in 1797 alone. Further creations followed almost as a matter of course, there were twelve in 1815 for instance. A number of these new peerages were rewards for military and naval service during the Napoleonic Wars, but the great majority were rewards for political services. Nevertheless, whatever the motives for their creation, these new peerages made almost no difference to the hegemony of the landed aristocracy. If anything the House of Lords was even more conservative in 1830 than it had been in 1714.

Similarly, there had been very little change in the institutions of local government. Counties were still administered by justices of the peace, who were still drawn almost exclusively from the landed gentry, and the practice which had become quite marked in some counties of appointing clergymen to the bench merely served to reinforce this. Enclosure followed by the commutation of tithes had made substantial landed gentlemen out of some clergymen and this had made them eligible to become justices of the peace. By 1831 something like a fifth of all magistrates were clergymen, although there were wide regional variations. It seems that they were commonest in those counties with the largest areas of parliamentary enclosure and hence tithe commutation. In Lincolnshire, for example, almost half of the magistrates were clergymen. These appointments served to increase the distance between such clergymen and their poor parishioners, since they had now to administer the game laws and the poor laws, obvious potential areas of conflict. County justices of the peace were gradually deprived of many of their administrative functions during the course of the nineteenth century, beginning with the Poor Law Amendment Act of 1834, but it was 1888 before elected county councils were created to take their place.

The administration of English and Welsh boroughs and of Scottish burghs also remained unchanged throughout the period. Some improvement in some towns took place in their physical appearance and amenities with the appointment of improvement commissioners under local and private acts of parliament. As we have seen, some of these commissioners did bring some improvement into the draining, lighting and paving of the main streets in a few towns, but the enormous physical expansion of the manufacturing towns went almost unchecked and it was long after 1830 before any concerted attempt was made at a national level to do anything to remedy the appalling conditions created by this expansion.

Ancient municipal corporations remained jealous of their rights and privileges. Their reform was one of the first issues tackled by the new parliament elected after the Great Reform Bill of 1832, and commissioners were sent to investigate the state of the administration and finances of these ancient institutions. A number considered the proceedings of the commissioners to be illegal. As the mayor of Arundel wrote, the commission was 'in violation of the Bill of Rights, an intrusion on the rights of Englishmen, and tending to encourage false representations by the administration of false oaths'. The commissioners in their turn often had scathing remarks to make about the corporations they visited. Of Bristol they wrote:

> the governing body of the corporation of the city of Bristol is constituted on the closest principles of self-election and irresponsibility; and it seems to us to offer a very unfavourable specimen of the results of such a system. . . . The ruling principle of the corporation appears to have been, at all times, the desire of power, and a watchful jealousy that nothing should be undertaken within the limits of the city over which they cannot, at pleasure, exercise control.

Whatever their defects, the ancient corporations did provide a minimum framework of local government. Some of the largest and most rapidly growing towns in the country were not boroughs, and so did not have even this. Instead they had to rely upon the parish vestry or a manorial court. Manchester, for example, was almost entirely without local administration for much of the eighteenth century. The Court Leet, which had been fairly active during the seventeenth century, had become moribund by the opening years of the eighteenth. Improvement acts were obtained in 1765 and 1776 but these also were largely ineffective. In 1792 a further act was obtained, providing for the creation of police commissioners. The act forbade bull- and bear-baiting, fireworks and football in the streets. The commissioners were authorised to provide street lamps and scavengers, water carts and fire engines. They could take in new streets, make drains and sewers, provide nightwatchmen, regulate hackney coaches and sedan chairs. The details of their powers throw a flood of light into the streets, squares and alleys of late eighteenth-century Manchester. The commissioners were also empowered to regulate certain aspects of building, including the proper construction of party walls, joists and chimneys, and appoint paid surveyors to see the regulations carried out. Only in the first years of the nineteenth century did the commissioners begin to make any impact, even within the restricted area of their competence, and all that they did was bitterly contested, first on the grounds of unnecessary expense and secondly from an intense dislike of anything that savoured of state interference.

The ancient boundaries of counties and boroughs remained quite without change during the eighteenth century. Some change took place in parish boundaries, but only at a purely local level, and an act of parliament of 1783 permitted the union of parishes for the purposes of poor law administration. By 1830 the traditional mosaic of boundaries and jurisdictions was clearly under considerable strain as a consequence of the rapid changes that were taking place, especially in the distribution of population, and alterations in ancient boundaries to take account of these changes could not long be delayed. St Helens, for example, finds no mention in the 1831 census because strictly it lay within the township of Windle in the parish of Prescot, a parish which also included the township of Widnes with Appleton. Footnotes on every page of the published abstract of the 1831 census are evidence of the nice attention that was everywhere given to the intricate network of overlapping boundaries and conflicting jurisdictions that were accepted as a matter of course as part of the fabric of eighteenth-century Britain. A single example must serve as an illustration. The borough of Thetford in Norfolk contained three parishes, two of which extended into Suffolk, but because they lay wholly within the borough their Suffolk inhabitants were returned as being in Norfolk. Such distinctions, tolerable in a traditional, rural, particularistic society, were by 1830 beginning to look out of place.

Change in the structure of social relationships was equally muted. Outwardly and formally society continued to be intensely hierarchical in its outlook, attitudes and expectations. Among the petitions received by the Colonial Office in 1827 for assistance in emigrating to Canada is one from a man in Aberdeen who had been a captain in the regular army. He wished to know 'if he can obtain a grant of land according to that rank.' The prestige and influence of the landed aristocracy continued almost unabated, although their political monopoly was increasingly resented by the newly rich industrialists and manufacturers of Birmingham, Manchester and Glasgow, and their ambitions form one of the threads in the parliamentary reform movement of the early nineteenth century.

Many old social ties were broken down by the drift of population into towns, although, as we saw in chapter six, kinship networks remained important for recruitment into factories. In the countryside enclosure was undoubtedly a contributory factor to the pauperisation of the agricultural labourer from the 1790s, and the night sky over southeastern England was ablaze with burning ricks in the autumn of 1830 as the Captain Swing riots released pent-up resentment. In Scotland the elaborate social hierarchy and traditional structures of the fermtoun were replaced by the purely commercial relationship of landlord, tenant farmer and labourer.

Although the social structure of Britain remained, formally at any rate, almost unchanged, the 1790s and succeeding decades saw a greater, more radical and more popularly based questioning of the whole fabric of society than had taken place in Britain since the period of the Commonwealth in the seventeenth century. This popular radicalism was feared because of its associations with the French Revolution, and for much of the period of the Napoleonic Wars almost every suggestion for reform, however mild, was condemned out of hand as savouring of Jacobinism. Nevertheless this radicalism was one of the contributors to the quickening of social awareness that is also discernible from the 1790s as the grim problems created by industrialisation become more and more apparent. The Utilitarian doctrines of Jeremy Bentham and James Mill as well as the Evangelical movement also contributed to this quickening of social awareness, but from profoundly different points of view.

Opposition to proposals for reform, from whatever source, was extraordinarily strong and emotionally deepseated in a way which is now very difficult to appreciate, and it was to be found in every rank in society. Even the agricultural labourers rioted for a return to traditional standards and relationships rather than for revolution. This opposition was often compounded of a reverence for the authority and teachings of the established church, a deepseated distrust of state interference in all save a very narrow range of affairs, of which foreign policy, defence and the administration of the law were the most important, and a view of society as an organism in which growth and change were not to be hurried. Such views find their most eloquent expression in the writings of Burke.

This quickening social awareness was coupled to a revival of moral earnestness and fervour, so that proposals for change were most likely to succeed if they could be shown to have some moral purpose. In 1787 George III issued a proclamation calling for the suppression of vice, profanity and Sabbath breaking. One of the reasons for the intense unpopularity of George IV was his dissolute private life. In 1802 the first act of parliament to attempt to regulate working conditions in factories was passed. It was called, significantly, the Health and Morals of Apprentices Act, and it was concern for the morals of the apprentices that was the more important reason for its passing. It laid down that pauper apprentices in cotton mills should work no more than 12 hours a day, but there was no provision made for its enforcement.

An act of 1799 finally brought to an end the 'arling' of Scottish coal miners, a system by which, if a miner worked for a year and a day in a pit, or took a present, 'arles', on taking an oath to serve, then he was bound for life to the colliery owner, and could be brought back if he ran away.

From the 1780s a variety of attempts were made to provide basic education in England. The first steps in this direction came with the Sunday school movement, more especially when it was taken up by Robert Raikes, a Gloucester printer. The Royal Lancasterian Society, Quaker in origin, was founded in 1810, the British and Foreign Bible Society in 1814, and the National Society for the Education of the Poor in the Principles of the Established Church, whose title is a succinct statement of its aims, in 1811. By 1830 these societies had managed to provide schools in most English parishes, although they were often small and poorly attended. Interdenominational bickering prevented any state aid to education until 1833.

Finally, this re-awakening of moral earnestness led to a change in the internal patterns of family relationships. The middle-class housewife, on the crest of the rising tide of her husband's prosperity, gave up all connection with his trade. No longer would a widow be able to carry on her husband's business after his death. Instead she became preoccupied with entertaining, gossip, clothes and child-bearing, the management of the household being entrusted to servants. Servants now become domestic servants, and cease to be

77 The Gothic screen and gateway to King's College, Cambridge, designed by William Wilkins in 1822

assistants in trade or manufacture. They no longer take their meals with the family, and the social distance between master and employee is noticeably increased, whilst the gap between a chambermaid and her mistress becomes enormous. The dominant position of the husband in the family is re-stated in much more authoritarian terms and his authority was given almost divine sanction since for many he was the embodiment of the will of God. The tyrannical Victorian husband and father had already arrived by 1830.

It is only fitting that this description of Britain in 1830 should come to an end with some account of the art and literature of the time, since the basic theme of this book is the close connection between the environment which men create for themselves and the way in which the ideals, beliefs and opinions which inform their lives find reflection in it. We saw in chapter 4 something of the sweeping changes which by 1830 had taken place in acceptable architectural practices. Perhaps the chief consequence of these changes was the disappearance of a standard style against which all building could be measured and evaluated. Palladianism, which, with its wealth of associations from the other arts, had fulfilled this function in the first half of the eighteenth century, was long outmoded by 1830, and instead of being replaced by another single style it was supplanted by an ever widening range of styles drawn from an ever widening range of geographical and historical sources. The Brighton Pavilion of John Nash is an exploitation of one, or rather several, of these styles. The Greek Ionic style which Robert Smirke used for the British Museum from 1823 is another, and the Gothic screen and gateway with which William Wilkins completed the court at King's College Cambridge between 1822 and 1824 is a third. That Wilkins could also work in Greek styles, as witness his buildings for Downing College Cambridge, is a measure of the extent of this fragmentation of artistic ideals.

Similar fragmentation had taken place in literature. The first draft of Wordsworth's greatest poem, *The Prelude*, was completed in 1805. When it was finally published, in 1850, shortly after the poet's death, it bore the subtitle 'Growth of a Poet's Mind'. Such a subject matter for a work with all the outward features of an epic – it is in blank verse in thirteen books – would have been quite inadmissible in the early decades of the eighteenth century. Its opening lines:

Oh there is a blessing in this gentle breeze
That blows from the green fields and from the clouds
And from the sky: it beats against my cheek
And seems half-conscious of the joy it gives

reveal the shift that has taken place in attitudes to Nature. Daniel Defoe, after visiting Westmorland early in the eighteenth century, wrote that it was 'the wildest, most barren and frightful of any that I have passed over in England, or even in Wales itself'. And yet this was Wordsworth's homeland. For him Nature was wholly beneficent, the source of his inspiration and the basis of his moral beliefs.

In the year in which the first draft of *The Prelude* was completed Sir Walter Scott published his first verse tale, *The Lay of the Last Minstrel*, followed by *Marmion* in 1808. In these poems and their successors Scott extended the range of poetry back into Scottish history, and, with the publication of his first novel, *Waverley*, in 1814 he gave an idealised, romantic, exciting portrait of a traditional society that was almost unknown to contemporaries, one that was in any case on the point of passing away. His books were enormously popular, and *Waverley* was the first best-selling novel.

The geographical and historical range and excitement of poetry was further extended by Lord Byron. The first two cantos of *Childe Harold* were published in 1812, and he became famous overnight. If the Scottish poems and novels of Sir Walter Scott described an almost unknown society and landscape, the poems of Byron transported their readers into an Oriental fantasy world of passion and intrigue, with the added spice that Byron had himself been to the places he describes, Greece and Albania, then almost totally inaccessible to Europeans, and wrote from first hand experience.

Both Byron and Shelley were forced into exile by the same moral earnestness that stamped out bull-running and cockfighting. The fully developed Byronic hero now emerged: the man of great sins and great virtues, the outcast and rebel against conventional society. When *Cain* was published in 1821 it was considered little short of blasphemous.

The discovery of the medieval 'Gothick' past in architecture is echoed in literature with the craze for 'horrid mysteries' at the end of the eighteenth century. Horace Walpole, whose house at Strawberry Hill contributed to the growing taste for Gothic, wrote one of the earliest of these stories, *The Castle of Otranto*, in 1765. His friend Thomas Gray wrote to him that the book had made all at Cambridge 'in general afraid to go to bed o'nights'. Mrs Radcliffe, Matthew Lewis and Charles Maturin exploited haunted castles, ruined abbeys, contracts with Satan, lonely and mountainous scenery, beautiful and persecuted heroines for all they were worth. The cult of the Picturesque is their architectural counterpart. *Northanger Abbey* pokes fun both at the novels and at the cult, not least when Catherine Morland dismisses the whole of the city of Bath 'as unworthy to make part of a landscape'.

During the years analysed in these pages, men acquired the capacity to modify their surroundings almost at will. Bath was a landscape of the mind projected with an obsessive intensity into brick and stone, streets and pavements, crescents and squares. So, too, were the parks of 'Capability' Brown and his contemporaries, who moved whole villages to make a more pleasing prospect. Less intentional were the human problems created by enclosure, by overcrowding in flourishing provincial towns and cities, or the new dimensions to human behaviour consequent upon the factory system. Underlying all these changes was a general unwillingness to accept a static state of affairs. The pace of change was erratic and uncertain, but new ideas were diffused and accepted, as a comparison in almost any field between the Britain of 1714 and 1830 will make clear. As Edmund Burke observed, 'a state without the means of some change is without the means of its conservation.' The true triumph of Georgian Britain was to accommodate that process of change without the destruction of the society which gave it birth.

Further reading

The reader approaching the eighteenth century for the first time may be forgiven his feeling of stunned bewilderment at the mountains of books, periodical articles, manuscripts, archives, artefacts and buildings that serve to illuminate every facet of the life and thought of this century. Fortunately there are a number of very good guides through this material. The most substantial bibliography, *A Bibliography of British History: The Eighteenth Century, 1714 –1789*, edited by S. Pargellis and D. J. Medley (1951) is still valuable in spite of its age. The following general surveys will be found useful:

Asa Briggs, *The Age of Improvement* (1959).
R. H. Campbell, *Scotland since 1707* (1965).
H. C. Darby (ed.), *A New Historical Geography of England* (1973).
W. Ferguson, *Scotland, 1689 to the Present* (1968).
D. Marshall, *Eighteenth Century England* (1962).
T. C. Smout, *A History of the Scottish People, 1560–1830* (1969).
W. A. Speck, *Stability and Strife: England 1714–1760* (1977).
J. Steven Watson, *The Reign of George III* (1960).
B. Williams, *The Whig Supremacy* (1939), 2nd ed. revised by C. H. Stuart (1962).

Much is to be learned from *The Regions of the British Isles* series, including for example *The Highlands and Islands of Scotland*, by A. C. O'Dell and K. Walton (1962), and from *The Regions of Britain* series, including those by R. Millward and A. Robinson on *The Lake District* (1970), *The Peak District* (1975), and *The Welsh Borders* (1978). The pioneer work in landscape history is, of course, W. G. Hoskins, *The Making of the English Landscape*, first published in 1955 and now a classic. A series with this title comprising a volume on each of the English counties is now in progress. In addition there is M. Williams, *The Making of the South Wales Landscape* (1975), R. Millman, *The Making of the Scottish Landscape* (1975), and M. L. Parry and T. R. Slater (eds), *The Making of the Scottish Countryside* (1980). In addition to these, and as an introduction to the now lively discussion of what the landscape historian is trying to do, *The*

Interpretation of Ordinary Landscapes, edited by D. W. Meinig (1979), can be recommended.

The Victoria Histories of the Counties of England are an indispensable series for reference purposes, and more recent volumes such as *Warwickshire*, vols VII and VIII, *Leicestershire*, vol. III, *Oxfordshire*, vol. X and *Staffordshire*, vols II and VI, include important and well-documented studies of agriculture, trade, industry and urban development.

The publications of the Royal Commissions on the Ancient and Historic Monuments for England, Wales and Scotland have also broken out of their old, conservative moulds and now include a great deal of value for the student of the eighteenth century. Among the more recent volumes may be mentioned P. Smith *Houses of the Welsh Countryside* (1975), E. Mercer, *English Vernacular Houses* (1975), three volumes on Argyllshire from the Royal Commission for Scotland, and R. S. Fitzgerald, *Liverpool Road Station, Manchester* (Royal Commission, Supplementary Series, 1, 1980).

Sir Nikolaus Pevsner's volumes on *The Buildings of England*, and the magisterial *Survey of London* are indispensable.

Among older publications may be mentioned the *Reports* to the Board of Agriculture, published at the end of the eighteenth and the beginning of the nineteenth centuries. Arthur Young wrote that for Suffolk, published in 1813, and for Norfolk, published in 1804. W. Pitt's volume on Worcestershire appeared in 1813 and that by Charles Vancouver on Devonshire appeared in 1808. That on Northumberland, published in 1805, is particularly important since its authors, J. Bailey and G. Culley, were themselves leading agricultural improvers. Inexhaustible, irreplaceable and indispensable are only three of the adjectives to be applied to *The Statistical Account of Scotland*, edited and published by Sir John Sinclair in twenty-one volumes between 1791 and 1799.

The remainder of this Reading List is divided up according to the chapters of this book. The list for each chapter has been restricted deliberately to about a dozen items which have proved to be particularly informative for the themes of the chapter. Those books and articles mentioned elsewhere in the text have not been included.

Chapter one

R. W. Brunskill, *Vernacular Architecture of the Lake Counties* (1974).

J. T. Coppock, *An Agricultural Geography of Great Britain* (1971).

J. R. Coull, 'The Island of Tiree', *Scottish Geographical Magazine*, 78 (1962) pp. 17–32.

M. Flinn, ed., *Scottish Population History* (1977).

R. Hatton, *George I* (1978).

G. S. Holmes, 'Gregory King and the Social Structure of Pre-Industrial England', *Transactions of the Royal Historical Society*, 5th Series, vol. 27 (1977) pp. 41–68.

D. Moore (ed.), *Wales in the Eighteenth Century* (1976).

R. M. Nance, 'When was Cornish Last Spoken Traditionally?' *Journal of the Royal Institution of Cornwall*, 7 (1973) pp. 76–82.

H. Shennan, *Boundaries of Counties and Parishes in Scotland* (1892).

L. Stone, *The Family, Sex and Marriage in England, 1500–1800* (1978).

A. E. Trueman, *Geology and Scenery in England and Wales*, revised ed. by J. B. Whittow and J. R. Hardy (1971).

J. B. Whittow, *Geology and Scenery in Scotland* (1977).

C. W. J. Withers, 'The Geographical Extent of Gaelic in Scotland, 1698–1806', *Scottish Geographical Magazine*, 97 (1981) pp. 130–9.

E. A. Wrigley and R. S. Schofield, *The Population History of England, 1541–1871* (1981).

Chapter two
D. A. Alexander, 'Settlement, Field Systems and Landownership in Teesdale between 1600 and 1850', unpublished MA thesis, University of Durham (1972).

A. R. H. Baker and R. A. Butlin, (eds), *Studies of Field Systems in the British Isles* (1973).

A. Fenton and B. Walker, *The Rural Architecture of Scotland* (1981).

H. Fairhurst, 'Scottish Clachans', *Scottish Geographical Magazine*, 76 (1960) pp. 67–76.

J. E. Handley, *Scottish Farming in the Eighteenth Century* (1953).

A. Harris, *The Rural Landscape of the East Riding of Yorkshire, 1700–1850* (1961).

J. G. Jenkins, *The English Farm Wagon* (1961).

M. M. McArthur (ed.), 'Survey of Lochtayside, 1769', *Scottish History Society*, 3rd Series, vol. 27 (1936).

R. Miller, 'Land Use by Summer Shielings', *Scottish Studies*, 11 (1967), pp. 193–221.

G. E. Mingay, *English Landed Society in the Eighteenth Century* (1963).

P. Roebuck (ed.), 'Constable of Everingham Estate Correspondence, 1726–1743', *Yorkshire Archaeological Society, Record Series*, vol. 136 (1974).

L. R. Timperley, 'Landownership in Scotland in the Eighteenth Century', unpublished PhD thesis, University of Edinburgh (1977).

Chapter three
T. W. Beastall, *The Agricultural Revolution in Lincolnshire* (1978).

J. Colville (ed.), 'Letters of John Cockburn of Ormistoun to his Gardener, 1727–1744', *Scottish History Society*, vol. 45 (1904).

E. R. Cregeen (ed.), 'Argyll Estate Instructions, Mull, Morvern, Tiree, 1770–1805', *Scottish History Society*, 4th Series, vol. 1 (1964).

A. Davies, 'Enclosure in Cardiganshire, 1750–1850', *Ceredigion*, 8 (1976), pp. 100–40.

A. H. Dodd, 'The Enclosure Movement in North Wales', *Bulletin of the Board of Celtic Studies*, 3 (1925–7), pp. 210–38.

H. S. A. Fox and R. A. Butlin (eds), *Change in the Countryside* (1979).

H. A. Fuller, 'Landownership and the Lindsey Landscape', *Annals of the Association of American Geographers*, 66 (1976), pp. 14–24.

H. Hamilton (ed.), 'Selections from the Monymusk Papers, 1713 –1755', *Scottish History Society*, 3rd Series, vol. 39 (1945).

R. A. C. Parker, *Coke of Norfolk* (1975).

N. T. Phillipson and R. Mitchison (eds), *Scotland in the Age of Improvement* (1970).

J. M. Robertson, 'Model Farm Buildings in the Age of Improvement', *Architectural History* (1976), pp. 17–32.

W. E. Tate, (ed.) M. E. Turner, *A Domesday of English Enclosure Acts and Awards* (1978).

B. M. W. Third, 'The Changing Rural Geography of the Scottish Lowlands, 1700–1820', unpublished PhD thesis, University of Edinburgh (1953).

M. E. Turner, *English Parliamentary Enclosure* (1980).

S. Wade Martins, *A Great Estate at Work: The Holkham Estate and its Inhabitants in the Nineteenth Century* (1980).

A. J. Youngson, *After the Forty-five* (1973).

Chapter four

H. Colvin and J. Harris (eds), *The Country Seat* (1970).

J. G. Dunbar, *The Historical Architecture of Scotland* (1966).

C. Hussey, *English Country Houses: Early Georgian, 1715–1760* (1955).

C. Hussey, *English Country Houses: Mid-Georgian, 1760–1800* (1956).

J. Lees-Milne, *Earls of Creation* (1962).

I. G. Lindsay and M. Cosh, *Inverary and the Dukes of Argyll* (1972).

R. Oresko, *The Works in Architecture of Robert and John Adam* (1975)

L. Schmidt, 'Holkham Hall, Norfolk', *Country Life*, 167 (1980), pp. 214–17, 298–301, 359–62, 427–31.

D. Stroud, *Humphry Repton* (1962).

D. Stroud, *Capability Brown* (1975).

J. Summerson, *Architecture in Britain, 1530–1830* (1953).

A. A. Tait, *The Landscape Garden in Scotland, 1735–1835* (1980).

C. Thacker, *The History of Gardens* (1979).

P. Willis (ed.), *Furor Hortensis* (1974).

K. Woodbridge, *Landscape and Antiquity: Aspects of English Culture at Stourhead, 1718–1837* (1970).

Chapter five

I. H. Adams, *The Making of Urban Scotland* (1978).

M. W. Beresford, 'The Making of a Townscape: Richard Paley in the East End of Leeds, 1771–1803', in C. W. Chalklin and M. A. Havinden (eds), *Rural Change and Urban Growth, 1500–1800* (1974).

C. W. Chalklin, *The Provincial Towns of Georgian England* (1974).

D. Fraser (ed.), *A History of Modern Leeds* (1980).

W. Ison, *The Georgian Buildings of Bath* (1948).

W. Ison, *The Georgian Buildings of Bristol* (1951).

B. Little, *Birmingham Buildings* (1971).

R. Neale, 'Society, Belief and the Building of Bath, 1700–1793', in C. W. Chalklin and M. A. Havinden (eds), *Rural Change and Urban Growth, 1500–1800* (1974).

G. Rudé, *Hanoverian London 1714–1808* (1971).

F. H. W. Sheppard, *London, 1808–1870: The Infernal Wen* (1971).

J. Summerson, *Georgian London* (1945).

T. S. Willan, *An Eighteenth Century Shopkeeper: Abraham Dent of Kirby Stephen* (1970).

A. H. Youngson, *The Making of Classical Edinburgh* (1966).

Chapter six

D. Alderton and J. Booker, *The Industrial Archaeology of East Anglia* (1980).

T. S. Ashton, *An Eighteenth Century Industrialist: Peter Stubs of Warrington, 1756–1806* (1939, 1961 reprint).

F. Brook, *The Industrial Archaeology of the British Isles, I; The West Midlands* (1977).

J. Butt, *The Industrial Archaeology of Scotland* (1967).

J. Butt (ed.), *Robert Owen, Prince of Cotton Spinners* (1971).

S. D. Chapman, *The Early Factory Masters* (1967).

S. D. Chapman (ed.), *The History of Working Class Housing* (1971).

A. J. Haselfoot, *The Industrial Archaeology of Southeast England* (1978).

A. H. John and Glanmor Williams (eds), *Glamorgan County History*, vol. 5, *Industrial Glamorgan, 1700–1970* (1980).

J. Langton, *Geographical Change and Industrial Revolution* (1980).

J. D. Marshall and M. Davies-Shiel, *The Industrial Archaeology of the Lake Counties* (1969).

F. Nixon, *The Industrial Archaeology of Derbyshire* (1969).

L. T. C. Rolt, *Thomas Newcomen* (1963).

J. Tann, *The Development of the Factory* (1971).

J. T. Ward and R. G. Wilson (eds), *Land and Industry: The Landed Estate in the Industrial Revolution* (1971).

Chapter seven

W. Albert, *The Turnpike Road System in England, 1663–1840* (1972).

W. G. East, 'The Severn Waterway in the Eighteenth and Nineteenth Centuries' in L. D. Stamp and S. W. Wooldridge (eds), *London Essays in Geography* (1951).

M. J. Freeman, 'The Carrier System of South Hampshire, 1775 –1851', *Journal of Transport History*, New Series, vol. 4 (1977), pp. 61–85.

C. Hadfield, *British Canals* (1950, 6th ed. 1979).

C. C. Owen, 'The Early History of the Upper Trent Navigation', *Transport History*, vol. 1 (1968), pp. 233–59.

J. D. Porteous, *Canal Ports: The Urban Achievement of the Canal Age* (1977).

D. Semple, 'The Growth of Grangemouth', *Scottish Geographical Magazine*, vol. 74 (1958), pp. 78–85.

G. L. Turnbull, 'Provincial Road Carrying in England in the Eighteenth Century', *Journal of Transport History*, New Series, vol. 4 (1977–8), pp. 17–39.

R. W. Unwin and R. G. Wilson, 'The Aire and Calder Navigation', *The Bradford Antiquary*, vol. 11 (1976) pp. 53–85, 131–86, 215–45, 332–69.

Chapter eight

J. Barrell, *The Idea of Landscape and the Sense of Place* (1972).

J. Barrell, *The Dark Side of the Landscape* (1980).

G. Best, *Temporal Pillars: Queen Anne's Bounty, the Ecclesiastical Commissioners and the Church of England* (1964).

P. Burke, *Popular Culture in Early Modern Europe* (1978).

O. Chadwick, *The Secularisation of the European Mind in the Nineteenth Century* (1976).

E. J. Evans, 'Some Reasons for the Growth of English Anti-Clericalism, *c*. 1750–*c*.1830', *Past and Present*, no. 66 (1975), pp. 84–109.

A. D. Gilbert, *Religion and Society in Industrial England, 1740–1914* (1976).

J. G. Jenkins, *Life and Tradition in Rural Wales* (1976).

F. D. Klingender, *Art and the Industrial Revolution* (2nd ed. 1968).

R. W. Malcolmson, *Popular Recreation in English Society, 1700–1850* (1973).

J. H. Plumb, 'The New World of Children in Eighteenth Century England', *Past and Present*, no. 67 (1975), pp. 64–95.

W. R. Rollinson, *Life and Tradition in the Lake District* (1974).

W. R. Ward, *Religion and Society in England, 1790–1850* (1972).

Chapter nine

R. J. Adam, 'Papers on Sutherland Estate Management, 1802 –1816', *Scottish History Society*, 4th Series, Vols 8 and 9 (1972).

E. Baines, *History, Directory and Gazetteer of the County Palatine of Lancaster*, 2 vols (1825).

British Parliamentary Papers: Comparative Account of the Population of Great Britain in the Years 1801, 1811, 1821 and 1831, *Parliamentary Papers*, 1831, vol. 18.

First Report of the Commissioners on the Municipal Corporations of England and Wales, *Parliamentary Papers*, 1835, vols 23–6.

General Local Reports of the Commissioners on the Municipal Corporations of Scotland, *Parliamentary Papers*, 1835, vols 29 and 33.

H. Fairhurst, 'The Surveys for the Sutherland Clearances of 1813 –1820', *Scottish Studies*, vol. 8 (1964), pp. 1–18.

M. Gray, *The Highland Economy, 1750–1850* (1957).

E. J. Hobsbawm and G. Rudé, *Captain Swing* (1969).

A. A. MacLaren (ed.), *Social Class in Scotland Past and Present* (1976).

H. Perkin, *The Origins of Modern English Society, 1780–1880* (1969).

Index

British Museum, 273, 292
Broadlands, Hampshire, 138
Brocklesby, Lincolnshire, 90, 93
Bromley, Kent, 86
Brown, Lancelot, (Capability), 118,
  137–40, 250, 294
Browne, Sir Thomas, 27
Brydges, James, Earl of
  Caernarvon and Duke of
  Chandos, 44
Brymbo, Denbighshire, 101
Buccleuch, Dukes of, 45, 87
Buckingham, 143, 214–15
Buckingham, Marquess of, 93–4
Buckinghamshire, 21, 35, 39, 52–4,
  59, 79–82, 92–3, 146, 178, 211,
  215–16
building materials, 14, 20, 21, 22,
  80–82, 92
  see also brick, clay lump and
  wichert
building regulations, 150, 287
Building Societies, 162
bull-baiting, 258, 287
bull-running, 258, 293
Burghley House, 137–8
burghs, Scottish, 36
  convention of, 36
  government of, 32, 36–7, 286
Burke, Edmund, 289, 294
Burlington, Richard, third Earl of,
  45, 116–18, 122, 131, 263, 266
Burnham, Norfolk, 238
Burns, Robert, 28
Burrell, John, 110
Burslem, Staffordshire, 221
Bury St Edmunds, Suffolk, 265
Bute, 32
Buxton, Derbyshire, 169, 213
Byron, Lord, 293

Caernarvonshire, 100
Caledonian Canal, 235, 242
Calgary Bay, Mull, 279
Campbell, Colen, 115, 118, 154
Camborne, Cornwall, 194
Cambridge, 226, 293
  university, 42, 291
Cambridgeshire, 81, 97, 210
Campagna, Italy, 49, 132
Campbell, Sir Duncan, 121
Campbeltown, Argyllshire, 224
Campsie Fells, 21
Canada, 277–8, 280, 288
canals, 213, 230–38

Cannock, Staffordshire, 86
Canisp, Sutherland, 18
Canterbury, Archbishop of, 41
Cape Wrath, Sutherland, 242
Cardiff, Glamorganshire, 24, 223,
  225
Cardiganshire, 64–5
Carlisle, 224
  Earl of, 45
Carmarthenshire, 136
Carr, John, 120, 170, 257
carriers, 110, 117, 216–19, 220, 224
Carsethorne, Dumfries, 238
Carshalton, Surrey, 257
Cartwright, Major, 202
caschrom, 67
Castleford, Yorkshire, 227
Castle Goring, Sussex, 128
Castle Howard, Yorkshire, 45–6,
  134, 168
Catrine, Ayrshire, 205
Caxton, Cambridgeshire, 210
Chambers, Sir William, 124
Champney, Thomas, 89
Charles II, 255–7
Chatham, Kent, 175
Chatsworth, Derbyshire, 46,
  129–30, 134
Cheddington, Buckinghamshire,
  92
Cheddleton, Staffordshire, 191
Chelsea, 172
Cheltenham, Gloucestershire, 173
Cheney, John, 257
Chertsey, Surrey, 220
Cheshire, 52, 62, 176, 225
Cheshunt, Hertfordshire, 220
Chester, 235
Chester canal, 234
Chesterfield, Derbyshire, 201
Cheviot sheep, 277
Chiltern Hills, 21, 60, 214
Chirk aqueduct, 235
Chiswick House, 116, 119–21
church attendance, 247
  building, 245–9, 262, 284
  clergymen, 38, 40–41, 245, 247,
  250, 285
  dioceses, 41
  endowments, 38–41
  patronage, 38
  teind, 40
  tithes, 39–40, 245, 250, 285
Church Building Commission,
  248–9

304

Ferrers, Earl, 39, 47
Ferrybridge, Yorkshire, 230
feu, feuing, 134, 161
field barns, 76
Finsbury, 256
Fisher, George, 56
Flintshire, 100
Flitcroft, Henry, 131
Fochabers, Morayshire, 134
Fonthill, Bedfordshire, 211
football, 252, 255–6
    Association, 256
Fordwich, Kent, 36
Fort Augustus, Inverness, 224,
    242, 264
    George, Inverness, 264, 266
    William, Inverness, 224, 235, 264
Fortescue, Francis, 53
Forth, Firth of, 24, 238, 242
fortifications, 262
Fountains Abbey, Yorkshire, 137
Fox, John, 220
France, 29, 129, 161, 194, 258, 264,
    270
Frithville, Lincolnshire, 98, 248
Frome, Somerset, 213
Fulham, 136
Fulmodestone, Norfolk, 91

Gabroc Hill, Ayrshire, 107
Gaelic, 28
Gaidhealtachd, the, 28
Gainsborough, Lincolnshire, 229,
    238
Gardenesque, 141
gardening, gardens, 128–42
Garstang, Lancashire, 36
Garston, Lancashire, 191
gas works, 147, 230, 268–70
Gatehouse of Fleet,
    Kirkcudbrightshire, 205
Gateshead, Durham, 197
Gayhurst, Buckinghamshire, 247
Georg Ludwig, elector of
    Brunswick Lüneburg, later
    George I, 13, 23, 27, 29, 31, 48,
    271
George III, 140, 264, 273, 283, 289
George IV, 169, 271–4, 290
Gibbon, Edward, 250
Gibbs, James, 245
Gillespie, Graham, 170
Glamis, Angus, 17, 181
Glamorgan, canal, 197
    vale of, 24, 64

Glamorganshire, 225
Glasgow, 24, 28, 36, 149, 161–3,
    170, 240, 242, 261, 277, 281, 288
Glencaple, Dunfries, 238
Glendale, Northumberland, 85
Glen Mor, 235
Gloucester, 234, 290
Gloucestershire, 33, 36, 86, 113,
    196, 202–203, 206, 211
Godwin, William, 269
Goethe, Johann Wolfgang von, 28
Goldsmith, Oliver, 134
golf, 257
Goole, Yorkshire, 230, 236
Gordon, Alexander, Duke of, 134
Gordon Castle, Moray, 134–5
Gordon Riots, 261
'Gothick', 115, 122, 126, 293
Gower peninsula,
    Glamorganshire, 65
Grafton, Dukes of, 45, 86–7
Grafton, Northamptonshire, 87
Grampound, Cornwall, 284
Grand Junction Canal, 214, 237,
    264
Grangemouth, Stirlingshire, 236
Grant, Sir Archibald, 72, 109–10
Grantown-on-Spey, Morayshire,
    111
Gray, Thomas, 293
Graystock, Cumberland, 50
Great Bowden, Leicestershire, 56
Great Crosthwaite, Cumberland,
    37
Great Gable, Cumberland, 37
Great Glen, the, 224, 235
Great Haseley, Oxfordshire, 52
Great Haywood, Staffordshire, 234
Great Limber, Lincolnshire, 90
Great Missenden,
    Buckinghamshire, 210
Great Ouse, river, 216, 226
Great Yarmouth, 146
Greece, 115, 293
Greenock, Renfrewshire, 37
Greenwich, 13, 257, 271
Grey, Earl, 271
Gribun cliffs, Mull, 17
Grosvenor, Dame Mary, 153
    Sir Richard, 153–4, 159
    Sir Thomas, 152
Guest, John, 206
Guildford, Surrey, 182
Gwydyr, Lord, 142

307

Haddenham, Buckinghamshire, 82
Haddington, East Lothian, 68, 276
Haddlesey, Yorkshire, 229
hafotai, 65
Hainault Forest, Essex, 275
Halifax, Yorkshire, 219
    second Marquess of, 45
Halstead, Essex, 191
Halton, Buckinghamshire, 60
Hamilton, Dukes of, 18, 105, 110
Hammersmith, 136
Hampshire, 58, 69, 94, 98, 124, 138, 191
Hampstead, 217
Hampton Court, Middlesex, 122
Handel, George Frederick, 116
Harborough, Earl of, 247
Harecastle tunnel, 234
Harewood House, Yorkshire, 124
Harleston, Norfolk, 145
Hartington, Derbyshire, 213
    Lord, 45
Hatshill, Warwickshire, 214
Hartshorne, Derbyshire, 191
harvest festivities, 112, 254, 260
Harwich, Essex, 182, 213
Haselbeach, Northamptonshire, 52
Hawick, Roxburghshire, 37
Hawksmoor, Nicholas, 122, 245
Hayton, Cumberland, 62
Haydock, Lancashire, 232
Hay Tor, Devon, 16
head dyke, 69, 108
Heathcote, Sir Gilbert, 134
Hebrides, 19, 278
Helensburgh, Dunbartonshire, 242
Helmsdale, Sutherland, 241, 278
Helpston, Northamptonshire, 28
Helvellyn, 37
Henderskelf, Yorkshire, 134
Henry II, 29
Henry VI, 262
Hereford, 213, 234
Herefordshire, 44, 86
    canal, 234
Herrick, Robert, 27
Hertfordshire, 209, 220
Hexham Manor, Northumberland, 97
High Wycombe, Buckinghamshire, 143–6
Highland Roads, Commissioners of, 214, 224, 241
Highlands, Scottish, 19, 24, 28, 35, 50, 67, 69, 86, 88, 105, 122, 175, 187, 223–5, 240, 275, 277, 280

Higgs, Thomas, 60
Hoare, Henry, 46–7, 131–2, 136
    Sir Richard Colt, 136
Holkham, Norfolk, 85, 91, 93, 102, 254
Holland Fen, Lincolnshire, 97–8
Holland, Henry, 102
Holt, John, 84
Holyhead, Anglesey, 226
    Road, Commissioners of, 214
Holyrood House, Edinburgh, 24, 164
Holywood, Dumfries, 70
Hopetoun, Earl of, 111
Hopton, Derbyshire, 78
Horace, Q. Horatius Flaccus, 131
horse gin, 100, 182–4, 192
horse power, 184
horse racing, 256–8
household, *see* under family
Huddersfield, Yorkshire, 219
Hull, Yorkshire, 238–40, 266
Humber, river, 222, 227, 237
Huntingdonshire, 210
Hurleston, Cheshire, 235
Hythe, Kent, 264

Idbury, Oxfordshire, 53
Idle, river, 222
industrial housing, 204–205
infield-outfield, 67–9, 277
Inivea, Mull, 277
Inveraray Castle, Argyllshire, 46, 88, 111, 126
Ivergordon, Ross and Cromarty, 240
Inverness 224, 242, 264, 266
Inverness-shire, 17, 111
Ipswich, Suffolk, 35–7
Ireland, 29
Irwell, River, 233
Islay, Earl of, 34
Islington, 171
Italy, 115, 121, 124

Jacobinism, 48
James, Edward, 86
James VI of Scotland and I of England, 30, 257
Jockey Club, 257
Johnson, Dr, 17, 28, 250
Johnstone, John, 121
Jones, Inigo, 115
justices of the peace, 30, 34, 105, 208, 216, 285

Kames, Lord, 67
Kedleston, Derbyshire, 125
kelp, 24, 276–7
Kemp, Thomas, 273
Kendal, Westmorland, 25, 217,
    250, 265
Kenmore, Perthshire, 106
Kennedy, George and Lewis, 141
Kennet, White, bishop of
    Peterborough, 41
Kent, 76, 97, 118, 120, 191, 261
Kent, William, 115–16, 122, 131,
    133, 263
Keswick, Cumberland, 37
Kew Gardens, 140
Kilmarnock, Ayrshire, 37
Kinfauns Castle, Perthshire, 103
King, Gregory, 23, 25, 35, 44
Kingswells Dyke, Aberdeenshire,
    108
Kinnaird Head, Aberdeenshire,
    242
Kinross, 32, 109
kinship, 44, 56, 207, 289
Kintyre, Argyllshire, 88
    Mull of, 242
Kip, Johannes, 117, 129
Kippford, Kirkcudbrightshire, 238
Kirby Stephen, Westmorland, 62,
    176, 217
Kirkby Overblow, Yorkshire, 217
Kirkcudbrightshire, 105, 178
Kirkharle, Northumberland, 136
Kirkwall, Orkney, 241
Knight, Richard, Payne, 127
Knottingley, Yorkshire, 227, 236,
    238
Knyff, Leonard, 117, 129

Lacock Abbey Wiltshire, 123
laithe houses, 74
Lake District, 16, 17, 28, 37, 50, 74,
    97, 181, 188, 206, 222
Lammermuir Hills, 108
Lanarkshire, 204, 225
Lancashire, 25, 36, 84, 92, 97, 162,
    176–8, 192, 199, 204, 207, 232,
    269, 282
Lancaster, 61, 217, 238
Land Tax Commissioners, 44
Langley, Batty, 122
Langriville, Lincolnshire, 98
Lasswade, Midlothian, 74
Latchford, Oxfordshire, 52
Launceston, Cornwall, 32
Laurie, Daniel, 162

Laverstoke, Hampshire, 191
Leasowes, the, Shropshire, 133
Lee, Edmund, 186
Leeds, 25, 160–62, 211, 219, 227,
    230, 236, 248, 284
Leeming Lane, Yorkshire, 219
Leicester, 35, 213
Leicestershire, 38, 52, 55, 62, 176,
    198
Leiden, Netherlands, 42, 121
Leith, Company of Gentlemen
    Golfers of, 257
Leoni, Giacomo, 116
Lewis, island of, 16
Lewis, Matthew, 293
Lhuyd, Edward, 29
lighthouses, 241–2
Lincolnshire, 89–90, 92, 96–8, 237,
    248, 274–5
Linton, Roxburghshire, 109, 113
    sheep, 277
Liskeard, Cornwall, 32
Literary and Philosophical
    Societies, 269
Little Drayton, 213
Liverpool, 145, 170, 172, 197, 214,
    217, 231, 235, 239, 242, 249, 266,
    271
Livingstone, David, 205
Llandyssil, Montgomeryshire, 65
Llangollen, Denbighshire, 29
Lochnell House, Argyllshire, 121
Locke, John, 30
Lombe, Thomas, 178, 198, 200
Lomond, Loch, 17
London, 13, 24, 62, 70, 87, 110,
    120, 144, 146, 149–59, 209, 213,
    216–19, 222, 225–6, 238, 245, 265
    Adelphi, 154
    Bishopsgate, 146
    Brook Street, 153, 159
    Brown's Court, 155
    Buckingham Palace, 169
    Burlington House, 116–117, 159
    Carlton House, 169
    Cheapside, 145
    Claridge's Hotel, 159
    Clifford Street, 159
    Cork Street, 159
    Covent Garden, 151
    Cumberland Terrace, 168, 169
    Davies Street, 158
    Dorset Square, 256
    Dunraven Street, 159
    Grosvenor Estate, 150–59, 162
    Grosvenor Square, 154–9, 161

Moray, Earl of, 165, 170
Moray Firth, 28, 235
Morayshire, 135, 261
Morvern, Argyllshire, 88
Moss, Edward, 55
Moxon, Joseph, 76
Mull, isle of, 17, 88, 278–80
Municipal Corporations,
  Commissioners, 286–7
Murdoch, William, 147
Murray, James, 205

Nailsworth, Gloucestershire,
  202–3, 206
Nairn, 28, 32
Nash, John, 128, 168–9, 273, 292
National Society for the Education
  of the Poor, 290
Neagh, Loch, 231
Netherlands, 79
Nether Winchendon,
  Buckinghamshire, 127
Newark, Nottinghamshire, 229
Newby Park, Yorkshire, 118
Newcastle, Dukes of, 44
Newcastle-under-Lyme,
  Staffordshire, 86
Newcastle-upon-Tyne, 25, 36, 197,
  217, 219, 224, 265–6, 269
Newcomen, Thomas, 180, 194–5
  engines, 49, 195
New Lanark, 200–4
Newport Pagnell,
  Buckinghamshire, 143, 216, 220
Newport, Shropshire, 86
Newry, Co. Down, 231
Newton Castle, Carmarthenshire,
  136
Nicholson, Peter, 240
nobility, 45–6, 285
Nonconformity, 41–2, 260–61
Norfolk, 46, 57, 85, 87, 91, 92, 103,
  118, 178, 238, 275, 288
Normanton, Rutland, 134
Northampton, 42, 216
Northamptonshire, 21, 28, 40, 52,
  54, 237, 247, 254, 263–4
Northern Lighthouses, Board of
  Trustees of, 242
North Merchiston, Midlothian, 132
North Uist, 70
Northumberland, 25, 61, 64, 84–5,
  96–7, 136
  Duke of, 126
Norwich, 25, 36, 144, 220

Le Nôtre, André, 129–30, 142
Nottingham, 149, 155, 161, 170,
  184, 200–1, 229
Nottinghamshire, 69, 198
Nuneham Courtenay,
  Oxfordshire, 134

Oakhill, Somerset, 94
Oakley, Buckinghamshire, 255
Oban, Argyllshire, 191
Ochill Hill, 21
Old Deer, Aberdeenshire, 196
Oldham, Lancashire, 204, 247, 249,
  282–4
Olney, Buckinghamshire, 143
open-field system, 52–61, 82–3,
  112, 274
  see also enclosure
Orford, Suffolk, 238
Orkney Islands, 187
Ormistown, Midlothian, 110–11
Ossian, 28
Osterley Park, Middlesex, 125
Otham, Kent, 76–7
Ottley, Suffolk, 112
Ouse, river, Yorkshire, 227
Overman, Mr, 238
Overstone, Northamptonshire,
  247
Owen, Goronwy, 29
Owen, Robert, 201–2
Oxford, 29, 216
  university, 42
  Magdalen College, 54
Oxfordshire, 21, 52–3, 131, 134

packhorses, 221–2
Packington, Leicestershire, 52
Padbury, Buckinghamshire, 59,
  215
Paisley, Renfrewshire, 172, 204
Paley, Richard, 162
Paling, Robert, 176–7
Palk, Sir Lawrence, 283
Palladianism, 49, 116–21, 123, 134,
  292
Palladio, Andrea, 116, 120, 124,
  133
Palmerston, second Viscount, 138
Palnackie, Kirkcudbrightshire, 238
Pangbourne, Berkshire, 229
Papplewick, Nottinghamshire, 196
parish ales, 253
  boundaries, 36, 287
  new parishes, 247, 249

311

wichert, 82
Wick, Caithness, 224, 241
Widnes, Lancashire, 288
Wigan, Lancashire, 231, 262
Wilkins William, 124, 291
Wilkingson, John, 101, 195–6
Willey, Shropshire, 196
Willington, Derbyshire, 221
Willoughby Waterless,
    Leicestershire, 57
Wiltshire, 47, 118–19, 131, 196
Winchcombe, Gloucestershire,
    110, 218
Winchester, Bishop of, 41
Windle, Lancashire, 288
windmills, 185–8
Windsor, Berkshire, 218, 262
    Castle, 273
Winslow, Buckinghamshire, 22, 79
Winter, Thomas, 109, 218
Wirksworth, Derbyshire, 200
Wisbech, Cambridgeshire, 238
Witney, Oxfordshire, 196, 200
Woburn Abbey, Bedfordshire, 102
Woburn Farm, Surrey, 132
Wolsingham, Durham, 98
Wolverhampton, Staffordshire, 86
Wood, John, senior and junior, 166
Wood, Robert, 124
Woodbridge, Suffolk, 188, 238

Wootton-under-Edge,
    Gloucestershire, 36
Worcester, 213
Worcestershire, 33, 94, 106, 113,
    191, 194
Wordsworth, William, 292
Workington, Cumberland, 85
Worsley, Lancashire, 92, 233, 240
Wren, Sir Christopher, 115, 245
Wrexham, Denbighshire, 24, 235
Wyatt, James, 220
Wyatt, Samuel, 101–102

Yarborough, First Baron and First
    Earl of, 90
Yarranton, Andrew, 209
yeoman, 45–7, 53–7, 76, 85
Yester, East Lothian, 68
York, 36, 120, 173, 217, 257, 265–6,
    282–4
    Archbishop of, 41
    Vale of, 17
Yorkshire, 25, 42, 57, 61, 89, 93, 97,
    116, 118, 122, 137–9
    East Riding, 25, 98, 139, 274
    West Riding, 25, 74, 97, 162, 204,
    227
Young, Arthur, 85, 87, 106, 112,
    238